Priorities in Marketing Series

Leonard L. Berry, general editor

Marvin A. Jolson, *Sales Management: A Tactical Approach*
Robert W. Joselyn, *Designing the Marketing Research Project*
Robert W. Haas, *Industrial Marketing Management*
Richard T. Hise, *Product/Service Strategy*

Sales
Management
A Tactical Approach

Marvin A. Jolson
University of Maryland

 PETROCELLI/CHARTER   NEW YORK 1977

Printed in the United States of America

1 2 3 4 5 6 7 8 9 10

Library of Congress Cataloging in Publication Data

Jolson, Marvin A
    Sales management.

    Includes indexes.
    1. Sales management.   I. Title.
HF5438.4.J65   658.8'1   76-51332
ISBN 0-88405-392-X
ISBN 0-88405-442-X pbk.

To the Memory of

Mother and Dad

Contents

Contents

List of Cases

Preface

The ideal sales-management text would serve the needs of management, students, instructors, and the academic institution. A book about the dynamic subject of sales management must kindle interest, inspire, correct misunderstandings, tell, teach, and demonstrate principles with a variety of realistic examples and lively copy. Finally, it should provide an organizing frame of reference to assist the reader in developing predictive generalizations. This book attempts to achieve this set of formidable goals.

Students in the sales-management area prefer a textbook that is simultaneously complete, comprehensive, understandable, and succinct. Thus, this book attempts to avoid the lengthy repetition of basic concepts and definitions from other business courses. It omits step-by-step mathematical and statistical discussions except in areas strongly tied to frequent sales management practices, for example, sales forecasting. The book's level of rigor, depth of coverage, and built-in redundancies are not uniform throughout the text and are related to the importance and complexity of the issue at hand and the adequacy of previous treatments. The length and content of the text are designed to encourage expansion by the professor or course leader and to generate intense participation and discussion in the classroom.

The material is intended to be eminently practical, stressing both the why and the how-to of effective sales management rather than abstract theories that have little relevance for the career-oriented student or practitioner. The tactical approach is action oriented, in that the reader is exposed to more than the firm's broad strategic selling plans. The execution and implementation of strategies are emphasized and illustrated by activities and dialogues practiced by sales managers. Scattered throughout are examples of successes, failures, and omissions that suggest new strategic and tactical opportunities for modern sales managers.

Hopefully, this book is particularly sensitive to the needs of students and of sales leaders who are on their way up, in that it takes into account the numerous frustrating steps that one must climb in order to be a successful sales executive. It directly attacks the anxiety-provoking elements of selling and sales management without attempting to offer rebuttals, overcome stigmas, and reverse the reader's beliefs or career plans. Instead, it attempts to face the realities of the sales world head-on, reflecting both positive and negative dimensions. Only then can the reader divorce himself from blinding influences which previously may have distorted his ability and his desire to view the field of sales management objectively and critically.

Despite the book's commitment to the reader's practical needs, it avoids the strong vocational orientation that could isolate a course in sales management from the rest of the academic program. The material includes challenging analytic areas and touches on several controversial issues such as consumerism, ethics, and social responsibility. It encourages the student to recall and apply successfully his prior learning and experiences. Finally, the book contains the subtleties which allow the reader to develop his thinking power and the attendant instinctiveness that is characteristic of most sales leaders.

The text, discussion questions, and cases present an assortment of fresh incidents or live situations taken from sales organizations. Perhaps no pedagogical technique is available to course leaders which stimulates more student or trainee interest and response than the incident method. It is hoped that the incidents, cases, examples, and poems contained herein will stick to the reader's ribs and that the book will serve as a ready reference long after the reader has fulfilled his role as a student or trainee.

It was my pleasure and good fortune to work with many who made strategic decisions in a great variety of sales-management situations when I served as a consultant to management and as a senior vice-president with Encyclopaedia Britannica, Inc. It has been my additional advantage to enjoy research experiences and stimulating exchanges with marketing students and academic colleagues. Hopefully, the book has captured some of the underlying patterns of these exposures.

The final preparation and form of this book have thus profited from the ideas generated by sales-minded business associates, other authors, and classroom exchanges. My special thanks are due to Charlotte Schisler, without whose patience and typing excellence my chicken scratchings could not have been converted into a legible manuscript.

Marvin A. Jolson

A Special Note to Readers

In this text, terms such as *salesman, he,* and *man* are used strictly for writing convenience. They are in no way inferences that women are less active than men in sales management.

Section I

Overview of the Selling Task

1

Personal Selling— a Subset of Marketing

It is not uncommon for practitioners, students, teachers, and journal writers to view marketing and selling as identical functions. This author is not one to quibble over definitions or refute personal viewpoints. However, it might be helpful at the outset of this text to clear up this misconception and establish the environmental setting in which salespeople, sales managers, and other marketing people must coexist with other entities and with each other.

The Marketing Concept

Marketing literature is rich with discussions of the marketing-concept philosophy of management, which, in general, emphasizes organizing and combining company resources to deliver customer satisfaction at an acceptable profit to the firm. Yet, a 1965 study designed to discover the currently accepted meaning of the marketing concept elicited (among many others) the following responses from marketing executives: [1]

> In my opinion, the meaning of the marketing concept is . . . all phases of sales management.

> Regardless of how you use the word *marketing,* regardless of how you define it, don't you really mean a simple five letter word—SALES? We do not use the word *marketing* in any way at our company. It is just

plain finance-production-sales and we fan out from there. We have no confusion or misunderstanding whatsoever by operating in this manner.

It is no doubt inappropriate to criticize the above responses on the grounds that the respondents are not profit minded or not consumer oriented. A more viable conclusion is that executives who fail to differentiate between marketing and selling do not think in terms of systematically dovetailing the numerous corporate functions, strategies, and tactics (including those related to selling) into a coordinated package which accomplishes simultaneously the objectives of the firm, its customers, and its employees.

One may assume that in most business organizations management thinks in terms of obtaining and retaining satisfied customers. It is even more certain that most firms concentrate heavily on profit making. However, while customer satisfaction and profitability are the desired results, the trick is how to achieve these often conflicting goals. In the opinion of the author, the solution calls for the skillful integration of all company functions so as to promote teamwork throughout the company by sound organizational structure, the cohesion of individual goals, and the avoidance of personality clashes and political intrigue.

The Marketing System and Suboptimization

Although marketing and selling exist in nonprofit as well as in profit-making organizations, it is convenient at this point to define marketing as *a total system of intersecting business activities designed to plan, price, promote, and distribute want-satisfying goods and services to household and organizational users.*[2] A system may be regarded as a nonrandom collection of interconnected and functionally related parts. The systems concept emphasizes optimal goal achievement for the entire system rather than for any of the individual parts. In practice, the goal-seeking actions taken by one entity in a system may reflect negatively upon the capacity of one or more of the remaining system parts to attain their desired levels of achievement. This condition may be referred to as suboptimization. A serious example of suboptimization occurs when the goals of one part of a system are optimized to the detriment of the goals of the entire system.[3]

To illustrate both conditions of suboptimization, when economic conditions are unfavorable, a credit and collection manager may decide to improve his collection performance by tightening up his credit-approval policy. However, as more orders are rejected, sales-force members whose compensation is tied to commissions may become disenchanted enough to seek employment elsewhere. The loss of sales manpower can result in an immediate reduction in sales and a vexing drop in market share and profits.

Hierarchy of Systems [4]

Figure 1.1 helps the reader to conceptualize the business firm as an operating system within a larger external environmental system. In turn, the business system can be divided into a number of subsystems including the promotional system. Finally, the promotional system has a number of parts of which the personal selling system is one.

The flow chart also demonstrates a logical sequence for management activities within the firm including those of general management, marketing management, product management, sales management, and others. Coordination of systems and parts of systems is vital if the goals of each entity are to be attained without chaos or conflict in a structure.

The sequence begins with an examination of the general environment (block 1), which includes pervasive background factors (social, political, governmental or regulatory, economic, technological) which now or in the future may affect the firm's undertakings. The next two considerations concern the operating environment (blocks 2 and 3), consisting of the company in interaction with other entities such as customers, competitors, suppliers, unions, investors, bankers, ad agencies, and so on. Realized market opportunities call for the firm's understanding of both the operating and general levels of the external (to the firm) environment.

Meaningful adoption and implementation of the marketing-concept philosophy demand that all levels of management be constantly aware of the current and potential whims, attitudes, opinions, and requirements of customers and the environmental factors that affect them. Customer orientation does not restrict itself to the firm's immediate customer but instead demands consideration of wholesaler, retailer, and consumer wants and expectations. Management must also keep abreast of competitive offerings, pricing, promotional efforts, and so on, especially in terms of unfilled wants of the marketplace.

Clearly, a number of internal factors (block 4) are high-priority considerations for the general marketing manager and his sub-managers. The marketing group must, of necessity, operate within the constraints imposed by top management, including budget requirements and compatibility with the firm's overall objectives. To assure an integrated effort, the marketing manager must be familiar

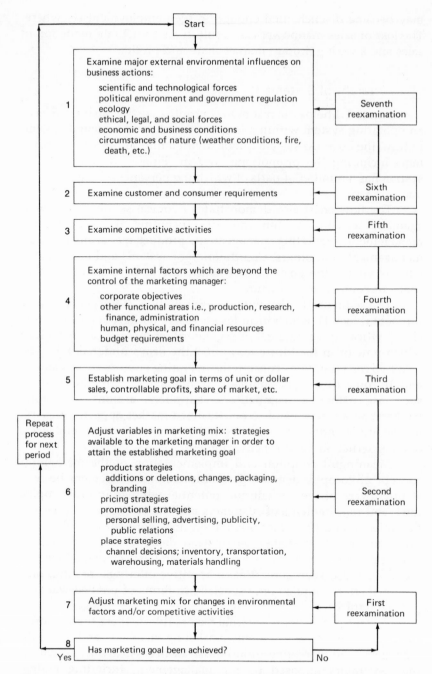

Figure 1.1 Sequence of marketing-management activities

Source: Marvin A. Jolson and Richard T. Hise, *Quantitative Techniques for Marketing Decisions* (New York: Macmillan, 1973), p. 7.

with weaknesses and limitations of personnel, techniques, policies, and other resources of all functional divisions within the firm. It is important for the reader to realize that goals or objectives (whether corporate, marketing, sales, or otherwise) should not be established until the available means or resources of the goal-setting unit have been considered adequate. In other words, it is logical to estimate the available inputs before establishing a desired output.

From the viewpoint of the marketing manager, the corporate system is external. Thus, a careful study of the physical and behavioral forces outside the firm, inside the firm but outside of the marketing division, and within the marketing operation should precede the setting of specific marketing goals.

The marketing goals (block 5) are therefore servile to those of the firm, which are, in turn, dependent upon the current objectives and constraints of the system external to the firm (general and operating environments). Following the establishment of a general marketing goal, the marketing manager is prepared to launch the plans of action (strategies) to reach his goal and the explicit procedures to execute these plans (tactics).

As shown in Figure 1.1, the marketing mix and its subelements (block 6) represent the set of controllable variables that are subject to simultaneous manipulation by the marketing staff. These numerous marketing-decision variables can be considered to be the strategies and tactics of marketing action. As previously mentioned, the marketing-mix instruments must be set simultaneously since they are interdependent. The setting of a single variable, say price, without consideration of its impact on other variables, say advertising and sales-force morale, can lead to suboptimization in its strongest form. For example, an arbitrary increase in price to cover rising costs could call for an accompanying boost in advertising support to make demand more inelastic. If the sales force perceives the price as a formidable sales hurdle, revenues may drop or not rise sufficiently to cover the cost increment. Moreover, disenchanted sales-force members could be permanently lost due to decreases in personal earnings.

It is seen that personal selling, advertising, and other elements are grouped under the promotional instrument. Thus, within the promotional system, the firm may employ one or more sales managers, directors of advertising, public-relations people, and others. Selling goals must concur with the broad promotional plan which, in turn, is subordinated to established marketing objectives.

The reader may now be in a better position to determine whether selling means marketing and vice versa. The foregoing discussion suggests that selling is but one part of the promotional system which, in turn, is a single element in the marketing mix of the broader marketing system.

THE PROMOTIONAL SYSTEM

Most marketing authorities will agree that promotion has to do with demand stimulation and persuasive communication. Yet, during periods of shortages of energy, supplies, and other resources, demand may exceed supply such that promotion may take the form of "demand management" and "creative demarketing" rather than stimulation and persuasion. Definitions of promotion include the following:

> Promotion refers to the means used to stir up interest and carry forward the furtherance of company goals through communications.[5]
>
> Promotion encompasses all the tools in the marketing mix whose major role is persuasive communication.[6]
>
> Promotion describes all types of marketing activities designed to stimulate demand.[7]
>
> Promotional strategy is a controlled, integrated program of communication methods and materials designed to present a company and its product to prospective customers; to communicate need-satisfying attributes of products toward the end of facilitating sales and thus contributing to long-run profit performance.[8]

Promotion and Other P's

It was previously indicated that promotion is but one of the four P's (product, price, place, promotion) in the marketing mix. Yet, several of the above definitions suggest that promotion spills over into almost all parts of the marketing mix. For example, a low price is a demand stimulator as is a high-quality product. An ideal retail location with a splendid assortment of products, sizes, brands, and colors is an excellent communicator and especially persuasive when information about the location is passed from one satisfied customer to friends or relatives who are prospective purchasers.

However, this text seeks to differentiate between demand stimulators in general and promotional tools (promotools) in particular. Succinctly put, *promotion is the process of persuasively informing prospects about the other P's in the marketing mix.* Thus, promotion is a planned, overt communication process directed from the seller to the prospective buyer. Obviously, one of its major purposes is to stimulate demand for a product, service, or idea.

Advertising: any *paid* form of *nonpersonal* presentation and promotion of ideas, goods, and services by an *identified sponsor*

Personal selling: *oral* presentation in a conversation with one or more prospective purchasers for the purpose of making sales

Publicity: *nonpersonal* stimulation of demand for a product, service, or business unit by planting commercially significant news about it in a published medium or radio, television, or live show that is *not paid for* by the sponsor

Sales promotion: those marketing activities, *other than personal selling, advertising, and publicity,* that stimulate consumer purchasing and dealer effectiveness, such as displays, shows and exhibitions, demonstrations, and various *noncurrent* selling efforts not in the ordinary routine

As indicated by one author, *sales promotion* is often considered a catchall for promotools that are not formally classified as advertising, personal selling, or publicity. Moreover, sales promotion was once viewed as an ad hoc, short-term stimulus. Recently, it has been more generally adopted as a true auxiliary and support activity for selling and advertising.[10] Accordingly, many marketers currently include as part of sales promotion such activities as the design and installation of point-of-purchase displays, the development of sales presentations, and the creation of descriptive booklets, brochures, flip charts, audiovisual materials, and selling broadsides.

The use of promotional tools to exploit the availability of other demand-stimulating variables in the marketing mix should be emphasized. For example, a high-quality product, an exceptionally low price, and an ideal retail outlet would produce negligible revenues or profits if the promotional system were not operating to inform prospective buyers of these benefits.

Promotional Tasks

Different firms employ personal selling, advertising, publicity and sales promotion in varying degrees. However, every company or institution that offers a product or service for sale has the same four sequential promotional tasks. These are (1) finding prospects (prospecting), (2) making contact with prospects (contacting), (3) stimulating desire for the firm's offerings (stimulating), and (4) closing the sale (closing). When repeat sales are involved, a fifth step emerges, (5) keeping the customer sold (retaining).[11] It is reasonable to assume that these identical steps are also required by nonprofit organizations such as fund raisers, adoption agencies, and recruitment arms of the military services.

Some organizations such as direct-to-home marketers of insurance, vacuum cleaners, and encyclopedias depend on personal selling efforts to accomplish most and sometimes all of the five promotional tasks. In other firms, such as retail establishments, the same five steps are pegged more directly to merchandising skills, price reductions, and mass-media advertising. Also, it is not illogical to assume that in many companies, personal selling may make a large contribution to some promotional tasks and a very small one to others.

Trade-offs within the Promotional Mix

The two major promotools, advertising and personal selling, are often complementary and frequently interchangeable. As previously stated, personal selling is sometimes responsible for almost the entire promotional load. In other instances, such as in the case of mail-order selling or automatic vending, advertising predominates.

Generally, however, advertising and personal selling are mutually interdependent and supportive of each other. When prospective purchasers are relatively unaware of a product's existence or major benefits, advertising is typically an effective and economical means of creating product awareness or functional comprehension. When detailed explanation or demonstration is called for, personal selling generally takes over. Advertising often reenters the exchange process to reinforce the buying decision and to prevent buyer's remorse, that is, to assure the purchaser that he made the correct buying decision. One group of authorities describes the buy-sell relationship as consisting of three phases, pretransactional, transactional, and posttransactional, and suggests that advertising is predominant in the pretransactional phase as a market-cultivating force and in the posttransactional phase by providing rationalization to the purchaser.[12] The use of advertising as a pretransactional instrument is recognized in the popular saying that *advertising leads the horse to water and personal selling persuades him to drink.* An example of advertising in the pretransactional phase is the widespread use of coupons and business reply post cards in magazines, newspapers, and direct mail to generate qualified leads for sales-force members.

The mutually supporting relationship of advertising and personal selling is also demonstrated by the salesman's use of advertising reprints and tear sheets in his sales presentation. Such reprints often lend support to salesmen's statements about product benefits and prices. Moreover, elaborate or expensive ads seem to suggest company bigness, success, and quality. They also suggest products with broad consumption patterns, since most prospective customers are aware that ads in national media are designed for use with a large number of prospects over time.[13]

Cash and Crissy reinforce the notion that advertising and personal selling can, in many circumstances, be substituted for each other. In their discussion of the similarities and differences between advertising and selling, five advantages of personal selling are highlighted: [14]

1. Two-way rather than one-way communication allows for and in fact encourages continuous feedback from the prospect. Thus, customer questions and misunderstandings can be cleared up on the spot since the salesman serves as a problem solver.
2. "Noise" is relatively absent, in that personal selling does not have to compete with other simultaneous messages or with surrounding editorial copy, photos of *Playboy* bunnies, and other entertaining features.
3. A sales message is more flexible, more personal, and more suited to the specific customer than an advertisement since the salesman can adapt his message to the thinking, needs, and mood of the customer or prospect at the time of the sales call.
4. Selling can penetrate a larger number of the audience's sensory mechanisms since, in addition to the visual, the senses of hearing, taste, smell, and touch can be enlisted.
5. Frequent repetition and reinforcement are possible such that the salesman is able to regenerate attention and interest when he detects that they are waning.

To the above list, we can add the following:

6. Selling efforts can be limited to qualified prospects, minimizing waste communication.
7. Selling can be a large- or small-scale effort. Advertising, on the other hand, must normally be conducted as a campaign on a reasonably large-scale.
8. Selling is capable of carrying the audience through a logical and persuasive reasoning process, and includes the use of rebuttals in response to objections.
9. Personal selling is much more effective than advertising in closing the sale, that is, in obtaining the customer's consent or signature.

The foregoing list of the advantages of personal selling does not establish selling as a universally superior promotional vehicle. The advantages of advertising are also numerous, although there is little value in citing them here. In terms of total dollar expenditure and number of people employed, personal selling is depicted in Table 1.1 as being more important than other elements in the promotional mix.

How Much for Promotion?

It is difficult to visualize the firm that has no promotional tasks to perform, that is, has no need to find prospects or make contacts with them, no need to stimulate desire for ownership or use of its products, no need to close sales or retain customers. Yet, firms may opt to allocate substantial funds and effort to product improvement, price reduction, employee development, or improved services, thus decreasing the level of resources allocated to promotion.

The level of the promotional budget as a proportion of the total marketing budget is most difficult to determine in practice. This is because sales response as a function of promotional input is one of the more elusive marketing phenomena. This is not true in all cases. For example, when direct-mail selling predominates, response rates for each mailing piece can be determined over time, thus allowing the marketer to relate sales volume to advertising costs with reasonable accuracy. It has also been shown that sales volume for many types of organizations is a linearly increasing function of the number of productive sales-force members.[15]

However, the reader should remember that individual marketing-mix variables do not have an independent effect on the level of sales. Similarly, it is unlikely in practice that any single promotional input will have a constant effect on sales volume. For example, a series of 10 percent increases in advertising level will surely not generate a series of equal increases in sales responses. At some point in time, further increases in advertising outlays will increase sales at a de-

Table 1.1 Relative importance of personal selling in marketing

	Total dollar expenditures ($ Billions)	Number of people employed (Millions)
Personal selling	60	7.0–8.0
Sales promotion	40	
Advertising	20	0.5

SOURCE: Gary M. Grikscheit and W. J. E. Crissy, "Personal Selling: A Position Paper," in Ross L. Goble and Roy T. Shaw, *Controversy and Dialogue in Marketing* (Englewood Cliffs, N.J.: Prentice-Hall, 1975), p. 272.

creasing rate. Thus, sales volume and attendant profitability will in   13
all likelihood be expressed as a nonlinear function of all marketing
variables acting in concert. This substitutability of one promotional
and demand-stimulating tool for another and the difficulty of predicting the joint effect on sales levels complicate the marketer's task
of determining the ideal promotional budget.

A number of guidelines have been offered to aid the marketing
manager in making decisions about promotional budgets. These include many factors, among which are competitive considerations,
especially the required level of product differentiation; [16] position of
the product in its life cycle; [17] number and types of intermediaries in
the distribution channel; carry-over effects of current promotional
expenditures; number and similarity of products carried by the firm;
current economic climate; and the indirect communication effects
sought by the firm (such as preconditioning for future market cultivation). The relevant criterion in determining the total promotional
allocation is how much and what type of promotional activity is
required to find prospects and make the necessary contacts with
them, to stimulate desire for ownership or rental, to close sales, and
to retain customers. At a given point in time, a firm may decide that
there is little need to seek new prospects. When buyers are expected
to contact sellers rather than vice versa, demand stimulation may
take such forms as allocating scarce goods, improving the facilities of
a store, and refurnishing a buying office. When store traffic is sufficiently heavy without additional advertising, stimulation of desire
and closing of sales may be accomplished by price reductions. Finally, many firms accomplish customer retention by focusing on
product quality, liberal warranties, and return privileges.

The Promotional Mix

Considering the large reservoir of promotional techniques
available to the firm, how does management divide up the total promotional dollars among advertising, personal selling, sales promotion, and publicity? Moreover, how should the subelements of the
promotional mix be subdivided? For example, once the advertising
budget has been established, what proportions of the funds should
be assigned to TV, radio, magazine, newspaper, and direct-mail
media? What is the optimal sales-force level? Should sales-force compensation costs be fixed or variable or a combination of each? Should
salesmen be supplied with leads, or should they be expected to
operate on a cold canvassing basis? Are advertising and personal
selling readily interchangeable in the given firm?

Much of the material in the chapters to follow speaks to many of

14   the above questions. It is probable that both the manager and the astute student will be convinced that the problem of predicting and measuring the results of using any single promotional tool or combination of tools is most complex, to say the least.

Despite the inherent difficulties present in listing the key factors and prescribing a systematic methodology for allocating the promotional budget and effort among the several promotional elements (largely personal selling versus advertising), several of the more important consideratons are discussed in the following sections.

The Product's Position in the Marketing Communications Spectrum. It has already been suggested in a previous section that some prospective buyers are quite aware of, familiar with, and sold on a given product, brand, or outlet. The complete continuum stretching from unawareness to action (brand insistence) is shown in Figure 1.2 and is considered by Colley to be a marketing-communications spectrum.[18] The brand-loyalty ladder is shown as a parallel continuum.

Those who are *unaware* have never heard of the product or firm. The *aware* prospect has heard of the product and will no doubt recognize or recall the brand or company name, saying something such as "The *Syntopicon* is a book of some kind, a little bit like a dictionary or encyclopedia." The prospect at the *comprehension* level of the continuum is not only aware of the offering, but recognizes the brand name or trademark and has some idea of what the product is and does. He might say, "The *Syntopicon* is a two-volume index to the *Great Books*. It cross-indexes ideas the way a dictionary indexes words and an encyclopedia indexes facts." *Conviction* is shown by a consumer who says: "The *Syntopicon* is a vital reference tool since it enables the reader to trace any controversial thought or idea from the beginning of time to the twentieth century. It refers the curious person to precise passages in such works as the Bible, *War and Peace, Romeo and Juliet, Moby Dick,* and *Crime and Punishment* that discuss the single idea of his interest. Thus, he can read *in* the Great Books tracing a given idea without reading *through* all the books. Someday I'm going to buy the *Syntopicon* and the *Great Books*."

The terminal position is *action*, where the prospect has initiated some form of buying behavior. He may have clipped a magazine coupon which offered buying information about the *Syntopicon*. He may have phoned the publisher's local branch office to request a visit from a salesman.

As indicated by Colley, direct-mail advertising, door-to-door selling, and street-corner and in-store demonstrators are among the very few single communication forces that can move a prospect from unawareness to action.[19]

In general, advertising is effective and relatively economical at the lowest end of the spectrum with selling more potent in generating conviction and buying action. One interesting research approach would be to determine the proportion of consumers (in a representative sample of the market) on each level of the continuum of Figure 1.2. For a given product, presume the following findings:

Action	5%
Conviction	5%

Figure 1.2 Marketing-communications spectrum

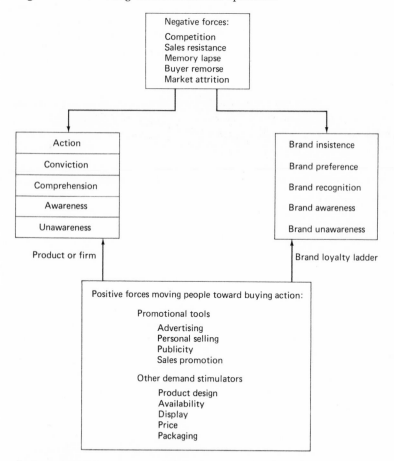

SOURCE: Modified version of diagram in "Defining Advertising Goals," Russell H. Colley, ed., *Defining Advertising Goals for Measured Advertising Results* (New York: Association of National Advertisers, 1961), p. 55.

Comprehension	10%
Awareness	20%
Unawareness	60%

The marketing manager's preliminary conclusion might be to emphasize a large proportion of advertising and a small proportion of personal selling. As a result of the ad campaign over time, consumers may be repositioned upward along the spectrum thus calling for a larger proportion of personal selling to enter the promotional mix.

Channel Level and Type of Customer. The previous analysis failed to consider the role of the seller, that is, is he a producer, wholesaler, or retailer? An associated question has to do with the type of immediate customer, that is, is he a producer, wholesaler, retailer, household consumer, or organizational user?

Consider the producer of a product such as potato chips which are stacked in space-saving, airtight, moisture proof, recappable, crush-proof canisters. Not so long ago, this product, because of its innovative packaging, was relatively unknown to both organizational buyers and consumers. Aggressive personal selling might be required by the manufacturer to convince large supermarket chains to carry such an item. However, part of the inducement could consist of a national advertising campaign with the producer sharing the costs of local advertising with the retail chain. In this example, as the saying goes, "personal selling puts the product on the retailer's shelves and advertising takes it off the shelves." The identical reasoning would follow as one traces the sale of a leisure suit from producer to retailer to consumer.

Often different brands of the same product will be sold through different channel systems, thus offering striking contrasts in promotional-mix strategies. For example, Hoover Vacuum cleaners and Helena Rubenstein Cosmetics are sold to consumers through retailers, while Electrolux and Avon sell similar products directly to consumers in their homes. In the first case, the producers and associated retail outlets emphasize advertising; in the second, they are personal selling experts.

Thus, the firm's channel position and customer target have an impact upon the required promotional mix. Consumer-goods producers may simultaneously feature strong personal selling, to establish a position with resellers, and heavy mass-media advertising, to stimulate consumer demand. Retailers will specialize in advertising when mail-order methods and self-service retailing are used and emphasize intensive personal selling efforts when direct-to-home marketing predominates. Finally, industrial marketers and distributors are likely to use trade advertising to pave the way for personal contacts by salespeople.

Brand Policy.[20] A producer's promotional mix is heavily dependent upon whether he chooses to distribute his product under his own brand or under the private brand of a middleman or by the simultaneous use of both branding policies. If a product bears the manufacturer's brand, the producer is assisted in gaining market control, since the goodwill of consumers who purchase the product at retail outlets is directed toward the producer.

Brand recognition, preference, and insistence (see Figure 1.2) are gained by continuous advertising in mass consumer media. When "pull through" advertising is successful in influencing shoppers to request a particular brand at the retail outlet, the retailer is, in turn, persuaded to request that brand from the wholesaler or manufacturer.

On the other hand, the promotion of private brands is the responsibility of the retail outlet, thus reducing advertising strains on the producer. This, in turn, permits the producer to offer lower prices and focus his promotional efforts on personal selling to middlemen with some support from trade-oriented advertising and sales promotion.

Price and Product Complexity. Products sold to industrial users are most often technical in nature and quite costly. Moreover, the number of industrial buying units is quite small in a given industry in comparison to the number of household prospects for a consumer product. Within a given geographical region, industrial firms are quite often located close together. Thus, promotional effort commonly features personal selling by technical personnel. Advertising in industrial publications is minimal but serves as an excellent supportive vehicle. Descriptive literature and technical specification materials are additional aids to sales personnel.

Often, a product may not be complex physically or functionally, but the communication requirements may be demanding. For example, although an expensive consumer product may have qualities superior to those of competitors, they may not be readily apparent without skillful explanation. The disadvantages of distributing such a product (encyclopedias, burglar and fire alarms, water conditioners, etc.) through in-store outlets are the dearth of skilled retail clerks, the difficulty of holding the attention of an in-store shopper for more than a few moments, the tendency for buyer procrastination due to confusion, the need for consultation with spouses, and the concentration of the store on numerous items rather than on a single product.

Herein lies the justification for direct-to-home personal selling. The direct seller depends on the relaxed feeling people have at home or the inherent courtesy extended to a guest. The in-home salesman is able to deliver his complete sales presentation in front of all family members with ample time to try to overcome buying objections. The direct seller usually carries only one product or line and thus is in a position to describe the features, benefits, and advantages of what he sells without simultaneous interference by competitive offerings or outside influences.

When complex and/or expensive products or services are being marketed, the salesman, in contrast to the advertisement, is more capable of responding directly and quickly to the prospect's information and problem-solving needs. Sellers of products with high-price images are ordinarily quite effective in training their representatives to spell out and justify their firms' pricing policies in terms of ultimate benefits and profitability to buyers.

Distinctive Competence of Seller. Not every marketing group has the human and other resources to implement a direct-selling program, launch a unique mass-media ad campaign, gain acceptance into an established distribution channel, or secure audiences with organizational buyers or merchandise managers. Thus, the appropriate promotional mix should take into consideration the marketer's unique skills in specialized personal selling, sales promotion, and advertising, as they apply to the promotional objectives of the firm.

The reader has no doubt read books or articles on marketing principles or marketing management wherein the authors have recommended the standard sequence for establishing marketing mix strategies: first product, then price, then promotion, and finally distribution. This author suggests that such programmed thinking is invalid and unreliable. The marketer's distinctive competence should predominate. For example, suppose Todd Ryan has held numerous positions as a commissioned direct-to-home sales manager and wishes to form his own company. His first decision may concern distribution, that is, he may decide to form a company that specializes in selling directly to homes or small business. Presume that Ryan holds a degree in electrical engineering. The product decision might then come next. Perhaps he will market systems for burglar or fire control. The pricing decision logically follows. He can choose either to sell or to lease his products. Advertising may or may not be used. Lastly, some sales-promotion support will be required to assist the personal-selling operation.

PROMOTION—MARKETER'S LINK WITH SOCIETY

It was shown earlier in this chapter that promotional communications consist of various flows of information and persuasive messages from the marketing organization to its channel members and ultimately to organizational and household consumers. In turn, a huge feedback network and attendant marketing dialogue are activated, which inform the firm about the relative success and acceptability of its market offerings, policies, and promotional undertakings.

Communications from the marketplace and other parts of the general or operating environment may be direct or indirect, positive or negative, visible or implicit. Communication may take the form of purchases, nonpurchases, favorable or unfavorable word-of-mouth exchanges, plaudits or expressions of disenchantment, the respect or disesteem of competitors, public acclaim or remedial activity.[21] The more direct vehicles of communication from the end user to the firm are the customers, sales figures, middlemen, facilitating agencies, and salespeople. However, the salesman has been frequently found to be a questionable source of market information due to his tendencies to suppress, delay, and distort information.[22]

Talking versus Listening

The promotional system is the arm of the firm that fondles or clouts society; the mouth that speaks to society; and, with the aid of market research, the eyes and ears that receive input from society. As in the case of some *people,* promotional programs often talk too much, say too little, and listen too infrequently. Proponents of consumerism claim that many corporate promotional programs are not providing the information necessary for meaningful choice, and they point to inaccurate, misleading, and inadequate information as the major reason for the demand for more protective legislation. Purportedly, a key reason for the communications gap is that in designing a promotional mix most of the emphasis is on one-way communication from the business organization to its target markets.[23] The reverse direction is frequently ignored.

The Societal Marketing Concept

Recently, one-way dialogue and limited listening have created serious complications for many firms. In addition, many authorities suggest that the marketing concept, with its inherent focus on satisfying the target market, may be indifferent to the broader demands of society in general.[24] Both the marketer and his satisfied users must be alert to the unintended linkages of the marketing mix with the environment, and the attendant forms of discomfort imposed upon nonusers and other members of society.

Marketing strategies that have undesirable effects on society are sources of a kind of environmental pollution that is subject to the same censure as that heaped on products and processes that produce smoke, noise, filth, waste, and other offensive results. Apparently, it is no longer enough to be sure that intended marketing communications satisfy a firm's target markets. Of equal importance is promotional conduct such that the entire spectrum of physical and psychological side effects will be tolerable for society.[25]

Control of Personal Selling

Both advertising and personal selling, because of their strong interface with markets and the broader society, have been subject to much criticism. Of the two, the ill effects of personal selling have been more damaging.

Advertising is a more structured mode in that the desired message is designed by many company executives, with the possible assistance of an ad agency. Moreover, the message is delivered in precise accord with company wishes. Thus, the company story is told the company way.

The sales presentation may also be highly structured or canned. But, since a salesperson is a more imperfect and less controllable vehicle than an advertisement, there are often discrepancies between the intended and actual communication. Salesmen forget; salesmen use puffery, exaggeration, and occasional misrepresentations in quest of sales and commissions. The sales interview is often viewed as a contest or conflict.[26] To many companies, salespeople are robots who are recruited, hired, trained, fired up, and evaluated in terms of how many orders they bring in.[27]

Social Neglect

In the drive for sales-force effectiveness and attendant profits, management sometimes overlooks some of its vital social responsibilities, both to users and nonusers. Conversely, the fashionability of criticizing selling programs, strategies, and tactics frequently requires that the firm be defended against unjustified claims of social peccadillos and irregular practices.

These ethical and social considerations crop up in subsequent chapters as the sales manager's various tactical approaches are dis-

Minimum-wage laws as applied to outside salesmen

The impact of compensation plans on selling behavior

Ethical considerations in designing the sales presentation

Full disclosure in recruiting and selling

Antiselling regulations

Confronting the salesperson with "easy-to-sell" prospects

The sales manager's role in community projects

Converting latent desire into a "now need"

The meaning of high-pressure selling

The salesman's grievance rights

The image of the salesman

Proselytizing of competitive sales-force members

SUMMARY AND CONCLUSIONS

The major blockage to the implementation of the marketing concept is the firm's inability or unwillingness to coordinate all marketing and nonmarketing activities. A nonsystematic approach to strategic marketing encourages suboptimization especially with regard to achievement of the firm's overall objectives.

Personal selling is an important but single unit in a massive system of systems which takes on the following schematic configuration: personal-selling system→promotional system→marketing system→corporate system→business system→social system. The promotional system is the firm's communication vehicle and serves as the primary interface with the marketplace and society. Advertising and personal selling, as the primary promotional tools, are always interdependent and quite often interchangeable. This substitutability complicates the task of determining the ideal promotional mix, which in turn is related to a multitude of interacting variables and parameters including the specific promotional needs of the firm at a given point in time.

Selling, more so than advertising, is perceived as offensive to society, since the former is less controllable by management. Responsiveness to the needs of sales employees, customers, competitors, suppliers, regulatory bodies, educators, and society in general is often incompatible with the firm's revenue and profit objectives. Accordingly, numerous strategic and tactical trade-offs are considered when sales-management procedures are examined in subsequent chapters.

NOTES

1. Martin L. Bell, *Marketing—Concepts and Strategy* (Boston: Houghton Mifflin, 1972), pp. 6–7.

2. This definition has been adopted with a minor modification from William J. Stanton and Richard H. Buskirk, *Management of the Sales Force* (Homewood, Ill.: R. D. Irwin, 1974), p. 4.

3. Suboptimization is discussed in detail in Edward M. Smith, "Systems Concepts and the Development of Marketing Strategies," *Southern Journal of Business* 5 (January 1970): 58–65 and David W. Miller and Martin K. Starr, *Executive Decisions and Operations Research* (Englewood Cliffs, N.J.: Prentice-Hall, 1965), pp. 40–53.

4. Much of this section was developed from Smith, op. cit., pp. 58–65 and Marvin A. Jolson and Richard T. Hise, *Quantitative Techniques for Marketing Decisions* (New York: Macmillan, 1973), pp. 6–8.

5. Frederick D. Sturdivant et al., *Managerial Analysis in Marketing* (Glenview, Ill.: Scott, Foresman, 1970), p. 392.

6. Philip Kotler, *Marketing Management—Analysis, Planning, and Control* (Englewood Cliffs, N.J.: Prentice-Hall, 1972), p. 646.

7. Bell, *Marketing—Concepts*, p. 765.

8. James F. Engel, Hugh G. Wales, and Martin R. Warshaw, *Promotional Strategy* (Homewood, Ill.: R. D. Irwin, 1971), p. 3.

9. *Marketing Definitions: A Glossary of Marketing Terms* (Chicago: American Marketing Association, 1960), p. 16.

10. Kotler, *Marketing Management*, p. 649.

11. Marvin A. Jolson, "Standardizing the Personal Selling Process," *Marquette Business Review* 18 (Spring 1974): 16–17.

12. Harold C. Cash and W. J. E. Crissy, "Comparison of Advertising and Selling," *The Salesman's Role in Marketing, The Psychology of Selling* 12 (1965): 56–75.

13. Sturdivant et al., *Managerial*, pp. 398–99 and Marvin A. Jolson, "The Underestimated Potential of the Canned Sales Presentation," *Journal of Marketing* 39 (January 1975): 77.

14. Cash and Crissy, *Comparison*, pp. 59–61.

15. Marvin A. Jolson, "How Important is Sales Force Size?" *Business Studies* 10 (Spring 1971): 31–40.

16. Richard Caves, *American Industry: Structure, Conduct, Performance* (Englewood Cliffs, N.J.: Prentice-Hall, 1967), pp. 110–111.

17. Kotler, *Marketing Management*, p. 651.

18. Russell H. Colley, "Defining Advertising Goals," in *Defining Advertising Goals for Measured Advertising Results* (New York: Association of National Advertisers, 1961), pp. 49–60.

19. Ibid.

20. Much of the thinking in this section was contributed by Stewart H. Rewoldt, James D. Scott, and Martin R. Warshaw, *Introduction to Marketing Management* (Homewood, Ill.: R. D. Irwin, 1973), pp. 271–72, 478.

21. Sturdivant et al., *Managerial,* pp. 380–82.

22. Gerald S. Albaum, "Horizontal Information Flow: An Exploratory Study," *Journal of the Academy of Management* 12 (March 1964): 21–33.

23. This thought is developed in Rolph E. Anderson and Marvin A. Jolson, "Consumer Expectations and the Communications Gap," *Business Horizons* 16 (April 1973): 12–13.

24. Leonard L. Berry, "Marketing Challenges in the Age of People," *MSU Business Topics* 20 (Winter 1972): 7–13; Leslie M. Dawson, "The Human Concept: New Philosophy for Business," *Business Horizons* 12 (December 1969): 29–38; Laurence P. Feldman, "Societal Adaption: A New Challenge for Marketing," *Journal of Marketing* 35 (July 1971): 54–60.

25. Etienne Cracco and Jacques Rostenne, "The Socio-Ecological Product," *MSU Business Topics* 19 (Summer 1971): 27–34.

26. Carl Rieser, "The Salesman Isn't Dead—He's Different," *Fortune* 66 (November 1962): 124–27.

27. Patrick J. Robinson and Bent Stidsen, *Personal Selling in a Modern Perspective* (Boston: Allyn & Bacon, 1967), p. xi; Marvin A. Jolson, "Salesman's Career Cycle," *Journal of Marketing* 38 (July 1974): 41.

QUESTIONS FOR DISCUSSION AND REVIEW

1. Do you think the advent of the marketing-concept philosophy of management has had a noticeable impact on the perceived prestige of the sales manager's job?

2. Defend or oppose the following statement: "A business should attempt to optimize its situation with regard to each specific objective as long as it does not affect adversely its situation with regard to any other objective."

3. In a recent study (see note 11), the total personal-selling task of life insurance companies was allocated to the five promotional functions as follows:

Prospecting	31%
Contacting	20%
Stimulating	6%
Closing	12%
Retaining	24%

Other (e.g., estate planning, proposal preparation, claims handling)	7%
Total	100%

a. Estimate the selling-task allocation for (1) distributors of gift items to specialty shops, (2) department stores, and (3) manufacturers of industrial packaging materials.

b. Support your estimated allocations and also those of insurance companies.

4. Are personal selling and advertising both interdependent and interchangeable in the following firms?
   a. A wholesale liquor distributor
   b. IBM
   c. Encyclopaedia Britannica, Inc.
   d. A marketer of management seminars to industry
   e. The publisher of this book
   f. The Baltimore Oriole baseball club

5. The joint impact of both advertising and selling input is illustrated by the firm whose monthly profits could be represented by the relationship:

$$\pi = 16A - 2A^2 - 10 - 4\,S^2 + 24S - 4AS$$

where A = ad expenditures in thousands of dollars

S = number of sales offices

π = profit in thousands of dollars

a. What is the maximum profit available to the firm? (ans: $30,000)

b. Suppose the firm arbitrarily opened four sales offices? How large an advertising expenditure would be necessary for the firm to at least break even? (ans: The firm would suffer a loss regardless of the level of advertising.)

c. How do you explain the answer to part b?
   (Note:The reader will find differential calculus helpful in solving this problem.)

6. Contact the chief marketing manager of three firms. Investigate the methods used by management to determine the total promotional budget and the proportion of the budget allocated to each element in the promotional mix. Criticize the methods used by each firm.

7. Suppose direct-to-home selling was banned. Suggest the promotional approach that should be employed by each of the following firms:
   a. Equitable Life Insurance Company
   b. Encyclopaedia Britannica
   c. Electrolux
   d. Avon

8. How can management encourage, persuade, or compel sales-force mem-   25
bers to exercise more fully their responsibilities to potential purchasers,
other firms, the community, and society?

Case 1.1 Bunky McFarland Appliance Manufacturing Company

Acquainting Employees with the Hierarchy of Business Systems

Lawrence Gomez is the newly appointed marketing vice-president of the above medium-sized producer of electric mixers, hair dryers, dishwashers, and electric fans. The findings of a study based on limited research disclose that as perceived by department-store buyers the firm has a high-quality product and unique advertising materials and provides suitable margins; but it is also perceived as being weak in providing merchandising assistance and necessary postsale services, as well as being overly aggressive, tardy in deliveries, and complacent.

During his investigation of the source of the above image, Gomez discovers that the six regional sales managers serving under him are of the opinion that marketing and selling are synonymous terms. He decides to write these managers a letter which will not only clear up the selling–marketing misunderstanding but will also supply them with some sophistication in understanding the roles of marketing and selling in the total system of business action. He feels his letter should include and demonstrate the interrelationships of the following:

Noncontrollables in the general environment

Customer needs and competitive activities

Elements of the marketing mix

Internal noncontrollable areas

Broad objectives of the firm

Marketing and sales goals

Gomez wants to take an approach that is decision oriented, so that his managers can be assisted in conceptualizing the totality of the marketing problem, the interaction of the above components, and the sequence in which they should be considered prior to formulating sales-management strategies.

1. Are the research findings related to the marketing/selling opinions of the managers?
2. Should Gomez be concerned about the opinions of the managers?
3. Do you think the letter should be written? If not, suggest an alternate approach.
4. Write the proposed letter or provide the details of the alternative approach.

Case 1.2 Surveillance Systems, Inc.

Determining the Optimal Promotional Mix for a New Product

In January 1975, Eric McNair started a burglar-alarm company in Pennsylvania with distribution and installation aimed at providing security measures for small retailers. The company leased conventional hardwire systems, including audible (bell and/or siren) and silent (direct-to-police) responses.

By January 1976, the business was growing at an accelerating rate. The firm had eight salespeople and was collecting an average of $25 per month from each of 320 accounts.

However, a major problem existed because as the number of clients increased, the required number of service calls also increased. McNair and his people had little knowledge of technical matters and electrical techniques, and they had considerable difficulty in hiring and retaining capable servicemen.

He was now interested in expanding his operation to other states via the franchising route. But he didn't feel conventional burglar alarms were unique enough for franchising. Also, he felt that perceived or actual servicing needs would be harmful to the effective recruitment and retention of franchised distributors.

Shoplifting and employee theft had become major sources of store shrinkage in early 1976. This convinced McNair to develop a simulated closed-circuit TV camera which was impossible to distinguish from a live camera. Even though the simulated camera could take no pictures, it was very real looking because of its perpetually flickering red light, its video cable, its heat vents, and the realism of its imitation lens.

Although McNair was mesmerized by his unique looking, low-cost camera, which would require little or no servicing, he wondered about its acceptance by retailers throughout the country. In particular, he was concerned about the appropriate promotional mix that should be employed by his company in launching the product in seven eastern states. However, he was willing to spend up to $5,000 for preliminary research information.

QUESTIONS AND ASSIGNMENTS

1. Do you think that McNair was an advocate of the marketing-concept philosophy?
2. Design a complete research project including the methodology, questionnaire, and method of analysis which would examine the proportion of prospective clients (franchisees and retailers) on each level of the marketing communications spectrum.
3. Assume that most retailers and prospective franchisees are found to be at a low level of awareness and comprehension with regard to the simulated camera. Given this finding, make specific suggestions as to the desired proportion of each element in the promotional mix of Surveillance Systems Inc. Further break down the proposed advertising and personal-selling components into specific subelements, showing the intended purpose of each.

2

Classification of the Activities of Sales Personnel

The systems approach of the previous chapter suggests that the goals of a firm's personal-selling unit form one terminal point on a continuum of goals that stretches from the goals of society to the goals of personal selling. Such a hierarchy, with typical goals inserted for each entity in the system, is illustrated by the model of Figure 2.1.

The adoption and implementation of the societal marketing concept demands that selling goals be subordinated to many other goals of business and society. As stated by one author, the primary responsibility of sales management is to plan and develop goals that will coincide with the broad goals both of top management and of those in the operating and general environments.[1] These broad duties fall under the umbrella of *sales administration* and include such planning and organizational activities as the determination of sales potentials, forecasts, and budgets, and the coordination of sales resources to correspond with planned outputs. Also included are selling research, communication with other company units, and the innovative contributions required to keep the selling activities abreast with internal and external dynamics.

Sales-force management is the means by which the plans of sales administration are carried out, and it consists of recruitment, selection, indoctrination, training, compensation, supervision, motivation, and evaluation of the field sales force. Back as far as 1960, writers indicated that many sales managers have done a better job of managing their sales force than they have of executing their sales-administration responsibilities.[2] The author's experiences as a consultant to various sales organizations indicates that the same still holds true.

Historically, sales managers at local or regional levels have been willing to delegate many activities of sales planning and organizing to home-office executives including policy-making officials, administrative planners, accountants, and marketing and financial specialists. Yet, effectiveness in implementing field-related sales-management actions depends on the field manager's understanding of corporate marketing and sales planning and of his own role in the planning sequence. Accordingly, even though this text devotes considerably more space to sales-force management than to sales ad-

Figure 2.1 The selling unit's view of the hierarchy of goals

ministration, many of the latter duties will receive substantial emphasis.

This chapter introduces the various areas of planning and manpower duties for both the home office and field sales managers. These are treated in more detail in later chapters. In addition, this chapter provides an in-depth classification of selling jobs so as to establish a needed framework for understanding the diverse activities performed by sales-management personnel.

MAJOR DUTIES OF SALES ADMINISTRATION

Market and Sales Potentials

The sales-planning process and goal development begin when the sales manager poses two questions: What is the maximum dollar sales volume available to all sellers of a particular product in a given time frame? What is the maximum dollar sales volume available to the firm in the same time frame? The answer to the first question is the product's *market potential*. The answer to the second question is the firm's *sales potential* for that product.

It is apparent that most industries rarely develop the market potential fully and that few firms realize their sales potential. However, most industries and firms are constantly striving for growth. When the economy is healthy, market potential is expanding and the market pie grows in size. Under such circumstances, there is enough for everyone and each firm's earnings per share are rising with the usual accompanying rise in share prices. Accordingly, marketers may be only mildly concerned with acquiring a larger proportion (market share) of the growing pie.

However, when growth slows down or the size of the pie shrinks, market share increases in importance, since each firm seeks a larger proportionate share of a smaller pie. In this situation sales planning for share of market calls for a stricter evaluation of competitive strategies, including the proselytizing of the competitor's key salespeople (to be discussed in Chapter 8) and dual distribution policies (competition with the seller's customers).

Sales Forecasts

Once the sales potential has been determined, and actual sales figures during earlier periods have been compared with perceived sales potential for those periods, the firm is ready to forecast sales for the forthcoming periods. This comparison will measure the firm's propensity to be optimistic or pessimistic. The sales forecast will in most cases be less than the sales potential for many reasons including the suspicion of limited production capacity; the fear of losing key sales-force members; potential shortages of product; likely difficulties with suppliers; conflicts with profit objectives, which might call for the discontinuation of the cultivation of smaller accounts; and other trade-offs between sales volume and profitability. Ideally, the sales forecaster should consider past, present, and future pricing of the firm's products, since dollar sales volume is made up of price and the number of units of product sold.

This is an especially ticklish problem for the forecaster when price-elasticity information is not readily available and he must guess the degree of customer sensitivity to price changes. A poor estimate of this response to price could result in a completely inaccurate forecast.

Sales Budgets

After the forecast in dollars and cents has been completed, the fixed and variable costs required to obtain the forecast may be determined. The budget, therefore, is the plan that assigns and authorizes the costs or expenses that are perceived as being required to generate the forecasted sales level.

The budget planner may or may not be the same person who spearheads the forecasting function. The functions are strongly interrelated since lowered costs may allow for lower prices, which in turn will increase revenues in an elastic market. But cost determination is highly dependent on forecasted sales units. This is because the spreading of fixed costs among the total units sold will help to determine fixed costs per unit. Thus, one should know unit costs before determining price. Price determines units sold, and units sold determine unit cost. This complex interdependency whereby one does not know where to start helps to explain why forecasting and budgeting should be almost simultaneous activities. Both are discussed in detail in Chapter 4.

Sales Territories and Manpower

A firm may view its market as consisting of all buying units in large or small areas such as the world, the United States, New England, the state of California, the northwestern suburbs of Chicago, and postal zip code 21204 in Baltimore. When the firm's market is so large, in terms of geography or numbers of prospects or diversity of types of prospects, that it cannot be managed efficiently as a single entity, it is advisable to divide the market into a number of submarkets or territories.

The division of the entire heterogeneous market into a series of relatively homogeneous units is a process of segmentation in that each submarket is composed of potential customers who have certain common characteristics. These characteristics may relate to geography, type of prospect, size of customer, customer habits and requests, or any other factor that will facilitate management's task in matching selling efforts with selling opportunities.

Territories may be assigned to regional managers, franchisees, distributors, sales managers, etc., who will then further subdivide their territories for assignment to submanagers and eventually to salesmen. Each territory or subterritory will have its own measured sales potential, forecast, and budget. In fact, the company's sales potential, forecast, and budget are computed by summing the sales potentials, forecasts, and budgets of all territories and subterritories. In general, the larger the sales potential of a territory, the larger the number of salesmen that will be assigned to the territory. In many organizations the reverse is true in that territory A may have less potential than territory B at one point in time. However, due to superior management, sales manager A may surpass sales manager B in developing a sales force of a size and quality that increases the potential of territory A relative to B. Territories, sales force size, and quotas are the subjects of Chapter 5.

Quotas

A quota is the performance goal that is assigned by management to each selling unit, usually the salesman, to aid in directing and controlling sales operations. Usually, the quota is expressed in terms of sales dollars or units, although it can take other forms.

The method of assigning quotas can be completely arbitrary, or it can be tied to a territorial estimate such as sales potential. In most cases, the summation of quotas for all sales personnel in a territory will exceed the territorial forecast. This is an aid in meeting forecasts even when many salespeople in a territory fail to fulfill their individually assigned quotas.

Some managers set quotas which are difficult to reach and which they realize will be fulfilled by few. These managers view quotas as motivators and incentive-producing instruments that compel those with low levels of aspiration to put forth special efforts. Another viewpoint is that quotas should be quite conservative and within the grasp of everyone. This approach is designed to prevent

in the field sales organization with periodic assistance from the sales-training manager and field-liaison staff. It is demonstrated in future chapters that many companies deviate sharply from the structure shown in this figure. However, the hypothetical network should serve as a useful reference to readers when administrative and field activities are discussed.

Figure 2.2 Marketing and sales organization reflecting the marketing-concept philosophy

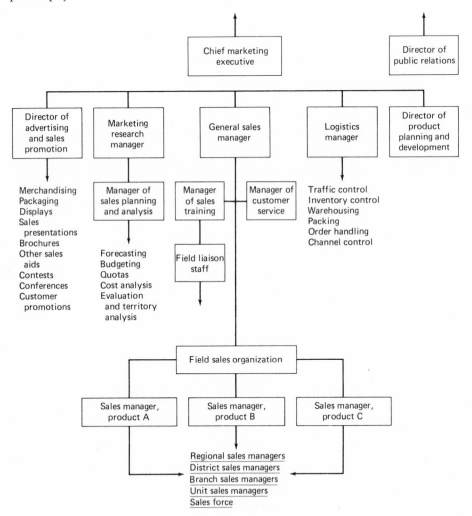

2. Classification of the Activities of Sales Personnel

Absence of the Marketing Concept

It would be naive to assume, even though the marketing concept is currently popular, that the organizational design of Figure 2.2 is predominant. Marketing and sales activities often fall under the domain of nonmarketing executives. Product planning and development is frequently assigned to the production manager, as are marketing research and logistics. Forecasting and budgeting are sometimes functions of the financial manager. In some firms, the recruitment, selection, and training of sales personnel are performed by the personnel department. There are still numerous cases where the chief marketing executive is the sales manager who in turn is responsible for advertising, sales promotion, marketing research, and most of the logistics functions.

Small versus Large Firms

It is interesting to note that some of America's largest firms condone highly fragmented marketing and selling activities while certain relatively small companies conform almost exactly to the highly coordinated marketing orientation suggested by the organization chart of Figure 2.2. An example of the latter is the Doughtie Food Company of Portsmouth, Virginia, whose net sales for 1975 were $21 million. They proudly promote their company slogan, POCOMO, meaning people oriented, customer oriented, and market oriented. Observers who are familiar with the Doughtie operation conclude that POCOMO is more than an acronym; it's a fully executed plan of action.

CLASSIFICATION OF SELLING JOBS

It is convenient for marketing authors to illustrate principles and general models by referring to the organizations of manufacturers or producers. This author attempts to be more versatile. Hopefully, as one studies Figure 2.2, one will have little difficulty in extrapolating to one's own organization or to that of a wholesaler, vending operator, fund raiser, medical supply distributor, or even to a "mom and pop" firm that employs only five salesmen. Marketing and selling organizations vary with the type of selling effort and the required management of that effort. Personal selling is an activity of great diversity. Thus a constructive analysis of the tasks of sales management requires some introduction to the numerous types of selling.

At least one-hundred methods of differentiating among sales jobs have been uncovered by the author. The more popular classifications are by (1) type of product sold, (2) type of employer represented, (3) type of prospect contacted, and (4) level of creative selling required. These are outlined below along with a brief identification of several others. The list is surely not exhaustive, and some factors appear in more than one classification.

I. Type of product or service sold
   A. Intangible service [7]
      1. For organizations
         a. Providing pure intangibles, e.g., security, franchising
         b. Providing added value to a tangible, e.g., consultation, advertising
         c. Making available a tangible, e.g., transportation, architectural design, contractual research and development
      2. For household consumers
         a. Providing pure intangibles, e.g., employment, travel, entertainment
         b. Providing added value to a tangible, e.g., insurance, repairs
         c. Making available a tangible, e.g., automatic vending, mortgages
   B. Tangible goods
      1. For organizations
         a. Infrequently purchased, e.g., computers, heavy machinery
         b. Rapidly consumed, e.g., light bulbs, office supplies
         c. For resale
      2. For household consumers
         a. Infrequently purchased
            (1) Real estate
            (2) Durables, e.g., washing machines, stereo systems
         b. Rapidly consumed, e.g., food, clothing

II. Type of employer and representative
   A. Manufacturer's or producer's salesmen
      1. Captive sales-force member
      2. Representative or agent
      3. Merchandising person, e.g., detail, missionary—see IV, D

2. Classification of the Activities of Sales Personnel

B. Wholesaler's salesman
C. Retail salesman
1. In-store
2. Route, e.g., for milk, bread, fuel oil
3. Direct-to-home, e.g., for encyclopedias, vacuum cleaners, etc.
D. Seller of professional services [8]
1. Equipment services: all services associated with installation, running, maintenance and repair of plant, accessories, and operating equipment, e.g., tools, instruments, furnishings, fittings
2. Facilitating services: all services that facilitate the productive operations of organizations, including finance, storage, transportation, promotion, insurance
3. Advisory and consultative services: all services providing general or specific technical expertise and intelligence, including advise on research, education, organization, marketing and the use and acquisition of resources

III. Type of prospect contacted
A. Industrial consumer
B. Organizational (nonindustrial) consumer
C. Reseller
1. Producer
2. Wholesaler
3. Retailer
a. In-store
b. Direct-to-home
c. Mail-order
d. Automatic merchandisers
D. Household consumers
1. In-store shoppers
2. In-home shoppers
a. By mail
b. From direct salesmen
c. By telephone

IV. Required creativity level and responsibilities [9]
A. Obtaining of new business, primarily from new customers
1. Creativity in presentation and/or demonstration of products or services
a. Direct-to-household items

      b. Direct-to-organizational consumers (e.g., for calculators, copying machines)

   2. Political, indirect, or "back-door" selling of big-ticket items with no truly competitive features; instead of selling product, salesman primarily sells himself as being uniquely capable of solving buyer's problem (e.g., for flour to a bakery, cement to a builder)

B. Technical selling, primarily for increasing business from present customers by providing technical assistance

   1. Major emphasis on salesperson's technical knowledge (e.g., engineering salesman who is primarily a consultant)

   2. Presentations to several people most of whom cannot say *yes* but all of whom can say *no* (e.g., in sale of components to an OEM account where key person may make buying decision jointly with engineering, research, production, and purchasing personnel)

C. Trade selling, primarily for increasing business from present customers by providing promotional and merchandising assistance; salesman largely outside order taker but also introduces new lines and expedites customer service (e.g., by deliveries, inventory control, displays, merchandising information); "hard sell" rarely if ever present (e.g., in sales to retailers, parts distributors)

D. Missionary selling, primarily for increasing business from present customers by providing personal selling assistance; salesman helps train and educate his customer's sales force or actual user (e.g., as with distiller's missionary man or medical detailer)

E. In-store selling

F. Route selling

V. Other criteria for comparing selling jobs

  A. Requirements for salespeople

   1. Degree of responsibility for actual transactions

   2. Degree of problem solving involved

   3. Number and complexity of nonselling duties

   4. Travel requirements and irregularity of hours

   5. Total time spent performing actual selling functions

   6. Amount and kind of education required

B. Company policies and parameters
  1. Method of compensating salesmen
  2. Company-generated leads versus self-generated leads
  3. Size of employing company
C. Selling Situation
  1. Typical selling results
     a. Conversion ratio (average proportion of sales presentations that result in orders)
     b. Size of average order
  2. Customer and market
     a. Reload versus one-time selling situations
     b. Relative positions of product and brand in marketing communications spectrum (proportion of buying prospects at levels of unawareness, awareness, comprehension, conviction, and action)
     c. Range and level of sophistication of persons called upon
     d. Where transactions occur
     e. Size of territory
D. Product and service features
  1. Nature and width of product line [10]
  2. New versus used products

Criticism of Selling Categories

Although groupings such as the above are acceptable, their originators are subjected to a number of challenges. For example, a number of authorities reject McMurry's ranking of sales jobs in terms of complexity, difficulty, and required creativity (see IV). Is it true, as he maintains, that obtaining new business is more difficult than providing technical assistance to industrial customers?

Few salesmen, including many who work in retail stores, see themselves as "order takers." Such a viewpoint is supported as one examines O'Shaughnessey's sophisticated application of the interpersonal influence process to retail selling.[11] On the other hand, some authors feel that department-store clerks should not be called salespeople because they do no creative selling. The same authors infer that it is silly to identify individuals who set up store displays as salesmen.[12] The argument is that the prestige of selling is going down because increasing numbers of people are being called salesmen when they have no legitimate claim to the title.

One authority argues that the primary responsibility of a salesperson is either to "increase business from present customers" or to "obtain business from new customers," but not both.[13] Yet a panel of sales executives at a 1975 Washington, D.C., conference winced at the thought that any sales force in any company would not be simultaneously concerned with both developing new customers and serving present ones. There are even arguments that no products are totally intangible in all circumstances, including services.[14] Despite strong arguments to the contrary, there are those who claim that required selling creativity is unrelated to product tangibility.

Impact of Variety in Selling Jobs

Chapter 3 suggests that the perceived prestige of a particular selling job is significantly related to the job's position in one or more of the above classes. Of more importance is the impact of the classifications upon sales-management requirements.

It was already mentioned (and Chapter 8 emphasizes) that prospective sales employees, especially those who have never sold before, have certain preconceived notions about job openings in selling. In general, applicants do not want to represent retailers, sell directly to households, travel, work evenings and weekends, be compensated through commissions only, work without company-supplied inquiries, or subject themselves to a substantial proportion of rejections.

When these perceived negatives are unavoidable, the burdens of recruiting, training, supervising, and motivating are increased, and sales managers who regard each obstacle as a challenge are required. The recruiter may prefer, for example, to withhold mention of the undesirable job requirements by using blind rather than full-disclosure help-wanted ads to attract applicants. Such a tactic will require an interviewer who is capable of composing a persuasive face-to-face presentation that will inform the applicant of the job requirements in both a logical and psychological sequence that will most likely achieve the desired effect.

The firm's mode of prospecting offers an interesting opportunity to examine another job classification and its impact upon the salesman, company tactics, and selling costs. Ask the sales recruit whether he would prefer to contact prospects on a cold canvassing basis or in response to voluntary inquiries, i.e., direct responses from national magazine ads or mail circularization. The latter method would be the overwhelming favorite.

But how much do qualified leads cost? Considering the costs of a direct-mail circular and the attendant costs of stamps, addressing, lists, stuffing, and mailing, the firm would be fortunate to put 1,000 lead-getting circulars in the mail for $100. If the rate of return is 2 percent, each lead would cost $5. If 1 out of 6 leads converts into a sale, then a promotional cost of $30 per sale must be added to the firm's sales-compensation payout. If the firm is to foot this cost, the commission rate will normally be affected. Moreover, careful supervision by management will be required to assure that the salesman does not "cherry pick" prospects on the phone or by mail since leads are free. For this reason, some firms sell leads to their salesmen with resultant improved rates of lead conversions and recovered costs by the firm. Obviously, some salesmen do not approve of this policy.

The efficiency of cold canvassing thus prevails for the hard-nosed salesman who develops an insensitivity to rebuffs or possesses a unique talent for cold calls. Such a person may look down on "lead hounds" as addicts who need a fix in the form of a lead. Clearly, however, a sales organization that stresses cold canvass prospecting demands leadership which differs considerably from that of a firm that supplies a large number of qualified inquiries to its sales force.

Classification by Promotional Activities

The previous discussion of prospecting suggests a typology of sales jobs which appropriately fits at the end of this section since it is a composite of many of the classification schemes already discussed. As noted in Chapter 1, in some firms (e.g., life insurance companies) most of the five promotional steps—prospecting, contacting, stimulating, closing, and retaining—are handled by salesmen. In other firms (e.g., department stores) few if any of these are assigned to salespeople. Thus a selling job could be classified in terms of what proportion of each promotional function is to be performed by a given salesperson.

Not so long ago, a group of major marketers of over-the-counter pharmaceutical products held a conference to discuss the overall performance of their sales representatives. The general opinion was that salesmen did very little to find prospects since their company supplied them with a list of established drugstore accounts when they began employment. The salesman actively contacted customers on a regular basis but did little to stimulate desire, since national advertising by the producer and local store ads created demand for the product. He did little to close sales, since no orders would be placed if the store shelves weren't half empty. Finally, since the salesman was quite likeable and cooperative, providing such services as counting inventories, straightening out displays, and expediting deliveries, it was concluded that he contributed somewhat to retaining the customer. However, it was more than likely that the drugstores would continue to buy the product with or without the salesman because a huge proportion of the store's customers preferred or insisted on the brand.

Although the logic of the conclusion is reasonable, this author would not agree or infer that drug-supply salesmen are inferior to people selling other products. The cited classification and example support the contention that competence in one type of selling does not guarantee equal competence in another.

> Success as an inside, route, or trade sales person does not necessarily qualify a person to engage in creative selling, or vice versa. The significance of all this is that each type of sales work requires its own unique combination of traits, attributes, and qualities in its practitioner. Hence, if a sales manager is to establish a productive sales force, his first and most fundamental step is to ascertain the category of sales to be undertaken and to prepare precise specifications covering the qualities the incumbents will need to assure success.[15]

INTERACTION BETWEEN SALESPEOPLE AND PROSPECTS

Seemingly, the five promotional tasks performed by salespeople have remained unchanged since time immemorial. Yet, since the arrival of the marketing concept, the salesperson has been described as being different—"a person with a softer touch and greater breadth, a new kind of person to do a new, more significant kind of job."[16]

Are Salespeople Different Now?

The new salesperson, supposedly, is one who introduces innovations to the market, conveys information to prospects, facilitates the consumption process, acts as an intelligence agent, helps solve customers' problems, carries feedback information to management, and manages a market area. Are these really new tasks or just a fashionable way of describing the old-hat functions of finding prospects, contacting them, stimulating them, closing sales, and retaining customers?

A number of authorities view much of the dialogue about the new, different salesperson as expository fashionableness. One marketing professor reacted rather strongly to certain textbook lists of the purposes of salesmen:

> I have my students take a big red pencil and under *purpose of salesmen* I have them write in "Get an Order—then if there is time—Do All Those

other Things"—My God—how far up in the tower can you get? Recessions like the one we're in now are caused by a lack of orders. Business doesn't go slack, demand does. If an epitaph is ever needed for American business, I'd suggest "they forgot to sell." [17]

Techniques Used by Salespeople

While terminology will vary from firm to firm, Figure 2.3 presents a reasonably complete summary of the major techniques used by field sales-force members. Although this is not a text on salesmanship, the list of techniques is important to the reader since it indicates what salesmen do and what field sales managers must get done.

A detailed description of every technique in the list is beyond the scope of this text. Many items appear in later chapters since they are directly related to the manager's task of developing the knowledge, skills, and attitudes that keep the sales force selling. Included in Figure 2.3 are the so-called new tasks of the salesperson and also the old tasks, which are as prevalent today as they were yesterday.

Total System Reliability

Let us assume that a distributor of duplicating equipment to business offices depends on the sales force to *find* a large proportion of territorial prospects by telephone solicitation and referrals from satisfied customers. Sales-force visits represent the only form of company *contact* with prospective customers. The firm does no advertising, so demand is *stimulated* largely by sales presentations. Salesmen *close* sales without assistance from management. Finally, salesmen are expected to supply continued instruction to the customer's staff and, if necessary, to provide entertainment and other social contact.

One of the company salesmen, let us call him Conrad Nave, does a very poor job of finding prospects. However, once he acquires a prospect's name, he visits him promptly, delivers an excellent sales presentation, and closes a high proportion of sales after his demonstrations. His customers like him very much, especially since he visits them often after the equipment has been delivered to make sure the employees know how to operate it.

Nave is one of the most likeable people in his organization and is always encouraging new salespeople and helping his peers improve their sales demonstrations. At the same time, Nave is looking around for another job since his commissions do not provide him with adequate earnings.

Finding prospects
   Cold canvass
   Telephone solicitation
   Referrals from customers and other sources
   Responses to mass-media advertising
   Responses to direct mail or circulars passed out
   Follow-up of will-call letters [a]
   Past call-backs
   Voluntary inquiries
   Outside bird dogs [b]
   Recommendations by suppliers
   Contacting customers who have already purchased another company
      product
   Trade shows and exhibits
   Specialty-advertising responses (matchboxes, pens, calendars)
   "Take-one" rack responses
   Friends and associates

Contacting prospects
   Unsolicited visit
   Announced periodic visit
   Visit following telephone appointment
   Visit following will-call letter
   Visit by prospect to salesman's place of business on voluntary, invited, or
      ad-response basis

Stimulating desire for ownership
   Personal sales presentation and demonstration
      Problem solving
      Demonstration of benefits
      Persuasion
   Preconditioning literature and materials
   Free-trial approach
   Sales presentation by telephone

Closing sales
   Demonstration of "now" need
   Price inducements
   Product-scarcity approach
   Two-man close [c]
   Trial order
   Selling oneself
   High pressure and gimmicks

Retaining customers
   Posttransactional service
   Supplying market intelligence
   Warmth and social contacts
   Return and exchange privileges
   Continuous customer contact

[a] An unsolicited announcement that salesman will call at some future date. Promotional literature may or may not be included.

[b] Outside canvasser or lead-getting organization paid to locate prospects for the firm.

[c] A salesman who is unable to close an order due to inexperience or a perceived personality conflict can solicit the aid of an associate or supervisor.

Figure 2.3 Major techniques used by salespeople to accomplish the five promotional tasks

The branch sales manager recognizes that Nave is strong in every task except prospecting. Nave hates telephone solicitation, refuses to use cold canvass, and acquires only a small number of prospects through referrals. It is not the company's policy to employ bird dogs (see Figure 2.3), and so the very popular Conrad Nave will soon be working elsewhere. How can this salesman's failure be explained?

The answer lies in the fact that within the selling system, a salesman's weakness in performing a single basic sales task can overwhelm his strengths in performing all other selling tasks. Reynolds discovered this when he applied Lusser's product law of reliabilities (developed during experimentation with the V-1 missile) to sales-force management.[18] Lusser's formula reads

$$R_{system} = R_1 R_2 R_3 \ . \ . \ . \ R_N$$

It indicates (1) that total system reliability is the product rather than the average of the reliabilities of the component parts; (2) the reliability of the individual components must be higher than the system reliability; and (3) the near or total failure of one component will result in a similar fate for the system.

In the case of Conrad Nave, if management were to quantify his performance in each of his five major tasks, his low rating in the prospecting function is predictive of his eventual failure with his firm. This does not mean, however, that he would fail in a firm that supplied prospects or used someone other than Nave to perform the prospecting task.

SUMMARY AND CONCLUSIONS

The functions of sales executives include administrative planning and field management. The former duties call for the determination of market and sales potentials, sales forecasts, sales budgets, territories, and quotas. Field-management responsibilities are largely concerned with salespeople and subordinate field managers and include sales-force recruitment, selection, training, compensation, supervision, stimulation, and evaluation.

Selling positions may be classified under various categories, including type of product sold, type of employer represented, type of prospect contacted, and required creativity level. These classifications convey certain messages to both prospective and incumbent salespeople. When these messages suggest negative perceptions of job duties and rewards, the impact upon management's recruitment and retention of salespeople is substantial.

The difficulty of the sales-management job is strongly related to the methods used by the firm's sales force in accomplishing the five promotional tasks—finding, contacting, stimulating, closing, and retaining. A salesman's total effectiveness can be measured by determining mathematically the product of his effectiveness in each of his tasks. Therefore, a salesman's weakness in performing any single task can be sufficient to outweigh his strengths in other areas of performance.

NOTES

1. Thomas R. Wotruba, *Sales Management: Planning, Accomplishment, and Evaluation* (New York: Holt, Rinehart, Winston, 1971), p. 12.

2. Eugene J. Kelley and William Lazer, "Basic Duties of the Modern Sales Department," *Industrial Marketing* XLV (April 1960): 68–83.

3. Marvin A. Jolson, "Minimum Wage Laws: A New Challenge for Sales Administrators," *Personnel Journal* 52 (April 1973): 279–87.

4. Gerhard W. Ditz, "Status Problems of the Salesman," *MSU Business Topics* 15 (Winter 1967): 68–80.

5. Robert N. McMurry, *How to Recruit, Select and Place Salesmen* (Chicago: The Dartnell Corp., 1964), p. 99.

6. Marvin A. Jolson, "The Salesman's Career Cycle," *Journal of Marketing* 38 (July 1974): 44.

7. For an excellent discussion of degree of tangibility see Aubrey Wilson, *The Marketing of Professional Services* (New York: McGraw-Hill, 1972), p. 8.

8. Ibid., pp. 2–3.

9. McMurry, *How to Recruit*, pp. 4–5.

10. Items 7 through 18 on this list were supplied by W. J. E. Crissy and Robert M. Kaplan, *Salesmanship: The Personal Force in Marketing* (New York: Wiley, 1969), pp. 31–60.

11. John O'Shaughnessy, "Selling as an Interpersonal Influence Process," *Journal of Retailing* 47 (Winter 1971–72): 32–46.

12. F. William Howton and Bernard Rosenberg, "The Salesman: Ideology and Self-imagery in a Prototypic Occupation," *Social Research* 32 (Autumn 1965): 277–29.

13. Derek A. Newton, *Sales Force Performance and Turnover* (Cambridge Mass.: Marketing Science Institute, 1968), p. 119.

14. Wilson, *Marketing*, p. 7.

15. McMurry, *How to Recruit*, p. 7.

16. Carl Rieser, "The Salesman Isn't Dead—He's Different," *Fortune* 66 (November 1966): 124.

17. Herbert J. Mossien, "I'm Too Busy Getting Orders, The Hell with Planning!" paper presented to American Marketing Association International Conference, New York, April 5, 1972, p. 3.

18. William H. Reynolds, "The Fail-Safe Salesman," *Business Horizons* 9 (Summer 1966): 19–26.

QUESTIONS FOR DISCUSSION AND REVIEW

1. Figure 2.1 illustrates a hierarchy of goals as viewed by the sales manager. How do you think the sales manager is informed of the goals of other units in the system?

2. Select any five sales organizations whose products and methods of selling are totally dissimilar. Rank these firms in order of the inherent difficulty in measuring or estimating sales potential for each.

3. It has been suggested that one should not restrict himself to a geographic definition of territory. For each of the following firms, show how the company's market could be segmented in nongeographic terms:
   a. Bethlehem Steel Co.
   b. Litton Industries
   c. Polaroid Corp.
   d. The largest university in your state
   e. The most prestigious ladies dress shop in your city

4. Comment on the following: If a given salesman fails, it is always the fault of sales management, since either the wrong man was hired or, if the right man was hired, he was managed improperly.

5. Obtain a detailed organizational chart (at least of the marketing unit) of any firm with an annual sales volume of more than $50 million. Speculate as to whether the firm has adopted and implemented the marketing-concept philosophy. What other information would you require to substantiate your answer?

6. Assume that you are the sales recruiter for the following firms, each of which offers a selling position with a perceived negative feature. Explain each feature in a way such that the applicant will not be discourged.
   a. The conversion ratio will be low, that is, many sales presentations will be required for each sale.
   b. Evening and weekend selling will be involved, but the salesman will work forty hours a week.
   c. The salesman will be required to perform many menial tasks, such as taking physical inventories for customers.
   d. The company will not provide the salesperson with prospects.
   e. Most of the company's prospects are unaware of the product's existence.

7. A sales manager reads the section of the text that deals with the reliability of the sales system. He asks you to design a method which will permit him to compare the reliability indices of all members of his sales force.

Advising Future Sales Leaders

The employment market for MBA's had dried up somewhat in March 1977. Bill Nagle was a bit concerned about his employment plans following graduation in May.

Bill was blessed with superior native intelligence and a 3.8 overall average in graduate school. He was an independent thinker with originality and imagination. He was an excellent writer and conducted himself well verbally, although in a low key.

Bill was 26, married, with a small child. His parents and wife had financed his schooling, and he was eager to go to work and earn the big dollar. He had been offered several sales positions which he was assured would lead to management opportunities. Before jumping headlong into a sales career, Bill decided to seek the advice of Dr. Clarence Hope, the head of the marketing department at his university.

BILL: Dr. Hope, I'm very much confused. When I started in the M.B.A. program, I had no intention of going into sales. Frankly, a lot of things about selling turned me off, and still do. For example, I doubt that I'd want to sell intangibles or be a servant to some buyer in a retail store. I'd hate being away from my family for long stretches, and I sure wouldn't enjoy talking people into buying something they didn't want. I don't know if I'm cut out for selling; but there's a lot of money in it, and not many other decent job offers exist.

DR. HOPE: Bill, are you considering sales now strictly because nothing else is available?

BILL: Not entirely. I took a couple of courses that caused me to really respect the salesman's role in society, and I think I'd be willing to work hard to manage a sales organization. I read every book and article about selling that I can. There are a lot of things about selling that sound great.

DR. HOPE: Where did you hear about all the selling negatives you mentioned? Have you ever done any selling? Was anyone in your immediate family involved in sales work?

BILL: No. I guess it's just what I've read or heard.

2. Classification of the Activities of Sales Personnel

1. Is Bill's attitude toward a selling career the typical student's attitude?
2. Why do you think Bill has received job offers from sales recruiters?
3. How should Dr. Hope respond to Bill's inquiry?
4. If you were a sales recruiter and Dr. Hope informed you of his conversations with Bill Nagle, would you be interested in hiring Bill?

3

The Environmental
Setting for
Field Sales Management

There is little doubt that many duties, responsibilities, and needs of the field sales manager parallel those of his counterparts in other functional areas. Successful management of any function on any level can take place only after the establishment of an environment which is favorable to the effective performance of an organized group.

However, the field sales manager is confronted with a number of problems not faced by managers of other company functions. These differences relate to the precise societal role of the salesperson, the dynamics of the sale itself, the impact of uncontrollable external influences upon the personal-selling system, the salesperson's personality traits and lack of conformity to rules of behavior, and the stigma that surrounds selling as an occupation.

This chapter centers on the inherent difficulties of establishing a favorable environment. Following a description of the setting in which the sales manager must perform, the reader is introduced to the field sales organization and to the primary job activities of the field sales manager. Later chapters present the underlying strategic and tactical approaches that support these activities.

PERSUASIVE SOCIAL INTERACTION

Does the Buyer Buy or Is He "Sold"?

It was inferred in Chapters 1 and 2 that salespeople are evaluated in terms of how many orders they bring in. This is surely true.

However, it does not follow that buyer-seller confrontation takes place in a battlefield framework of kill or be killed.

The real innovation in modern sales thought is that selling, instead of being something the salesman does *to* the prospect, is something the salesman does *for* the prospect. Some practitioners give lip service to this philosophy, but their actions indicate a lack of real acceptance of it, especially when the prospect is a household consumer or an unsophisticated organizational buyer. The potential purchaser is often characterized as the target of the salesman's pitch which is "well calculated" to make the prospect buy.[1] There is nothing wrong with finding the buyer's "hot" button and pushing it. It is also reasonable to assume that many buyers' motives are based on unconscious fears, irrationality, cupidity, and other psychological (Freudian) factors. When relatively naive buyers are involved, the selling plan (especially the presentation) may be viewed as a well-organized offensive action designed to overcome the prospect's poorly organized defense. As put by one sales manager: "A powerful sales presentation is like the Green Bay Packers playing against a high school team."

In a speech before national sales executives, Thomas Gordon confirmed the fact that sales managers have traditionally trained and motivated salespeople to influence prospects by communicating, that is, by telling, advising, suggesting, appealing, teaching, and ultimately controlling and persuading. A more recent and more fashionable approach conceives of goods as being bought rather than sold. "The buyer is the actor, the salesman a more or less passive reactor who hastens to supply the buyer with what the buyer *really needs.*" [2]

Finding Prospects Who Are Already "Sold"

In comparing the two caricatures of the salesman, one may view the salesman's role of influencer and changer of attitudes and behavior as giving way to the role of caterer to existing attitudes and needs. This new concept sees the salesman as a value creator rather than a need creator. Presumably basic needs are latent and do not have to be created. These needs particularize themselves and attach themselves to any product or service whenever the prospect can see that the product or service represents value to him—either for subsistence or self-growth.[3]

This shifting approach does not mean that the modern salesman is an *order taker* rather than an *order maker*. It does suggest a stronger emphasis on the *prospect finding* and *prospect contacting* tasks rather than on *stimulating the prospect* and *closing the sale*. This has been true for some time in organizational selling and is growing in importance within creative direct-to-consumer selling firms. Stimulation takes place as prospect and salesman interact, as the salesman searches for the prospect's problems, as the prospect weighs the potential benefits of the salesman's offerings.

Finding prospects who have needs is often considerably more difficult than creating new needs by aggressive and persuasive selling. Prospects are not sufficiently rational to seek out products when they want and need them, nor have they been programmed to do so. Often the desire for ownership is latent and requires awakening by means of a sales presentation that demonstrates the power of certain products to satisfy needs. Stimulation thus becomes the process of converting a latent desire into a "now need." The sale should be closed when the benefit/price ratio of the salesman's product is perceived by the buyer as being satisfactory or superior to that of competitive offerings.

Sales Resistance

The reader should reread the last sentence of the previous section, particularly the words "should be closed." Logically, if the offering is perceived by the prospect as being capable of improving his present situation, if he likes the firm and the salesman, and if the benefit/price ratio is acceptable, the sale *should* be closed. But people resist change. They do not act hastily to improve themselves. They are procrastinators. Prospects often want to think it over, to sleep on it. The prospect has a natural desire for power and may prefer to buy at his own convenience rather than at the convenience of the salesman. He may ask the salesman to leave his card or to phone him in a few days.

Some organizational buyers resent the attempt of an outsider to solve their company's problems. Other purchasers lack confidence in their own ability to make the proper buying decision. Certain prospects display their level of interest or disinterest openly. In other situations, the salesman is at a loss to figure out where he stands. A potential buyer may also display a variety of moods, pleasant and receptive one day, skeptical and belligerent when the salesman calls again.

Many firms make elaborate attempts to teach salesmen how to classify prospects both before the sales call is made and also during an early stage of the sales visit. Other companies discourage the salesperson's attempt to size up or prejudge potential customers. For example, is it important for the automobile salesman to be able to tell the difference between a looker and a buyer? Should the salesman alter his presentation sequence when the buyer says "Quote the prices before you demonstrate the product" or "I only have five minutes to talk to you today." Should an encyclopedia salesman avoid elderly prospects and those with poor command of the English language?

SELLING WHEN TIMES ARE BAD

Penny Pinching

An examination of personal-consumption expenditures as a percentage of personal income discloses that in 1974 only 28 percent of the consumer's disposable income was available for unplanned purchases (see Figure 3.1). During times of inflation and recession, money becomes even more tight and money fears increase. During the business recovery in the middle of 1975, the penny-pinching mood continued, with consumers inclining toward bargains, shunning frills, and trying desperately to save more of their rising incomes. Even the consumer's tax rebate was saved instead of spent.[4] Consumer penny pinching had its impact all the way up the channel of distribution, as retailers' open-to-buy and manufacturers' output

Figure 3.1 Personal-consumption expenditures as percentage of disposable personal income: United States, 1974

SOURCE: *Survey of Current Business*, U.S. Department of Commerce, Office of Business Economics, Washington, D.C. 1974.

NOTE: Interest payments and personal foreign transfer payments were excluded and remaining proportions were normalized so that total equals 100 percent.

were closely guarded. The impact on the sales-force members of all firms in the channel was apparent as evidenced by increased sales resistance.

In times of troubled economic conditions, consumers are not reluctant to criticize the programs of government and political leaders, the quality and price of products, the policies of labor, etc. As expressed by S. F. Marino, president of Penton Publishing Company:

> I define inflation as a frenetic phenomenon by which the worker receives a greater number of dollars for producing a smaller quantity of inferior quality products and with those dollars purchases fewer goods and services which, in turn, were produced by higher paid workers who labored only half as productively as they could while being paid twice as much as they should be.

Wooing Consumers in Times of Recession and Inflation

As the consumer's expectation for and realization of satisfaction become incongruous, smaller and less expensive products are in demand and sales forces must shift to products with fewer features. Advertising and personal selling must provide consumers and middlemen with more factual and helpful buying information to meet the demands of more rational and less emotional buying. The seller will be required to stress economy in the purchase and use of products, and dependability and efficiency in their operation. Retail salesmen will be advised to trade up less frequently. As buying becomes less automatic, persuasive selling, including the effective use of rebuttals and clever closing techniques, will become more important.

With increased unemployment, more new candidates for selling jobs will become available but the screening of applicants will be more intensive. Those schooled in the newer methods of marketing management and their intricacies will be favored.[5]

Whereas some sales organizations suffer severe setbacks when economic conditions are unfavorable, others are aggressive in opening up new markets when the chips are down. Gordon T. Williams, chairman of Stihl American Chain Saws, supplied his salespeople, his customers, and anyone else who wanted one with a free 1 3/4-inch lapel button emblazoned with the slogan "I Refuse to Participate in the Recession!" Halfway through 1975, Stihl sales were running 20 percent ahead of the previous year.[6] Seemingly, some sellers are inspired to step up their efforts when blockages become more formidable.

STATUS OF SALESMEN IN SOCIETY

Image of the Salesman

When society is ailing, it is difficult for business to be healthy.[7] In particular, actions by salesmen are so visible that the image of the firm and its product is often formed by impressions left by salesmen. Seldom is an organization judged by its administrators or production people.[8] Even in the often criticized field of direct-to-home selling, the consumer's overall image of the salesman was found to be significantly less favorable than his image of the salesman's firm or product.[9]

Criticism by Insiders

Understandably, various members of the operating and general environments are quick to criticize salesmen. It is unfortunate that the status of selling as an occupation is openly questioned by many practicing marketers, marketing teachers, authors of books on marketing and selling, and even by those who are devoted to the field of selling.

One academician blames the complacency of marketing teachers and practitioners and states that if his daughter were to date or seriously consider marrying a marketing major, he would chase him off the premises rather than acquire a huckster as a son-in-law.[10] A noted British industrial marketing consultant points out that people who enjoy buying often do not welcome salesmen.[11] His explanation of this anomaly is that there still hangs over all selling transactions a veiled suspicion that the salesman is attempting to obtain money from the unwary buyer by some trickery. This is because there is a "natural and irremovable difference of interests between seller and buyer, based largely on the view that the seller is more expert and better informed on the subject of the sale than the buyer, who is an amateur."[12]

In the following statement by Robert M. McMurry, one of America's authoritative scholars of selling, the implications for sales management are obvious.

> As many of the most productive salesmen are immature or neurotic and, in addition, some are not too well endowed intellectually, a number are chronic problems. Included are many prima donnas with their frequent total disregard for reality. Because of this, they are not to be regarded as wholly rational and responsible citizens. Instead, they may best be described as high-spirited wayward children.

Since they are completely selfish, they are incapable of loyalty to anyone: their employer, their associates, their supervisors or their prospects. They are, almost without exception, "lone wolves" of the first order.

Their primary motivation is an amalgam of greed and hostility. Their hostility is directed principally toward their supervision and toward the public to whom they sell. Their attitudes toward authority are those typical of adolescents—extremely ambivalent. On the one hand, they resent being told what to do; on the other, they are dependent and have a constant need for help and guidance, which they feel impelled to deny as unmanly—as unworthy of their images of themselves. In consequence, they are chronically dissatisfied. Nothing that can be done for them will please them or awaken their loyalty.[13]

Student Attitudes toward Selling

In a number of research projects, the attitudes of college students toward personal selling as an intended occupation have been investigated, and most of the attitudes have been unfavorable.[14] How did students develop these negative attitudes? By listening to salesmen or former salesmen? By listening to friends or relatives who never worked in selling but did not want their children to enter a selling occupation?[15] By reading articles in newspapers and magazines? By holding part-time jobs as salesmen? By listening to professors or reading textbooks? Following many informal studies and lengthy conversations with students, this author has concluded that most student input comes from people who have little or no personal experience as salesmen. The author has also conducted several before/after studies at several colleges and universities and observed that when salesmanship or sales management courses are taught by qualified academicians with a substantial, successful background in sales, student attitudes toward selling as an occupation are significantly improved.

Regardless of the source of student attitudes, unless young people of today become inclined toward sales careers, tomorrow's qualified sales recruits and managers will be few. The best approach may be to raise the prestige of selling, since occupational preference has been found to be strongly related to perceived status.[16]

Determinants of Occupational Prestige

Although a number of authors have attempted to explain the elements contributing to the occupational prestige of personal selling, one more logical approach is Mason's development[17] of five criteria borrowed from the field of sociology.[18] Listed in the order of their importance, as perceived by many analysts, they are as follows:

1. Distinction between white-collar and blue-collar occupations
2. Income
3. Freedom of action
4. Power
5. Education and training

White-Collar Versus Blue-Collar. There is considerable evidence that the extensive shift of manual workers into selling is perceived as a major improvement in status for those workers. In a study involving a sales force of four hundred people, the largest single proportion of the sales force (26 percent) originally worked in the plant.[19] Since immediate monetary advantages were negligible and employment security was reduced, the major attraction was the workers' contact with managers, technicians, business owners, and professionals in lieu of contact with other factory workers.

It has been shown, however, that it is often difficult to convert manual workers into salesmen. For example, at one time the sales force at Kawasaki Motors Corp., U.S.A., was made up of mechanics who liked to ride and repair motorcycles. It was theorized that their dedication would be enough to sell the product. In time, the mechanics were replaced by experienced salesmen who knew how to sell to retail dealers. Marketing-services director Graham Kerk discovered that it was much easier to teach the facts about motorcycles to salesmen than to teach salesmanship to motorcycle buffs.

The white-collar versus blue-collar distinction should be viewed as a continuum rather than a dichotomy. For example, an ad agency's account executive is viewed as considerably more in the white-collar class than is a route salesman for a bread company and, accordingly, the account executive has more status. Another related indicator has to do with required physical activity and, indirectly, with tangible versus intangible products. For example, physical activity is a factor in selling parts over the counter for auto dealers and plumbing-supply distributors, walking from office to office in a high-rise office building, and carrying heavy samples rather than a brief case.[20]

Company house organs often print stories about such cases as former security guards who become leading burglar-alarm salesmen, former printers who become advertising-space salesmen of the month, and former plant workers who sell more cars than their colleagues. Such publicity is widely used to convince potential applicants and mediocre producers that the company's business is so great that *anyone* can be successful.

Income. In general, the relatively high income of salesmen serves as a prestige-producing factor; yet the variance in their income is probably greater than in other occupations, due to the existence of many salespeople whose earnings are low.[21] The higher earner's compensation is ordinarily tied to commissions, while the lower earner, for example, the in-store salesman, is typically paid on straight salary.

The incentive of a straight commission plan is viewed as incompatible with the security of a straight salary plan. Thus many firms prefer to combine both objectives in the form of a draw or a guarantee against commissions.

It has been shown that the salesman's strong interest in money is related to his desire to buy the symbols of status, for example, luxury clothing, expensive cars, boats, and homes in exclusive neighborhoods. If these purchases are made on credit, they often constitute overspending and create pressures for continuous high earnings which may not be forthcoming on a straight commission plan.[22]

Yet selling offers more immediate opportunities for "near instant" earnings than other occupations do, even for those with little prior experience and training and with limited financial resources. Moreover, most successful commissioned salespeople associate security with the potential for unlimited earnings based on high selling productivity. Conversely, they view the salaried employee as relatively insecure because of the ceiling on his income and his perceived servility to the whims of management.

Freedom of Action. In terms of the freedom from close supervision and the flexibility of working hours, conduct, and activities, the outside salesman is purported to enjoy many of the advantages of self-employment. More than most inside employees, the field salesman can sleep late, enjoy the midweek golf game, and participate in other status-generating activities.

Often he has little contact with management. The high-producing, relatively indispensable salesman is less obsequious, less docile, less submissive, and less responsive to management's requests than other employees. As a result, the salesman is often in the driver's seat, and management is compelled to win his goodwill by appeasement tactics.[23] In referring to the demands of his star salesman, one industrial field sales manager said: "When George Clark tells me to eat crow, I look for the nearest salt and pepper shaker."

3. The Environmental Setting for Field Sales Management

Power. The salesman is a middleman in the company/customer relationship. As such, his occupational prestige is related to his control relationship with these channel entities. Does he control their behavior or they control his?

Although it has been shown that the supersalesman can often buck management and get away with it, power is not considered a positive contributor to the prestige of the selling occupation. Ordinarily, the salesman has few or no subordinates reporting to him and has little or no control over prices, product line, deliveries, other salesmen, company inadequacies, etc. He must sell at his prospect's convenience, thus suffering the discomforts of travel and evening and weekend work, and he must cool his heels in waiting rooms and endure the many nos that are sprinkled in with the yeses.[24] The salesman's required insensitivity to rejection operates to reduce perceived occupational prestige since he is expected to accept rebuffs as a matter of course.

Education and Training. The lengthy, formalized, and expensive education and training required by custom, practice, or law for entry into various occupations constitute prestige factors. To say that a person is a physician, professor, or lawyer, implies a specific, formalized educational preparation, especially on a college level. To say that a man is a salesman makes no educational implication whatsoever.[25]

Some companies have lengthy sales-training programs such as the unique, sophisticated, in-residence program of Bethlehem Steel Company. Other firms can effectively train a sales recruit in a few days or few hours. The point is that there is no standardized, universally recognizable educational program to prepare one for salesmanship. This helps explain the negative attitudes of college students toward salesmen and selling reflected in such remarks as "Salesmen don't require much education" and "After all these years of schooling, why should I become a salesman?"

Summary of Factors that Produce Prestige. The previous discussion leads one to conclude that white-collar positioning, income, and freedom of action are variables that are generally favorable as determinants of the prestigiousness of selling as an occupation. The absence of formal education and training and the limited power and control the salesperson has over others are the major reasons for the relatively low occupational prestige of salesmen.

It should be clear, however, that the five factors that produce prestige do not combine or summate to produce an overall prestige index for a given selling position. A single positive or negative factor may be potent enough to override all other factors. Evaluation of prestige necessarily takes place within the value system of the evaluator. One might conclude, for example, "The hell with prestige— give me the money."

In most cases, salesmen are confident and happy individuals who love their work. However, studies of their attitudinal patterns have disclosed some examples of self-deprecation, self-pity, inverted occupational prejudice, and in extreme cases occupational hatred.[26] Salesmen, jokingly or otherwise, refer to themselves as "peddlers" and "men with larceny in their souls." One highly successful regional sales manager with a well-known firm spoke to selling applicants as follows:

> Most people who answered our ad are here because they have been unsuccessful in their previous jobs. They have tried every other kind of job and failed at all of them. Therefore, before jumping headlong off the Chesapeake Bay Bridge, they will even try selling.

One does not require a license or permit to assign a low prestige or status rating to personal selling as an occupation. In fact, the rater may have no personal experiences or other valid evidence to back up his judgment. Even more detrimental, however, is the condemnation of selling by salespeople, sales managers, and educators. Although occupational prestige is an inexact, intangible measure, its impact upon recruiting effectiveness is substantial.

THE FIELD SALES MANAGER

In Chapter 2, the reader was introduced to the typical alignment of the sales organization (see Figure 2.2) and the major administrative and repetitive management duties of the sales manager. The preceding sections of this chapter described many areas of controversy in selling which affect relationships between the customer, salesman, and manager. In contrast to other employees, whose experiences are within the company and who generally conform to behavioral rules, the salesman encounters and reacts to unique external situations daily. He is hindered by changing economic conditions, criticism of his occupational status, and shifting perceptions of his precise role. He associates with his fellow employees infrequently, and is thus deprived of the opportunity to share his rejections and successes with others. Even the more successful salesman lives on an emotional escalator. Is it any wonder that he is difficult to manage?

Unique Leadership Requirements

It is within this environment of change, challenge, and stress that the field sales manager must assemble, train, supervise, and stimulate a group of often criticized human beings and create an exciting, purposeful, cohesive, productive selling unit. Some of his duties will be routine and repetitive. Most will be unique, one-time, emergency tasks that demand leadership skills based on instinct, that is, the ability to respond promptly and effectively to unexpected situations. This ability is difficult to learn, impossible to teach, and is developed gradually as the sales manager experiences some successes and numerous failures. Many books and articles have been written about instinctive sales leadership, and the following guidelines, discussed briefly below, are especially important for sales managers: [27]

Spend the majority of your time with your salesmen.

Give up all work that can be delegated.

Be a constructive critic.

Set an example in the field.

Plan your work, and work your plan.

The field sales manager must spend considerable time with salesmen in their territories, visiting them and their families, holding local sales meetings and clinics, analyzing call reports, and responding to their personal needs. To make the necessary time available, certain paperwork must be avoided or delegated to administrative assistants or secretaries. This includes evaluating expense accounts, writing newsletters, proofreading bulletins and house organs, reading and responding to routine correspondence, and generally warming the executive chair. The sales manager should train others to assume certain inside responsibilities and free himself for more creative activities, for example, for developing the latent abilities of submanagers and sales-force members.

Many years ago, Burton Bigelow recommended a three-pronged approach for the sales manager to use in reprimanding salesmen: a copper-toed boot, a well-sharpened prod, a bottle of balm. The boot, he pointed out, is used to administer a good kick to the salesman in the seat of his "can'ts"; the prod is used to needle the straggler; the balm is for managerial bruises and needle pricks and the self-inflicted wounds incurred in the course of the salesman's work.

A sales manager must anticipate that salesmen will misunderstand instructions, become careless and indifferent, and partially succumb to the drag of mental and physical inertia. Thus, he must inspect continuously and correct promptly. But praise should usually precede reprimands and suggestions since the carrot is usually more inciting than the stick. The sales manager must help his salesmen to dream the right dreams, and he must help make these dreams come true.

It has been said that a salesman can fail for only two reasons: either he does not work or he does not work right. The same holds for the sales manager. As indicated by Merle Thorpe, former editor of *Nation's Business Magazine:*

> The first quality of leadership is an ability to see the completed task before a project is begun—a capacity to project oneself realistically into the future.

Included in the sales manager's plan should be his organization's precise sales goals; methods of achieving these goals, including an outline of procedures; appropriate assignment of responsibilities to the people who must achieve these goals; and devices for monitoring the activities of these people in order to anticipate and correct procedural deviations. If salesmen are doing well, there is a natural tendency for the supervisor to somewhat ignore their procedures or tactics. If they are doing poorly, their techniques, behavior, and call reports are examined with more care. When confronted by a salesman who was producing poor results and who complained because he was being closely supervised while one of the top producers was not, one sales manager replied:

> If you're doing okay, you'll hardly know I'm around. But when you begin to falter, I'm going to make sure you fail my way.

In summary, the required leadership qualities of the field sales manager include the willingness to center all activities around the needs of sales-force members; the capacity to apply the proper combination of reprimand and praise; self-discipline; persistence; sensitivity to the first sign of an emerging problem; and the instinctiveness to respond effectively to unexpected situations.

Organization of the Field Sales Organization

Field sales managers have been identified as line officials who operate between the sales force and the home-office executives.[28] As shown in Figure 3.2, field managers hold various titles that may or may not be related to geographical, or territorial, responsibilities. Some firms use the term "division manager" instead of "regional

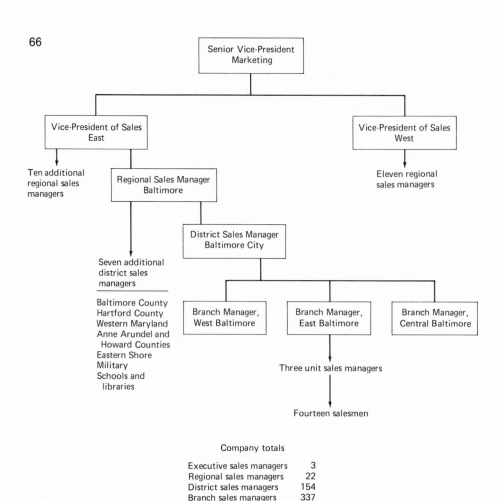

Figure 3.2 An example of a field sales-management hierarchy

manager.'' Often senior salesmen serve as unit managers and supervise four to six field salesmen. Sometimes branch managers or district managers are more toward the top of the hierarchy than regional managers are.

The hierarchy depicted in Figure 3.2 is that of a publishing company with over 1,300 field sales managers supervising more than 4,000 salespeople. It will be noted that within each of the twenty-two regional territories, separate sales operations exist to service the specialized military, school, and library markets. All salespeople and field sales managers are compensated on the basis of commissions.

Therefore, every time a sale is made, commissions must be paid to the salesperson and four layers of field sales managers. In this company, the total of commissions paid out is almost 50 percent of the selling price. A similar hierarchy exists for each of the company's three products.

In other firms, all salespeople and all field managers may be responsible for all products. Consider the case of the textbook publishers whose salespeople contact college professors in an effort to encourage textbook adoptions and solicit new manuscripts. Most salespeople for these companies call on professors in all disciplines throughout a school and discuss the firm's entire range of texts covering subjects from marketing and early-childhood education to biology. Some inefficiencies are introduced since a sales-force member cannot be expected to be familiar with this broad spectrum of academic disciplines and the unique features of each text, including those of competitors. If a single salesman called only on business professors, he would be more familiar with this specialized literature; however, this would entail additional travel costs since the salesman would probably be required to visit many more institutions. Moreover, several company salespeople would be operative in a single university.

The field sales organization can be based on geography, product, customer, span of control, functional specialization, or combinations of these. The appropriate choice is dependent on such factors as the need for specialization, selling cost considerations, competitive organizational structures, the range of offerings, and sales-force preferences.

Primary Job Activities

It has already been indicated that field sales managers manage salespeople in the field, perform administrative functions, engage in inside personnel duties, and solicit personal sales. It is also clear that many field sales managers are engaged in marketing activities beyond those strictly related to personal selling. The field sales manager's allocation of time among these duties varies considerably among companies and even within the same company.

Figure 3.3 summarizes the findings of one investigation of the job activities of field sales managers. Seemingly, field sales managers see themselves spending a major part of their time in the field, either selling or assisting salespeople. Yet, these same managers perceive that over 43 percent of their time is spent performing inside marketing, administrative, and financial activities. When MacDonald and Bailey [29] investigated the primary responsibilities of the field sales

Marketing activities (18.1%) [a]

  †* Analyzing sales data
ᵠ†* Communicating corporate information to salesmen
ᵠ†* Digesting information from management
     Summarizing sales and customer data for management
   † Reviewing competitive activity
     Forecasting future sales in his district
     Reviewing district sales coverage and salesmen's territory alignment
     Advising on changes in price, delivery, arrangements, products or on new
        product development
     Managing advertising and/or other non-selling promotional activities
     Participating in the formulation of overall marketing policy

Selling activities (36.6%)

ᵠ†* Making sales calls with salesmen
ᵠ†* Personal selling to his own accounts
   * Handling problem accounts
     Deciding on a customer's request for special terms of sale
     Expediting customer orders

Administrative activities (18.2%)

ᵠ†* Managing the field office
     Keeping records
     Working with dissatisfied customers
 ᵠ† Writing reports on various aspects of district operations

Personnel activities (20.4%)

ᵠ†* Training salesmen
  †* Establishing standards of performance
ᵠ†* Planning and holding sales meeting
     Advising salesmen on personal problems
     Handling problem salesmen
   ᵠ Recruiting and selecting new salesmen
     Revising man specifications for field sales
     Reviewing compensation programs for salesmen
     Forecasting future personnel need in his district

Financial activities (7.4%)

  †* Analyzing selling expense data
   * Controlling inventory and warehousing costs
   * Controlling costs of branch office operation
     Watching trend of costs expended in relation to profits generated in his
        district
     Preparing budgets
     Advising on the need for additional capital expenditure in his district

Figure 3.3 Ranking of job activities by field sales managers

supervisors in 223 companies, 28 percent of the firms indicated that the major responsibility was to develop salespeople. Ranked next in importance were to plan and monitor territorial sales effort (25 percent) and to motivate salesmen (15 percent). Only four of the firms felt that the field supervisor's primary responsibility was to acquire personal sales.

Personal Selling by Field Sales Managers

This author has led, participated in, and overheard numerous discussions on the subject of whether the field sales manager should sell, and there is the same lack of agreement now as there always was on this question. Perhaps by presenting the major arguments in support of and in opposition to the issue, this text will assist the reader in reaching a conclusion as it applies to specifically defined selling frameworks.

Albert Dunn took a firm stand when he stated, "With a few exceptions, the sales manager should get out of selling altogether." [30] Dunn's argument was that the manager, unlike the salesperson, does not derive his job satisfaction from what he does himself, but from what his subordinates do. The sales manager is evaluated, rewarded, and punished on the basis of his department's (rather than his own) sales performance. This role is analogous to that of the football coach: he does not punt, pass, and block, and he may not be competent in any mechanical skills, yet he may be an eminently successful coach.

Another author supports this negative position by referring to the case of a strong salesman who is promoted to sales manager. [31] He argues that if management allows this sales manager to do what he undoubtedly does best, he will tend to ignore the managerial aspects of his job. Overall, the results may be satisfactory, but the performance of individual salesmen assigned to the field office will be below their own and the company's expectations.

---

[a] Mean percentage of time spent on job activity as seen by field sales managers.

Most time-consuming activities:

* As seen by field sales managers

† As seen by salesmen

φ As seen by top management

SOURCE: Adapted from Rodney Earl Evans, *An Empirical Analysis of the Function and Role of the Field Sales Manager* (East Lansing, Mich.: Michigan State University, 1968), unpublished dissertation, appropriate pages.

The above modified version appears in H. Robert Dodge, *Field Sales Management* (Dallas: Business Publications, Inc., 1973), p. 16.

3. The Environmental Setting for Field Sales Management

Those who condone limited personal selling by the sales manager offer only two reasons in support of the question: (1) the purchasing agents of certain key accounts may insist on dealing with a manager, and (2) the sales manager may be the most effective field trainer of sales recruits. The latter is one of the most important reasons for encouraging the field manager to engage in personal selling.

As will be shown in Chapter 9, classroom instruction can only partially prepare the new salesman to face his first prospect. Most companies send the new salesperson into the field to observe sales presentations as they are made by an experienced person, such as a senior salesman or a manager. If the company or local operation is relatively new or undeveloped, senior salesmen may not be available for field-training duties. Thus, the field manager may serve as field trainer. When a sales district has been operating successfully for some time, the district manager may delegate field training to branch or unit managers (see Figure 3.2). But the reader must remember that branch or unit managers are also field sales managers.

It is not enough to tell a new sales-force member what to do. He must also be shown how to do it. Above all, he must be taught how to do it. The newcomer's attitude is often "How can I be expected to do it if I've never seen it done?" This attitude is conveyed by the following poem which has been widely distributed at sales seminars.

SERMONS WE SEE

I'd rather *see* a sermon than hear one any day;
I'd rather one should walk with me than merely tell the way,
The eye's a better pupil and more willing than the ear,
Fine counsel is confusing, but *example's always clear;*
And the best of all the preachers are the men who live their creeds,
For to see good put in action is what everybody needs.

I soon can learn to do it if you'll let me see it done;
I can watch your hands in action, but your tongue too fast may run.
And the lecture you deliver may be very wise and true,
But I'd rather get my lessons by observing what you do.
For I might understand you and the high advice you give,
But there's no misunderstanding how you act and how you live.

When I see a deed of kindness, I am eager to be kind.
When a weaker brother stumbles and a strong man stays behind
Just to see if he can help him, then the wish grows strong in me
To become as big and thoughtful as I know that friend to be.
And all travelers can witness that the best of guides today
Is not the one who tells them, but the one who shows the way.

One good man teaches many, men believe what they behold;
One deed of kindness noticed is worth forty that are told.
Who stands with men of honor learns to hold his honor dear,

For right living speaks a language which to everyone is clear.
Though an able speaker charms me with his eloquence, I say,
I'd rather see a sermon than to hear one, any day.

Edgar A. Guest

It is as important to show the slumping salesman how to do it right as it is to tell him what he did wrong. Consider situations involving changes that have been introduced by the firm. The salesman may have to contact new types of customers; introduce new products, revised prices, and unique applications and alter his sales presentation. For example, a company that has been selling its product outright may be in the process of switching to a leasing arrangement. Without thorough preliminary indoctrination, coaching, and field example, drastic changes are capable of stirring up negative thoughts and poor morale among sales-force members.

It is probably inappropriate to compare salesmen to football players who have demonstrated that they have the necessary skills to become members of the team. The coach can have organizational, motivational, and supervisory skills even though he may never have been a player. A sales manager may have more difficulty in understanding all the complex details of interaction between customer and salesman if he has never grappled with these situations himself or if his experience is not relatively recent. Without a familiarity with the daily field problems of the salesman, the armchair manager may be an inadequate coach, critic, and leader. Accordingly, many salesmen resent the sales manager's override on their business unless the sales manager has earned the right. There is an important need for the sales supervisor to earn the respect of his people. Except in a few sales settings, there is no known correlation between the personal selling ability of a field sales manager and his success as a manager. What is important is the manager's ability to transfer his selling skills to his subordinates.

Often the sales manager seeks personal sales to contribute to the overall sales of his operation or to his personal income. This is a weak argument. A sales manager may receive 18 percent as commission on his personal sales and only 2 percent overwrite on his men's sales. The strong salesman who is a weak manager may say, "Why should I spend my time struggling with these helpless new salespeople when I can earn the big dollar selling personally?" This type of manager often allows his salespeople to sink or swim. He wants the title of sales manager only for prestige purposes and in order to enjoy some overrides on a few self-starters in his organization.

Although this author has reaped numerous benefits from field managers who also sell, it is recognized that each selling situation and each set of company resources demands a different strategy with respect to allocation of the field sales manager's time. One must, however, challenge the unequivocable statement that the sales function should be controlled by insights, concepts, and office training—and not by personal example in front of the prospect.

Moving up from Salesman to Field Manager

The opportunity to advance in his organization is a major incentive to the salesman. He may discuss management possibilities as early as during his first interview with the firm's recruiter. As he masters the selling requirements, he thinks in terms of going up or out. If he's not promoted when he thinks he should be, he's all ears to competitive offers.

Few who are promoted to management positions admit that they inherited healthy situations. There is some unpublished evidence that most newly appointed field sales managers do, in fact, take over ailing operations or have the task of building entirely new sales teams. In either case, the new manager takes over in an atmosphere of urgency or even crisis. His management development program takes place in whirlwind fashion and he finds himself involved in many management functions for which his experience as a top salesman did not prepare him. He may have the additional burden of relocating his family and adjusting to an unfamiliar location.

Incumbent sales-force members may resent having been overlooked for promotion. Better salesmen may become concerned if policy or tactical changes hamper their activities. Weaker sales-force members may expect the new manager to be a "messiah." He will be required to meet the spouses of his salespeople and office staff. He must find out about the peculiarities and unique needs of certain customers. He will be compelled to attend meetings at the home office or at district or regional headquarters.

His thinking changes as he becomes more concerned with company needs. He may defend company policies that irritated him when he was a salesman. He may ask salespeople to be more considerate of customers than he was when he was a salesman. He assumes the viewpoint of a manager.

SUMMARY AND CONCLUSIONS

Ideally, the modern salesman solves problems and answers needs instead of influencing and persuading prospects to purchase products and services whose ultimate benefits may be suspect. This shifting emphasis dictates management's need to develop salesmen's prospecting skills, to create low-cost lead-getting vehicles, and to encourage work habits that help sales-force members locate prospects who are already sold. Such an approach is especially challenging in times of troubled economic conditions which introduce new forms of sales resistance.

The salesman's status in society has always been challenged by those not engaged in personal selling. More recently the salesman has been severely criticized by insiders, including teachers, writers, managers, and salesmen themselves.

Concerning occupational prestige, salesmen are viewed as white-collar employees with relatively high incomes who enjoy considerable freedom of action. Negative factors focus around the salesman's ability to succeed without high-level education and training, the variability of his earnings, the lack of subordinates under his control, and his required insensitivity to rejection.

The major requirement for field sales managers is an orientation to people rather than to functions. Field managers display effective leadership in many ways, including their personal selling ability. However, opinion is divided as to whether the sales manager should personally sell and whether the top salesman is a viable candidate for promotion to management.

NOTES

1. Robert A. Whitney, et al., *The New Psychology of Persuasion and Motivation in Selling* (Englewood Cliffs, N.J.: Prentice-Hall, 1965), pp. 204–05.

2. Ibid.

3. Ibid., pp. 207–08.

4. "Socking It Away," *Wall Street Journal* (21 July 1975), p. 1.

5. J. S. Schiff and Daniel Caust, "Strategies for Recession," *Marketing Times* 22 (January/February 1975):5–7.

6. "The Stubborn Man from Stihl," *Sales Management* 104 (2 June 1975):12.

7. Peter F. Drucker, "Business and the Quality of Life," *Sales Management* 102 (15 March 1969):31–35.

8. William J. Stanton and Richard H. Buskirk, *Management of the Sales Force* (Homewood, Ill.: R. D. Irwin, 1974), p. 19.

9 .Marvin A. Jolson, *Consumer Attitudes toward Direct-to-Home Marketing Systems* (New York: Dunellen Publishing Company, 1970), pp. 88–90.

10. Richard N. Farmer, "Would You Want Your Daughter to Marry a Marketing Man?" *Journal of Marketing* 31 (January 1967):3.

11. Aubrey Wilson, *The Marketing of Professional Services* (London: McGraw-Hill Book Company (UK) United, 1972), pp. 15–16.

12. Ibid.

13. Robert M. McMurray, *How to Recruit, Select, and Place Salesmen* (Chicago: Darnell Corporation, 1964), pp. 7–8.

14. For example, see William M. Barton, "What's Wrong with the Way We're Selling Sales Careers to Collegians?" *Sales Management* (15 March 1957):50; John L. Mason, "The Salesman's Prestige: A Reexamination," *MSU Business Topics* 10 (Autumn 1962):76–82; David L. Kurtz, "Student Attitudes toward a Sales Career: A Re-examination, *Journal of College Placement* 30 (December 1969–January 1970):85–86; 88. The Kurtz study yielded more favorable results.

15. In addition to Farmer, see J. Donald Staunton, "I Didn't Raise My Boy to be a Salesman," *Management Review* (March, 1958), p. 9.

16. Theodore Caplow, *The Sociology of Work* (Minneapolis: University of Minnesota Press, 1954), p. 39.

17. John L. Mason, "The Low Prestige of Personal Selling," *Journal of Marketing* 29 (October 1965):7–10.

18. See Edward Gross, *Work in Society* (New York: Crowell, 1958), pp. 147–48; and E. Wright Mills, *White Collar: The American Middle Class* (New York: Oxford University Press, 1956), pp. 256–58.

19. Gerhard W. Ditz, "The Internal-External Dichotomy in Business Organizations," *Industrial Management Review* 6 (Fall 1964):51–57.

20. Gerhard W. Ditz, "Status Problems of the Salesman," *MSU Business Topics* 15 (Winter 1967):70–71.

21. Gross, *Work in Society*, p. 117.

22. Ditz, "Status Problems," p. 72.

23. McMurray, *How to Recruit*, pp. 9–10.

24. The salesperson who uses the cold canvass prospecting method has been known to suffer as many as 179 "turndowns" to acquire one sale. See Marvin A. Jolson, "Direct Selling: Consumer vs. Salesman," *Business Horizons* 15 (October 1972):9.

25. Mason, "The Low Prestige," p. 9.

26. Robert N. McMurray, "The Mystique of a Super Salesman," *Harvard Business Review* 39 (March–April 1961):113–22.

27. These suggestions have effectively guided the author during his own career as a sales executive and their original source is unknown. Some are discussed by James F. Bender, "Six Challenges for Sales Management," in *Solving Manpower Sales Problems* (New York: Sales Management, Inc., 1959), pp. 22–25.

28. Robert T. Davis, "The Field Sales Manager and His Place in the Organization," in Albert Newgarden, ed., *The Field Sales Manager* (New York: American Management Association, 1960), p. 13.

29. Morgan B. McDonald, Jr., and Earl L. Bailey, "The First-Line Sales Superior," EMM, no. 17 (The Conference Board, 1968).

30. Albert H. Dunn, Eugene M. Johnson, and David L. Kurtz, *Sales Management—Concepts, Practices, and Cases* (Morristown, N.J.: General Learning Press, 1974), pp. 438–43.

31. H. Robert Dodge, *Field Sales Management* (Dallas: Business Publications, Inc., 1973), pp. 20–21.

QUESTIONS FOR DISCUSSION AND REVIEW

1. Is it possible for a salesperson to convert a prospect's latent desire into a now need and still meet with sales resistance? Explain.

2. Why is it that people who enjoy buying do not welcome salespeople? Is the prospect really concerned with the trickery or expertise of the salesperson.

3. If you were a sales manager, how would you respond to McMurry's hard-hitting attack on salesmen? (See page 58.) If you are a college student, what impact does his statement have on your present level of interest in pursuing a sales career? Does it discourage or encourage you?

4. Why should a salesperson be concerned about the prestige of his occupation? Suppose you wished to measure the relative prestige of various types of selling jobs. Design a research project which would develop this information.

5. The National Cash Register Company's branch manager's creed reads:
   I must possess the ability to multiply my own efforts through the selection, training, and motivation of an organization that will ensure adequate and profitable territory coverage.
   After reading the statement, one sales executive used it in support of the proposition that field sales managers should refrain from personal selling. Comment.

6. Support and criticize each of the following methods of developing field sales managers:
   a. Promoting the star salesmen
   b. Promoting an ordinary salesman who appears to have executive abilities
   c. Hiring an experienced sales manager presently employed by a company whose business is only moderately related to that of the firm seeking the sales manager
   d. Promoting an executive who has never been directly involved in selling or sales management

Case 3.1 Breakstone Advertising Agency

Top Salesman Becomes Manager

Breakstone Advertising sold prepackaged advertising programs to automobile agencies and banks. The program consisted of a time-tested collection of advertising software including newspaper advertising copy, point-of-purchase displays, radio and TV tapes, and unique offers of customer premiums. The average annual fee for this program was $6,600 with the regional manager receiving 32 percent of the sale price out of which he was obligated to pay the salesman 22 percent.

The average salesman sold two units per month, and the 1974 sales volume for the region in the southeastern United States was $1,225,000. Sales volume in 1973 was about $800,000 and the increase in volume was largely attributable to the fact that Leroy Saine had become the regional manager in December 1973. Saine had personally sold 47 units in 1973, which amounted to about half of the 1973 regional volume. During that year he had grossed almost $70,000 in earnings, of which approximately $15,000 had to be paid out in travel and entertainment expenses.

Saine had worked as a car salesman to help himself complete college. He was graduated with a B.S. degree (marketing major) in 1970, at age 27, and joined the Breakstone organization immediately. He had strong native intelligence and was an original thinker and a splendid oral communicator. He was aggressive and would not hesitate to drop in on owners of auto agencies and on bank executives without making an appointment. He was somewhat blunt in that he would not hesitate to point out to prospective clients the weaknesses of their promotional programs.

As a regional manager, Saine spent little or no time in his office, disliked paperwork and written communication, often disregarded appointments with everyone except prospective clients. In increasing sales, his approach was to "put himself in a copying machine and run off another Leroy Saine." His recruiting and selection approach was to take an applicant who looked promising out on sales calls for a day or two. Saine felt that applicants would be impressed by his selling success and would be eager to join the company. He reasoned that if they declined employment because they observed sales resistance in the field, the company would be better off without employees who were so easily discouraged.

During 1974, the southeastern region had a net increase of three producing salesmen but the sales-force turnover rate was about 120 percent. Saine was not responsive to requests from the home office for information such as hiring reports, sales and profit data, news for the company house organ. He was difficult to reach by telephone since he was almost always selling or involved in field training. Many of his former salesmen complained that he was impatient with slow learners, and some prospects complained of a high-pressured approach.

Peter Bowles, national sales manager, admired Saine's progress but felt that Saine was somewhat of a maverick who would never become a polished manager unless the company took steps to change his approach. He also felt that Saine was building sales but was not building an organization. Seemingly, if Saine became ill or disabled, his whole operation would fall apart. Bowles also hated to think of what would happen to the southeastern region if Leroy Saine ever left the company.

QUESTIONS

1. Was Leroy a good field sales manager?
2. Should Peter Bowles have attempted to change Saine's approach? If so, what methods could the home office have used to effect the necessary changes?

Case 3.2 Louis Meyer Insurance Company

Management's Response to Termination by Proxy

Henry Woytowicz had been employed by Martin-Marietta Company as a production worker for 5½ years. In January 1975 he was permanently laid off because a contract with the government had ended.

Henry answered a blind newspaper ad and was hired to sell health and accident insurance to farmers. He had done well as a salesman, as evidenced by his earnings of $4,240 for his first three months in the business. His total 1974 earnings with Martin's had been $9,000. Louis Meyer, the owner of the insurance company, was quite pleased with Henry and he was thinking about asking Henry to take on the field training of some rookie sales people.

On May 12, 1975, Mr. Meyer was in his office when Louise Woytowicz, Henry's wife, walked in.

MR. MEYER: Why hello, Mrs. Woytowicz. It's really very nice to meet you. What brings you to our part of town?

LOUISE: Mr. Meyer, Henry and I had a long talk over the weekend and we decided that Henry should go out and look for a regular job.

MR. MEYER: A what?

LOUISE: A regular job—a job where he would earn a steady income. So I brought in his sales kit.

MR. MEYER: Are you saying this is not a regular job just because our people work on commissions?

LOUISE: It's not only that. We just aren't sure how much money is coming in each week, and with a new baby on the way we feel insecure. And besides, I don't think there's too much of a market for insurance these days. People don't have much money and the last thing they're interested in is insurance.

MR. MEYER: Are you an experienced market researcher, such that you are an expert analyst of the insurance market?

LOUISE: Look, Mr. Meyer, I don't expect you to get smart about it. I just don't want Henry to be a salesman. I want him to have a regular job like other people.

QUESTIONS AND ASSIGNMENTS

1. Try to reconstruct the chain of events and the conversations that took place at the Woytowicz household over the weekend.
2. Why would Henry quit his job before he found another one? Why didn't he resign himself, instead of allowing his wife to take over?
3. What's a regular job?
4. Had Henry been managed properly during his employment with the company?
5. What should Louis Meyer do now? How can he prevent this from happening with another employee?

Developing the Sales Plan

4

Forecasting and Budgeting

A sales forecast is a prediction of a firm's sales (dollars or units) during a given period of time in the future. The forecast takes into account the possible impact of uncontrollable factors in the environment and within the firm. If management is displeased with the forecasted sales volume for the forthcoming year, certain actions can be taken now which will call for a readjustment of the forecast. Thus, forecasting compels management to think carefully and systematically about future periods and to design present actions that will bring about favorable future results.

THE FORECAST AS AN AID IN PLANNING

The sales forecast is a tool that assists planning in all functional areas of the firm. The firm uses the forecast to plan production schedules and inventory levels. An accurate forecast will reduce the likelihood of both stockouts and excessive inventories. Stockouts can cause the temporary loss of sales and the permanent loss of customers. Also, in some companies, sales-force members are continuously disturbed by the company's inability to deliver orders placed by customers. When forecasts are too optimistic, the company is confronted with additional costs due to obsolescence, slow-moving inventory, and underutilized resources.

The sales forecast affects the accounting and financial areas of the firm, in terms of anticipated rates of revenues, expenses, and cash flows. If the firm engages heavily in leasing or installment sales, the forecast is an important instrument in determining accounts-receivable levels, credit and collection needs, and required periodic borrowings.

Forecasts aid the personnel manager in planning for hiring, training, supervision, and termination of employment. Forecasts are important in planning for purchases, transportation and warehousing systems, advertising and other promotional efforts, preparation of the annual report, and other activities by top management.

The Profit Formula

Almost all forecasts of future sales volume are related, either directly or indirectly, to future profits. Suppose a firm is interested in forecasting the present value of the cash-profit contribution (π) of a relatively new product over the next two years:

$$\pi = \frac{Q_1(P_1 - C_1)}{1 + \rho_1} + \frac{Q_2(P_2 - C_2)}{(1 + \rho_2)^2}$$

where, for years 1 and 2, Q = forecasted sales units
P = average price during years 1 and 2
C = average unit cost during years 1 and 2
ρ = average cost of capital during years 1 and 2

It is difficult enough to forecast unit sales two years hence (Q_1 and Q_2). The problem becomes even more difficult when one considers the complex relationships among the variables in the profit formula. For example, as unit costs are reduced by spreading the fixed costs of existing resources among newly introduced products, price reductions may be introduced. Under elastic conditions, demand may be substantially increased. Thus, demand is a function of both price and cost. Yet unit costs depend on the number of units over which fixed costs may be spread. Thus, where does one start in forecasting sales volume?

The forecaster must also be concerned with the length and shape of life-cycle variations among products and the fact that incoming products may have either helping or hindering effects on the sales and profit contribution of existing products. As forecasting requirements leap periods ahead, the level of uncertainty increases and consensus among decision makers becomes most difficult to achieve. Accordingly, the techniques available to deal with the future are more plentiful and sophisticated than those covered in this single chapter.[1]

Responsibility for Forecasting

Is sales forecasting usually the direct responsibility of the General Sales Manager rather than his field sales managers? The answer is a vague "sometimes" or "partially" or "It depends on the size, type, needs, or level of sophistication of the firm."

The hypothetical organization shown in Figure 2.2 assigns the responsibility of sales forecasting to the manager of sales planning and analysis, who reports to the chief marketing executive through the marketing-research manager. These are the people who are most aware of both external and internal conditions, including the general environment, competitive actions, customer attitudes, opinions, and beliefs, and current company goals and interrelationships among functional divisions.

Larger firms may use staff or consulting economists to aid in the forecasting process. Some firms enlist the help of venture teams, or panels consisting of corporate executives and/or outside experts. In smaller organizations, the president, marketing manager, or general sales manager may serve as a one-man forecaster.

In some firms, the sales manager has little responsibility for forecasting but total responsibility for carrying out the sales plans which emerge from the final forecast. For example, in the Black and Decker organization, the sales-forecasting manager reports to the logistics manager who, in turn, reports to the vice president of marketing. The logistics function includes the forecasting of sales for more than two thousand catalog items for eighteen months into the future.

Inventory planning is designed to "smooth" the supply of products between the factory and the firm's customers. The sales-forecasting manager at Black and Decker acts as an interface with other managers and draws sales predictions from all product sales managers. He is expected to spot changing market trends by consulting sources within and outside of the firm. He is considered to be the firm's analytical specialist and uses a wide variety of forecasting techniques including exponential smoothing, statistical time series, Delphi Techniques, and other computer-related methods.[2]

BASIC FORECASTING TECHNIQUES

Forecasting methods can be grouped into two broad classes,[3] quantitative methods and qualitative methods. This classification generally reflects the extent to which a forecast can be based directly on historical data in a mechanical way. Those techniques that start

84   with a series of past data values and follow a given set of rules to predict future values are classified as quantitative methods. Qualitative methods are called for when such data are not readily available or when past relationships between sales results and demand determinants are not perceived as relevant for the future. In the latter case, management relies heavily upon the judgment and experience of both company employees and outside experts.

QUALITATIVE OR JUDGMENTAL FORECASTS

Sales-Force Composite

This method solicits forecast information from those who will be expected to produce the sales results. If the entire sales force consisted of five salesmen reporting to the national sales manager, each man would be sent an appropriate form and asked to fill in his estimate of sales in units or dollars. Often the salesman is requested to break down his estimate by product, customer type, territorial subdivision, etc. Usually the forecast will cover a period of a year and will include quarterly, monthly, or weekly totals as required by management. The salesman may or may not receive assistance from management in the form of a reminder list of demand determinants and other variables to be considered. The total forecast is the summation of the five individual forecasts.

Suppose, however, there are several layers of field sales management as shown in Figure 3.2. In all likelihood, the sales vice-presidents will request forecasts from the firm's twenty-two regional managers, who will, in turn, route the request down the management hierarchy to the next level, until eventually it is in the hands of the salesmen. Once completed by sales-force members, the forecasts are forwarded upward for scrutiny and possible modification by successive levels of field management. The sales vice-presidents in the home office will also have the opportunity to review and revise the field forecasts.

Although forecasting may occupy some of the salesman's free time, he is normally willing and frequently anxious to cooperate. First, he is pleased that his input is desired. Second, the forecasting process compels the salesman to do some thinking and planning of his own activities, schedules, needs, hoped-for results, and earnings for the forthcoming season or year. Finally, he develops more confidence in the fairness of the quotas which evolve from these forecasts.

Seemingly the accuracy of the forecast is assured by the sales force's proximity to and familiarity with local markets. But salesmen, who are often optimistic wishful thinkers, frequently do not concern themselves with emerging trends which have not as yet touched local markets. A producer of household equipment offered the following comments about the sales-force composite method:

> If we produced the number of units forecasted by the sales force, we'd have product crawling out of our ears. However, the sales-force estimate is a good way to start.

Executive Opinion

The sales estimate may also be based on the judgment of one or several company executives. It may be the results of pure intuition or it may be supported by facts, results of other forecasts, or follow-ups to results such as those elicited by the sales-force composite method. Eliciting executive opinion is inexpensive and generally speedy. It has the advantage of interdisciplinary decision making, in that some of the participants will be associated with functions other than personal selling.

This method is often used by relatively small organizations. It often lacks a scientific orientation. Also, when many executives are consulted, meetings can be frequent and prolonged, and consensus of opinion is often difficult to reach. Committee meetings are often dominated by those who have more power and authority and a better gift of gab than others. The result is often frustration and indecision with an attendant waste of executives' time and energy.

Nominal Group and Delphi Techniques

These are really group processes which offer more scientific approaches to the method of eliciting executive opinion. The Nominal Group Technique (NGT) is a structured face-to-face group meeting which follows a prescribed sequence of problem-solving steps. It overcomes the disadvantages of difficult-to-control committee meetings in that it features silence, independently generated forecasts, thinking, enforced listening, and a round-robin procedure which includes supporting one's forecast. Equality of participation prevails, and NGT meetings tend to conclude with a perceived sense of closure, accomplishment, and the desired consensus.[4]

In the Delphi process, the input consists of anonymous written responses from qualified panel members who are separated by distance. Hence, the conflict between executives, inherent in face-to-face confrontation, is avoided. Participants submit their forecasts, with appropriate support, by mail or via computer terminals. The

Delphi leader summarizes the estimates and sends the median or mean forecast for each period back to each panelist. He may or may not include supportive statements. Respondents are asked to revise their forecasts and submit them along with supporting arguments. The process stops when consensus has been approached among participants.[5]

The advantages of NGT and Delphi as judgmental forecasting devices are numerous. However, the methods are less useful when sophistication, finances, and processing time are not sufficient.

Buyers' Indication

In some industries, it is reasonable for the seller to ask customers for an estimate of buying intentions for the period to be included in the forecast. This approach is appropriate when the buyer-seller relationship has been firm and long-lasting and when reorders occur periodically and automatically. Such relationships frequently occur when vendors sell consumer goods to department-store buyers and when manufacturers sell equipment, such as fire- and burglar-alarm panels and auto accessories, to resellers. This method is obviously restricted to customers who can structure buying plans in advance and who are willing to disclose them to vendors. As in the case of the sales-force composite, customer estimates of past years must be compared with actual purchases to determine whether the forecasts were regularly optimistic or pessimistic.

When a salesman gathers this information from customers, management must be concerned with his propensity to flavor customers' estimates with those from his own imagination.

Market-Research

The research method considers the buying intentions of both customers and potential customers. It is obviously restricted to situations where potential buyers are limited in number and capable of ordering substantial quantities. The survey can be conducted either by field sales personnel or by members of the marketing-research department.

Other Qualitative Approaches

Within the past few years, a number of more sophisticated judgmental methods have been used with some frequency. These include scenario writing, envelope curves, credence decomposition, logistic and S curves, relevance trees, and several others. The limited

QUANTITATIVE FORECASTS

Aside from pure intuition, hunches, and educated guesses, the most popular base for sales forecasting is past sales performance. Extrapolation from the past into the future is a reasonably sound approach when conditions affecting sales performance are relatively stable. Drastic changes in the general or operating environments and unexpected upheavals within the firm can seriously weaken the validity of such forecasts. The following forecasting methods rely on the availability of a series of values from historical sales data.

Simple Moving Averages

Table 4.1 shows data received from the branch office of a firm that sells educational cassette programs directly to household consumers. Column 3 is the three-month moving average forecast using the sales data of the three preceding months of the same year. The forecast of 61 units for month 4 (April) was developed by averaging the sales for months 1, 2, and 3. Similarly, the forecast of 57 units for month 5 is based on the average sales for months 2, 3, and 4. Column 4 was calculated in the same way except that the sales of five previous

Table 4.1 Forecast of sales by the moving-average method

Month (1)	Observed unit sales (2)	Forecast with 3-month moving average (3)	Forecast with 5-month moving average (4)
1	73	—	—
2	58	—	—
3	52	—	—
4	62	61	—
5	67	57	—
6	74	60	62
7	80	68	63
8	85	74	67
9	62	80	74
10	70	76	74
11	92	72	74
12	80	75	78

months are used to forecast sales for the following month. The value of 62 units for month 6 (June) was found by averaging actual sales performance for months 1 through 5.

The method of moving averages is a short-term method, in that forecasts are developed for only one period in advance. As the forecaster increases the number of observations in the moving average, there is a greater *smoothing* effect, that is, a greater removal of random deviations in the sales data. Column 3 has a range of 23 units (80–57), while the range of column 5 is 16 units (78–62). Thus, a smoother forecast is derived from a five-year rather than a three-year moving average.

If we desire a smoother value, either because we think the historical observations contain considerable randomness or because we think there is little change in the underlying pattern, a large number (N) of observations should be used to compute the moving-average forecast. On the other hand, if we feel that the underlying pattern in the data is changing (and we want to react to fluctuations more rapidly) or that there is little randomness in the observed values, a much smaller number (N) of observations can be used.[7]

In calculating the mean absolute deviation and the mean squared error for three-month and five-month moving averages, the latter usually will be more accurate. However, as the number of observations increases, the accompanying costs of storing data increase. Therefore, when management is required to prepare forecasts for a large number (perhaps hundreds) of items in a product line, storage cost becomes a consideration.

Exponential Smoothing

The two major limitations of the moving-average method are, first, the cost of storing data and, second, the fact that equal weight is given to each historical observation used.

The exponential smoothing method overcomes these limitations by applying a correction that is determined by the amount of error in the previous forecast. In essence, a proportion of the error is added to the previous forecast to get a forecast for the next period. This proportion is called the smoothing constant, usually designated by α and somewhat analogous to $1/N$ where N is the number of observations used in the moving-average method. Thus a large α is the equivalent of a small N such that smoothing is minimal and correction is immediate rather than long term. In formula form

$$F_{t+1} = F_t + \alpha(X_t - F_t)$$

where $F_{t+1}=$ desired forecast for the next period
$F_t=$ forecast for the previous period
$X_t=$ observed sales for the previous period
$\alpha=$ smoothing constant
$(X_t-F_t)=$ error in the previous forecast

Table 4.2 uses the example shown in Table 4.1 to forecast sales by the exponential smoothing method with several assumed values of alpha. For example, to calculate the forecast for month 9 with $\alpha = .3$:

$$F_9 = F_8 + .3\ (X_8 - F_8)$$
$$F_9 = 71 + .3\ (85 - 71)$$
$$F_9 = 75.2 = 75 \text{ units}$$

In examining the relative accuracy of the forecast, it was found that in this example, the smallest value of alpha yielded the most accurate forecast. An exercise at the end of this chapter suggests that the reader verify this by considering the mean square error and the mean absolute deviation.

Table 4.2 Forecasting sales by the exponential-smoothing method

| Month | Observed unit sales | Forecast with smoothing constant (α) | | |
		$\alpha = .1$	$\alpha = .3$	$\alpha = .8$
1	73	—	—	—
2	58	73 *	73 *	73 *
3	52	71	69	61
4	62	69	64	54
5	67	68	63	60
6	74	68	64	66
7	80	69	67	72
8	85	70	71	78
9	62	72	75	84
10	70	71	71	67
11	92	71	71	69
12	80	73	77	87

* Since no previous forecast is available, the observed value is used.

4. Forecasting and Budgeting

Moving Average versus
Exponential Smoothing

The exponential-smoothing method usually but not always develops a more accurate forecast than the moving-average method. Seemingly, the former method is preferred because it requires only the most recent forecast and a value for alpha. However, both methods are effective for only single-period forecasts. Neither method is truly effective when the historical data are complex. The determination of the proper value of N or α is subjective, and is properly decided by experimentation. The results are often improved by using higher forms of smoothing such as double moving averages, double exponential smoothing, or more elaborate smoothing methods.[8]

Time-Series Analysis[9]

The arrival of the computer has simplified management's employment of forecasting methods which overcome many limitations of the techniques discussed above. This section illustrates the extension of historical data into the future by the use of linear regression analysis. Unlike most treatments in sales-management texts, the example to follow covers in great detail the methodology used in developing a trend line after removing seasonal variations in a four-year data series. Although the end result could be quickly obtained by the use of a computer, the longhand process below is an aid in understanding the method, especially for readers who are unfamiliar with it.

The data in Table 4.3 extend the data base to a four-year period for the same firm used above, a company selling educational programs to household consumers through a direct-to-home sales force. The data disclose a sales peak during the Christmas selling season and during the summer months, when students and teachers are available for recruitment. The first step is to remove these seasonal variations, and also those resulting from calendar inconsistencies and holidays.

A four-year monthly average is computed for each month and average monthly sales volume is calculated for each year. As shown in Table 4.3, a deseasonalizing index (DI) is derived for each month. The historical data are leveled or deseasonalized by dividing each monthly sales total in Table 4.3 by the DI for the appropriate month. For example, the figure of 78 units (rounded off) (month 1, year 1, in Table 4.4) is computed by dividing 73 (month 1, year 1, in Table 4.3)

Table 4.3 Historical sales data for four-year period by months

Month	Year 1	Year 2	Year 3	Year 4	4-Year monthly average	DI *
1	73	70	97	106	86.5	0.940
2	58	47	58	90	63.3	0.688
3	52	52	60	86	62.5	0.679
4	62	56	73	80	67.8	0.737
5	67	68	80	74	72.3	0.786
6	74	70	97	88	82.3	0.895
7	80	82	110	97	92.3	1.003
8	85	97	120	127	107.3	1.166
9	62	90	110	112	93.5	1.016
10	70	127	140	146	120.8	1.313
11	92	137	156	177	140.5	1.527
12	80	130	130	120	115.0	1.250
Total	855	1,026	1,231	1,303	1,103.8	
Average monthly sales	71.3	85.5	102.6	108.6	92.0	

* DI stands for deseasonalizing index. For example, for month 1, the DI is equal to the average sales for month 1 divided by the average monthly sales for the entire four-year period, or 86.5/92.0 = 0.940.

Table 4.4 Deseasonalized sales data

Month	Year 1	Year 2	Year 3	Year 4	
1	78	74	103	113	
2	84	68	84	131	
3	77	77	88	127	
4	84	76	99	109	
5	85	87	102	94	
6	83	78	108	98	
7	80	82	110	97	
8	73	83	103	109	
9	61	89	108	110	
10	53	97	106	111	
11	60	90	102	116	
12	64	104	104	96	
Total *	882	1,005	1,217	1,311	4,415

* Although the four-year total of 4,415 coincides exactly with that in Table 4.3, the column totals are slightly different because of rounding in calculating deseasonalized data.

4. Forecasting and Budgeting

by the DI for month 1 of 0.940. From the deseasonalized data of Table 4.4, the following totals emerge:

$\Sigma(x)$ sum of months $(1-48) = 1+2+ \ldots +48 = 1{,}176$
$\Sigma(y)$ total sales $= 855 + 1{,}026 + 1{,}231 + 1{,}303 = 4{,}415$
$\Sigma(xy)$ sum of (month $\times$ sales) $= (78 \times 1) + (84 \times 2) + \ldots +$ $(96 \times 48) = 117{,}220$
$\Sigma(x^2)$ sum of squares of months $= 1^2 + 2^2 + \ldots +$ $48^2 = 38{,}024$
$n = 48$

The above totals may now be substituted into the standard linear regression equations.

$$\Sigma(y) = na + b\Sigma(x) \tag{1}$$
$$\Sigma(xy) = a\Sigma(x) + b\Sigma(x^2) \tag{2}$$

where a is the y-axis intercept of the trend line and b is the slope of the trend line. The completed equations are

$$4{,}415 = 48a + 1{,}176b \tag{1}$$
$$117{,}220 = 1{,}176a + 38{,}024b \tag{2}$$

The solutions are $a = 67.9$, $b = 0.983$; and the straight line that best approximates the linear trend is $y = 67.9 + 0.983x$. The logic of this method of least squares is that the distance between each leveled observation and corresponding points on the trend line should be minimized.

To forecast deseasonalized sales for the 58th month, let $x = 58$ and substitute into the above equation such that

$$y + 67.9 + 0.983\ (58) = 125 \text{ units}$$

The corresponding DI for month 58 is 1.313. Thus, to convert the deseasonalized estimate back into a raw forecast for the month

$$125 \times 1.313 = 164 \text{ units}$$

The forecast may now be similarly completed for years 5, 6, etc., assuming the forecaster concludes that no drastic environmental or company conditions will arise in the future. This may be an unreasonable assumption for direct sellers who are now subject to cooling-off periods and who may be affected by other types of legislation in the making.

In Figure 4.1, the historical data, leveled data, and trend line have been plotted around the four-year monthly average of ninety-two units. The reader can observe the smoothing effect of deseasonalizing; the fluctuations of the leveled data around the average monthly sales line are substantially lower in amplitude than those of the raw data.

The seasonal pattern and trend have been analyzed. Cyclical variations and noise, or undetermined variation, have not. Figure 4.1 does not suggest a cyclical influence, but the relatively short time span of the data base does not permit a proper analysis. Noise is normally quite small and will not be considered in this example.

Multiple-Regression Analysis

In the previous section, it was assumed that unit sales are a function of only one independent variable—time. Surely, in the sample company and in all companies, many other variables are suitable predictors of sales volume. When management wishes to base its forecast on more than a single independent variable, multiple regression is a useful approach.

Suppose, for example, that the company feels that such variables as the number of college graduates (G), average rate of unemployment (E), and average household income (I) are closely corre-

Figure 4.1 Historical and leveled sales data

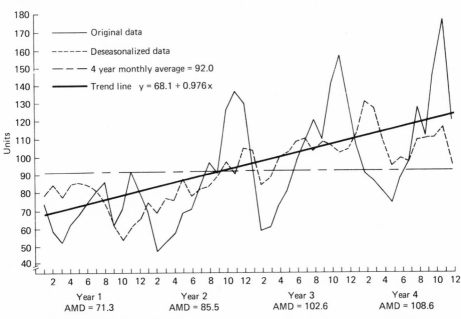

————	Original data
- - - - -	Deseasonalized data
— — —	4 year monthly average = 92.0
———	Trend line $y = 68.1 + 0.976x$

Year 1
AMD = 71.3

Year 2
AMD = 85.5

Year 3
AMD = 102.6

Year 4
AMD = 108.6

AMD = Average monthly demand

lated with the company's sales (S) for the following year. Expressed mathematically

$$S_{t+1} = f(G_t, E_t, I_t)$$

Through multiple-regression analysis, the forecaster attempts to produce the predictive equation that would define the above functional relationship. The equation may take the following linear form:

$$S = aG + bE + cI + d$$

where S = annual sales in year $(t + 1)$
G = number of college graduates in year (t) (000's)
E = average rate of unemployment in year (t)
I = average annual income per household in year (t)
a, b, c, d = coefficients to be found

The forecasting procedure begins when the company compiles a list of historical values of $S, G, E,$ and I for several past years. Using this historical information and a multiple-regression computer program, coefficients $a, b, c,$ and d may be determined and the final equation for forecasting sales is established.

ESTABLISHING THE SALES BUDGET

Once the sales forecast has been completed, management's immediate task is to figure out how much it will cost to reach that sales level while earning a satisfactory profit and achieving other company goals. The budget is the forecast of expenditures that will be required to buy the projected revenues.[10] The budget is the formal expression of managerial plans. Its purpose is to coordinate and control company resources over the time frame of the sales forecast.

The Budget as a Plan

Earlier chapters discussed the strong need to coordinate company activities to achieve the firm's hierarchy of goals without excessive suboptimization. Accordingly, company operations are subject to a hierarchy of budgets of which the sales budget is but a single entity. One handbook lists and discusses nineteen separate budgets within a firm.[11]

It was indicated in Chapter 1 that goals, including the sales goal as quantified by the forecast, should not be established until the available resources of the goal-setting unit are considered adequate. The budget is the instrument for establishing this adequacy. When resources are lacking or required costs are viewed as excessive, the forecast must be reduced. In many instances, goals for net earnings or ROI objectives may dwarf the objectives for sales, share of market, and sales-force morale.

Thus the sales forecast and sales budget operate in concert, as each is adjusted to accommodate the other. They are so interdependent that one writer makes little distinction between the two:

> The sales forecast is the estimate or prediction which may or may not become the *sales budget*. The forecast becomes the budget only if management accepts it as an objective. Often, the forecast leads to adjustments of managerial plans, so that the final sales budget differs from the original sales forecast.[12]

An example may be helpful in demonstrating the interrelationship of sales volume, costs, and company resources. Assume that the sample company in this chapter sells an audio educational program for $399. The contractual arrangement with the customer calls for a $39 deposit and thirty-six monthly payments of $10. As soon as an order is received, verified, and shipped, the company is committed to the following out-of-pocket cash outlays:

Commissions to salespeople	$ 80
Commissions to various field sales managers	100
Average lead-getting cost	30
Cost of product	90
Total	$300

This does not include administration, logistics, and other costs. Nevertheless, every time an order is received, $39 comes in and $300 goes out, so that the immediate net cash outflow is $261. Therefore, if it is forecast that the firm will sell 3,000 orders a month, the net cash outflow will be $783,000 per month. This is a sizeable cash requirement each month, and the budget must account for the source of these funds. If the firm has been established for years, considerable cash will be generated by accounts receivable. If the firm is publicly listed, another source of funds is available. Often the firm must depend on short-term borrowing or factoring. These sources are available if the lending institution is favorably impressed with the flow of cash from the collection of receivables. Collection efficiency is strongly related to the level of customer satisfaction, both with the buying transaction and the product itself, and is also related to the credit-approval policy of the company. Thus a loose credit policy, a poor product, and salesmen who exaggerate product benefits could be responsible for poor collections which, in turn, could diminish the firm's borrowing power. This is but one of a number of examples that illustrate the overwhelming scope of budgeting and the potential disasters that can and often do arise when coordination is poor or when the company information system is weak.

The foregoing illustrates the planning needs of management on a home-office level. Budgeting also takes place on regional, district, and branch levels. This is sometimes difficult due to the widespread resistance of field sales managers to calculations and cost considerations. Yet it has been shown that when employees participate in establishing a budget, they are more likely to accept the related plan of action as their own. Although the district manager, or his equivalent, is seldom responsible for financing, borrowing, or cash flows, the field-office sales budget cannot be separated from the field-office sales forecast.

The district manager should at least have the responsibility of planning for costs that are subject to his own control. Suppose a district manager in our sample firm works on a 35 percent procurement contract. The home office charges his account with $90 for each product package sold and $3 for each direct-response inquiry in his territory that is generated by national magazine advertising. Based on past experience, the district manager presumes that every ten inquiries will be converted into a $399 sale. He develops the following sales budget for his operation:

Fixed costs (monthly)

Rent	$ 600
Telephone	400
3 clerks or secretaries @ $700	2,100
Other administrative costs	500
	$3,600

Variable costs per order

Salesmen's commissions (20 percent)	$ 80
Unit manager's overrides (5 percent)	20
Lead costs	30
Product cost	90
	$ 220

Using the above figures, the district manager's calculations indicate that he will require eighteen monthly orders to break even. He then forecasts an average of fifty orders per month, which will yield a monthly district profit of $5,350. The reader should verify these calculations by using the relationship

$$PQ = FC + vQ + \pi$$

where P = average price per unit sold (dollars)

Q = number of units sold
FC = fixed costs (dollars)
v = variable costs per unit (dollars)
π = profit (dollars)

The district manager's budget requires home-office approval even though the costs are charged to the district manager's account. Obviously the firm's ad campaign must be large enough to supply the district with five hundred inquiries per month. Moreover, rental, telephone, clerical, and administrative costs can be prohibitive if a large number of the 154 district sales offices operate below the break-even volume or below the level of acceptable earnings to the district manager. When field sales managers are compensated by salary, bonus, or overrides instead of the described profit-sharing plan, the home office's scrutiny of planned costs becomes more severe.

The Budget as Control Mechanism

When actual performance differs substantially from budgeted and forecasted performance, management is in a position to pinpoint the precise areas of deficiency with an aim to ultimate improvement. Variances may be due to unanticipated changes in conditions that call for forecast and budget revisions. In fact, it is quite normal for the firm's marketing and sales vice-presidents to take up a substantial portion of the first quarter's board meeting with presentations in support of forecast and budget revisions, in either upward or downward directions.

It is seen that the sales budget is far more than a mechanical accounting process. It is an ideal troubleshooting technique, which astute field sales managers accept as constructive. However, many sales managers see budgets as a continuous monitoring system which informs top management of field weaknesses. Often budgets are perceived as restrictive and penny pinching. One authority likens the unpopularity of the word *budget* to that of terms such as *layoff, strike,* and *pay decrease*.[13] Thus, subordinates must be carefully informed regarding the value of budgeting for all levels of management.

Similarly, marketing people and top sales executives in the home office submit their budgets to the president in competition with budgets submitted by managers of other functional areas including production, engineering, research and development, personnel, logistics, etc. Thus, an elegant sales presentation is often required to "sell" top management on the merits of accepting a given budget proposal.[14]

SUMMARY AND CONCLUSIONS

The sales forecast initiates the budgeting process since production, inventory levels, promotional endeavors, etc., are ordinarily pegged to the rate of sales activity, except in periods of shortages. In addition to the master budget for the entire firm, budgets are prepared for each part of the firm and by the various levels of the sales organization.

Budgets specify the expected costs of achieving the forecasted sales volume. When these budgeted costs or anticipated cash needs are looked upon as excessive, sales forecasts are often reduced. Thus the budget serves as a device to help management in planning profits and other management goals. Budgets also serve to detect deviations from the performance plan and to suggest specific areas of improvement.

Judgmental forecasting methods are qualitative in nature and depend on data submitted by sales-force members, field sales managers, home-office executives, and current and prospective customers. Quantitative methods attempt to extrapolate past performance into the future by using moving averages, exponential smoothing, and regression analysis. The method of time-series analysis presumes that sales volume is a linear function of time. This chapter demonstrated the popular method of developing a trend equation after raw data have been deseasonalized.

Often sales volume is looked upon as being affected by a number of independent variables. Multiple-regression analysis enables the forecaster to compute a predictive equation which conveys the relative sales impact of each of these variables.

The level of complexity of the firm's forecasting and budgeting procedures will depend upon the size of the firm, the relative importance of long-range planning and cost control, the degree of sophistication of management on all levels, and the perceived usefulness of the process. In general, the availability of the electronic computer has encouraged more elaborate forecasting and budgeting systems. Yet, numerous instances can be cited where companies do not prepare forecasts or budgets of any kind.

NOTES

1. Several of these techniques are discussed in Marvin A. Jolson, "New Product Planning in an Age of Future Consciousness," *California Management Review* 16 (Fall 1973):25–33.

2. The author is grateful for the information provided by Richard B. Rosecky, Sales Forecasting Manager of the Black and Decker Manufacturing Company, Towson, Maryland 21204.

3. Steven C. Wheelwright and Spyros Makridakis, *Forecasting Methods for Management* (New York: Wiley, 1973), p. 4.

4. For detailed examples of this method, see Andre L. Delbecq, Andrew H. Van de Ven, and David H. Gustafson, *Group Techniques for Program Planning* (Glenview, Ill.: Scott, Foresman, 1975): pp. 15–82.

5. For a detailed explanation of the Delphi method, see N. C. Dalkey, *The Delphi Method: An Experimental Study of Group Opinion* (Rand Corporation, June 1969). For an example of Delphi used in sales forecasting, see Marvin A. Jolson and Gerald Rossow, "The Delphi Method in Marketing Decision Making," *Journal of Marketing Research* 8 (November 1971):443–48.

6. See Wheelwright and Makridakis, *Forecasting,* pp. 177–94; and Jolson, "New Product Planning," 25–33.

7. Ibid., p. 32.

8. Ibid., pp. 41–47, and the bibliography that follows, for an explanation of more complex smoothing methods.

9. For a more detailed explanation of this method, see Chester R. Wasson and David H. McConaughy, *Buyer Behavior and Marketing Decisions* (New York: Appleton-Century-Crofts, 1968), pp. 526–39, which suggested part of the format for this section.

10. Thomas R. Wotruba, *Sales Management: Planning, Accomplishment, and Evaluation* (New York: Holt, Rinehart and Winston, 1971), p. 118.

11. Lillian Doris, ed., *Corporate Treasurer's and Controller's Handbook* (New York: Prentice-Hall, 1950), pp. 106–07.

12. Charles T. Horngren, *Cost Accounting: A Managerial Emphasis* (Englewood Cliffs, N.J.: Prentice-Hall, 1963), p. 175.

13. Ibid., pp. 165–66.

14. Richard R. Still and Edward W. Cundiff, *Sales Management: Decisions, Policies, and Cases* (Englewood Cliffs, N.J.: Prentice-Hall, 1969), pp. 420–21.

QUESTIONS FOR DISCUSSION AND REVIEW

1. Dick Grey, national sales manager of the health care division of Johnson and Johnson, said, "If a brand has 8 percent of the total sales, then it should get 8 percent of the sales budget" (*Sales Management*, May 19, 1975, p. 10). Support or reject this statement.

2. In 1976, the Michelle Toy Company enjoyed net profits of $200,000 on a sales volume of $2,000,000 through wholesalers. Because of the huge growth of discount retailing, the firm is considering the possibility of

eliminating the wholesalers and selling directly to retailers. It is estimated that sales volume will drop 40 percent, but net profits will be $180,000 because there will be no wholesaler's markup. If the change is made, fixed costs would increase from the 1976 level of $200,000 to $300,000 in 1977 because of the need for additional warehousing, materials-handling equipment, and sales branches. What sales volume, in dollars, would be required in 1977, under the proposed plan, to equalize the level of 1976 profits? (ans: $1,250,000)

3. If you were a field sales manager, would you welcome the responsibility of preparing forecasts and budgets, or would you be content to leave these matters to the home office?

4. As a sales-management function, *control* involves three distinct kinds of activity. Identify them as they apply to sales budgeting.

5. Discuss the value of forecasting and budgeting in each of the following types of firms:
   a. Vending machine operators (such as Macke Corp.)
   b. Major department stores
   c. Producers of women's pants suits
   d. Textbook publishers
   e. Producers of hand-held calculators
   f. Sellers of duplicating machines

6. After you have completed assignment 4 of Case 4.1, plot the raw data, leveled data, trend line, and the four-year monthly average. Offer your analysis of the exhibit.

Case 4.1 Harris Wiping Cloth Company

Comparing Methods of Sales Forecasting

Historical sales data for the Harris Wiping Cloth Company are as follows:

	Year			
Month	1971	1972	1973	1974
Jan.	362	336	380	384
Feb.	336	309	344	362
Mar.	394	416	438	418
Apr.	441	416	434	507
May	449	441	453	450
June	409	402	446	455
July	356	336	389	376
Aug.	432	420	427	452
Sept.	438	451	472	471
Oct.	481	502	531	520
Nov.	554	538	578	584
Dec.	839	912	940	932
Total	5491	5479	5832	5911

ASSIGNMENTS

1. Prepare a set of deseasonalized data.

2. With the data from the previous assignment, prepare a monthly forecast for 1974 using three-month and five-month moving averages.

3. Repeat the above using the exponential-smoothing method where alpha equals .2, .5, and .8.

4. Prepare a monthly forecast for 1977 using linear time-series analysis.

5. Compare the accuracy of the forecasts in assignments 2, 3, and 4 for the year 1974 using both the method of mean square error and the method of mean absolute deviation.

5

Territories,
Sales-Force Size,
and Quotas

In the previous chapter, it was assumed that for the most part the firm's total area of marketing opportunities was already divided into field-management subdivisions, salesmen's territories, and other manageable work units. Accordingly, it was demonstrated that home-office sales planners benefitted from the input of field managers and sales personnel when formulating forecasts and sales budgets.

Since forecasting and budgeting are properly related to submarkets, or territories, as well as to the firm's total market, decisions on sales-force allocations are central for planning and setting sales objectives. In this chapter, decisions pertaining to territorial boundaries, sales-force size, and frequency of calls are discussed. Included are elements of quota setting that guide field sales managers and salesmen in allocating their efforts.

CONCEPT RELATIONSHIPS

As indicated in Chapter 2, a territory is a segment of the firm's total market composed of potential or actual customers who share certain common characteristics relevant to buying behavior. Although territory often has a geographical connotation, the basic definition is related more to a grouping of accounts rather than an area of land.[1] Thus territories may be designated by location, customer type and size, product, and any other characteristics that facilitate management's task in matching selling efforts with selling opportunities.

Territories may also be subdivided in terms of two or more joint characteristics. For example, many insurance companies divide their markets into geographical subdivisions and then further divide these by using separate sales forces to sell individual product lines such as casualty, life, health, and accident policies. Within the existing geographic and product boundaries, one group of salespeople may sell only to household consumers while others might specialize in selling to organizational accounts.

The established territories may be compared in terms of sales potential, which in turn, will govern the required frequency of calls, sales-force size, and resultant sales forecasts and budgets. Whereas forecasts and budgets focus largely on financial planning, quotas are motivational targets that are assigned to field units and/or individual sales-force members.

Figure 5.1 assumes that sales quotas have been assigned to the managers of the company's three sales territories with quotas weighted in terms of the proportion of the total sales forecast expected from each territory. Each territory must employ a given number of salespeople (n_1, n_2, n_3) to achieve its forecasted sales volume. Thus, the total company forecast $(F) = p_1F + p_2F + p_3F$, and the total number of required company salespeople $(N) = n_1 + n_2 + n_3$.

TERRITORY DECISIONS

Number and Size

It is commonly argued that the sales potential of a given territory is fixed during a specified time frame. The reader will recall that

Figure 5.1 Relationships between territory, quota, and sales-force size

Territories	Territorial quota (Dollar sales)	Number of salespeople
A	p_1F	N_1
B	p_2F	N_2
C	p_3F	N_3
	F	N

NOTE: F = total company forecast (sales dollars)

p_1, p_2, p_3 = proportion of total forecast planned for each territory

n_1, n_2, n_3 = number of salespeople required in each territory

N = total number of company sales-force members

sales potential refers to the maximum dollar sales volume available to a territory within the time frame. It should therefore be apparent that this maximum volume will be achieved *only* if the best available field sales manager is managing the territory. Thus, even if the sales potential of the state of New York far exceeds that of Kentucky, it is conceivable that a superior field sales manager, operating in Kentucky, could achieve a larger sales level than a poor sales manager in charge of the New York territory.

One of the fallacies of allocation of geographical territories to field sales managers is that many firms will attempt to equalize the sales potential of each assigned territory. Such an arrangement will automatically determine the size of each geographic territory. Thus, one determinant of territorial allocation is sales potential, or the number of prospect/customer units.

Two additional commonly used criteria are the accessibility of prospect and customer units and the required level of customer service. These factors are closely related in that the territory's field sales manager is normally required to develop and maintain a sales force that is capable of both procuring sales and servicing present customers. Sales procurement consists of selling to new customers and reselling to old ones.

Territories that are equivalent in terms of sales potential may be vastly unequal as measured by work load. For example, the sales potential for the state of Colorado may equal that of upstate New York for a given firm. However, the relatively high travel requirements for salesmen in Colorado surely diminish the time that can be spent contacting prospects and/or servicing customers.

Territorial work load is also increased when small, rather than large customers predominate and when customers require frequent service, advice, and other contacts with salespeople. In other words, the frequency of required calls varies among territories.

From management's point of view, the best territorial arrangement is the one that is most effective in accomplishing the territorial profit objectives.[2] This is true in opening up new territories for the first time and also in adjusting territories in the light of new profit constraints or demands. For example, the business equipment division of Pitney-Bowes has successfully increased its pretax profit from 7.3 percent in 1972 to 11.0 percent in 1974 by making every branch sales office a profit center while pruning the number of branches from 146 to 133.[3]

Satisfying the Company

One specialist in developing computer systems for territorial decisions relates the firm's allocation questions as follows:

The most profitable size of the sales force depends on how well the territories are aligned. Profitability of territory alignment, in turn, is related to how many calls should be made on each account and prospect. The number of calls that should be made depends on the size of the sales force and territory alignments.[4]

As the analyst applies marginal analysis principles to the sales-force allocation problem, he frequently finds that the sales potential of assigned territories should not necessarily be equal. Instead, there should be more territory for more talent. Managers and salesmen should not be boxed in if they are capable of meeting their sales forecasts or quotas and if they can provide the required level of customer service and develop the targeted territorial profits. The field manager's task of determining the most profitable sales-force size will be developed in a subsequent section.

Satisfying the Sales Employee

Not all salespeople are satisfied with or effective in a given territory. A salesperson with a pronounced southern accent may have difficulty selling in New York City. Conversely, a number of salesmen who have been quite productive in New York have not been well received in Alabama and Kentucky. There is also evidence that white salespeople are not well received by black prospects, and vice versa.[5] Some salesmen seek to avoid the competition of salesmen from rival firms by moving to remote, untapped territories or to international markets that are as yet unexposed to the firm's product offerings or selling approach. Thus a major requirement of the field sales manager is to match a given salesperson's abilities, effectiveness, and desires with the characteristics of particular locations or customer groups.

In general, salesmen and their field managers crave more territory, even though they may not be adequately covering the territory they have. Since salespeople are inherently optimistic, they anticipate that they will soon be ready to expand. Consequently, they seek to reserve or lock in more sales potential to avoid being locked out by a peer. Accordingly, one of the sales manager's major chores is to dissuade subordinates from creating underutilized territorial resources. A desirable approach is to assign small territories and expand the boundaries in concert with improved performance.

One of the greatest fears of the commissioned salesperson is that after building up a highly profitable sales territory for himself he will have it removed or reduced at some later date to accommodate the firm's profit motives. Unfortunately, this happens frequently, especially when a firm decides to switch from outside commissioned sales agents to a captive sales force whose compensation plan is more fixed than variable.

Satisfying the Customer

Salespeople must work at the customer's convenience. Customers may be categorized on the basis of convenient call times and required call frequencies. High-priced direct-to-household products must often be demonstrated on weekends or during evening hours so that husband and wife may make a joint decision. Some prospects are converted into customers on the first sales call while others require two, three, or even more meetings with the salesperson.

Many organizational buyers fail to recognize that the salesman's time is a limited resource. Often, the salesperson is required to repeat the same sales presentation or demonstration to several people in the same organization. The seller often finds it difficult to identify the decision maker in the firm diplomatically. The problem is compounded when those without the power to make purchasing decisions insist on screening the product offering before referring the seller to those with the power to buy. The astute representative can remove many of these inefficiencies by better preparation for calls, including the collection of information about the account, its markets, its needs, and the people who influence and make decisions.

Recent profit squeezes have resulted in an increased desire for sales service by customers. Retailers may depend upon the vendor's sales force for inventory control, display assistance, and merchandising suggestions. The salesman's neglect of these duties can result in the loss of a key account to a more obsequious competitor.

Callbacks and customer service chores are costly in terms of time and money, especially when long distances are involved, and when the reorder cycle is short, deliveries are slow, and home-office customer-service personnel are indifferent and ineffective.

In short, customer demands for posttransactional services have reached an all-time high. Salespeople are expected to be installers, troubleshooters, advisors, merchandisers, trainers of the buyer's personnel, expediters, and dinner hosts, and to serve in a vast variety of other functions. Moreover, a faithful customer may be indifferent to the salesperson's other commitments when the above needs arise. Such demands, reasonable or not, have telling effects upon the seller's capacity to serve the needs of all his clients and simultaneously pursue new business.

Territorial Specialization

The question of whether to specialize field sales units and representatives by product should be decided by both customer needs and cost considerations. As was indicated in Chapter 3, at one time textbook publishers employed sales representatives who were specialized in specific disciplines, for example, business and economics, history, psychology and sociology, etc. A representative would travel from school to school, calling on professors in a certain discipline. More recently, a publishing rep calls on all the professors in a given university, regardless of discipline. The end result is reduced travel costs, a less-informed representative, and some communication inefficiencies between buyer and seller. At one time, Encyclopaedia Britannica, Inc., sold *Encyclopaedia Britannica, Britannica Junior, Compton's Encyclopedia,* and *Great Books of the Western World* by using four different sales forces in a single territory. Although the operation was relatively effective as measured by sales volume, the huge sales and administrative manpower needs and the duplication of resources compelled the company to use a single sales force to distribute three of the products.

There are examples where a given prospective purchaser is subjected to sales calls by different salesmen distributing different products for the same company. For example, organizations often purchase a combination of policies for their employees, such as group life, hospitalization, health, and accident insurance. Retail buyers frequently buy several fashion, food, and drug items from the same firm. These buyers, to conserve time, have a preference for one-stop shopping. On the other hand, buyers often require special advice about the use, merchandising, reselling, and servicing of certain products. Thus there are advantages in having specialized salespeople who have acquired expertise about their assigned products and/or their application.

Sales specialists are popular with buyers in certain industries and distasteful to others. Almost always, specialization results in increased sales costs because of increased sales-force size, the need for more field sales managers, higher travel expenses, duplicated facilities, and administrative functions. Yet specialization may result in increased revenues since a salesman handling a single product devotes all his time to that product. When a single salesperson handles many items, his loyalty to and familiarity with any single product may suffer and the warehouse may become overloaded with slow-moving products.

SALES-FORCE SIZE

How many salesmen does a firm need in a given territory? Previous discussions in this chapter have at least flirted with some answers to this question. As in the case of most business decisions, the answer depends on the specific goals of the enterprise and the factors that currently inhibit the achievement of these goals.

Profit Maximization

Most models for determining the optimal sales-force size follow the profit orientation suggested by Semlow:

> Since the direct and indirect cost of maintaining a field sales organization is often the major part of total selling expenses, a method of determining the optimum number of salesmen required to develop the most profitable selling effort is most desirable.[6]

Table 5.1 approximates the territorial performance of an actual company whose territorial sales-force size ranges from one to twenty people. It is useful to examine these data to determine the ideal sales-force size from the point of view of controllable profit dollars. Each sales territory is purported to have the same sales potential.

An examination of the data indicates that annual sales dollars, or total revenue (TR), is a function of the number of salespeople (n) in the territory: $TR = 200,000 \sqrt{n}$.

There are both fixed and variable costs of keeping the sales force in the field. Sales commissions (to salesmen and field sales managers) as a percentage of dollar sales volume may be expressed as v. The average fixed cost of maintaining each salesperson in the field may be expressed as c, and consists of items such as travel and entertainment expenses, the salary portion of salesman's compensation, as well as the costs of administration, supervision, clerical help, sales samples, etc. Thus the total sales cost (TC) may be expressed

$$TC = nc + 200,000 \, v \, \sqrt{n}$$

Since profit in dollars (π) equals total revenues (TR) minus total costs (TC),

$$\pi = 200,000 \sqrt{n} - nc - 200,000 \, v \, \sqrt{n}$$

This equation reduces to

$$\pi = 200,000 \sqrt{n} \, (1-v) - nc$$

In order to find the setting of n (sales-force size) that will maximize profits, this last equation is differentiated with respect to n and set equal to zero:

$$\frac{d\pi}{dn} = \frac{100,000 \ (1-v)}{\sqrt{n}} - c = 0$$

The final solution is

$$n = \frac{10^{10} \ (1-v)^2}{c^2}$$

If $c = \$20,000$ per year and $v = 35$ percent, n is approximately equal to 11 salespeople per territory. This will maximize the profits that are controllable by the territorial sales manager.

Sales-Volume Objectives

As in the case of most profit-maximizing models, the above solution to the question of sales-force size is based on several highly restrictive assumptions, which limit its practical use in actual territorial situations. Among the variables that have been neglected or assumed away are such factors as the quality of the salesmen and sales management, the turnover rate, recruitment and training costs, opportunity costs associated with poor salesmanship, the degree of market satiation, competitive effects, and customer service requirements.

In practice, sales volume, rather than profits, is predominant in dictating sales-force additions or deletions. It has been shown that under certain circumstances the objective is to develop as large a sales force as possible with no upper limit. For example, the follow-

Table 5.1 Relationships of sales volume, profits, and number of salespeople

Number of sales-people	Territory	Annual sales volume	Annual controllable profits	Annual costs	Annual sales volume per man
		(Thousands of Dollars)			
20	A	895	180	712	45
10	B	630	211	420	63
5	C	450	191	256	90
2	D	283	145	140	141
1	E	200	110	90	200

5. Territories, Sales-Force Size, and Quotas

ing circumstances appear quite regularly in many traditional sales organizations: [7]

1. The major element in the promotional mix is personal selling rather than advertising, packaging, sales promotion, etc. Put another way, few if any sales are the result of voluntary inquiries or automatic reorders. The seller arranges to contact the prospect in order to create a sale instead of waiting for the prospect to come to him at a store or seller's place of business.

2. The market is unsatiated such that substantial increases in sales volume are possible and desirable.

3. The effects of competitive reactions to sales increases are negligible.

4. Sales personnel are generally compensated on a straight commission basis and must adjust their work schedules to the convenience of the prospective or actual customer.

5. The salesman requires little or no technical ability or prior product knowledge; therefore the training period is brief.

6. Sales-force turnover is high and terminated salesmen are difficult to replace.

It has been shown, for circumstances such as the above, that sales volume is a linearly increasing function of the number of active sales representatives.[8] This research result suggests that the average sales-volume performance of sales-force members is fixed over a given time frame, regardless of territorial boundaries or sales-force size.

Semlow has suggested that the average salesman will produce about the same volume of business regardless of variations in the size of the territory.[9] Adding more territory or more sales potential will not increase a given salesman's volume, since he probably would not work any harder or put in any more selling time or effort than he does now. An expanded territory may result in "instead" rather than "plus" business as the salesman picks up the easy sales in his new territory.

The data of Table 5.1 show a different pattern, in that sales productivity per man is inversely proportional to sales-force size. First of all, this company's sales potential is obviously limited such that as the sales force increases in size, the potential per salesman decreases. Also, there are fewer easy sales for each salesman. Finally, since the reservoir of good salesmen is far from bottomless, it is reasonable to assume that under certain conditions of employment, successively lower-caliber people are hired, as sales-force size increases.

Apparently there is no simple formula that will indicate how much additional sales volume will be contributed by an additional salesman. However, as previous discussions in this text indicated,

Customer Requirements

As in the case of territorial decisions, the goals of customers may conflict with those of the firm. Designated levels of sales volume and profitability may not be reachable when customers' service needs are not satisfied. It has already been indicated that sales-force members must be available to perform many nonselling chores for retailers and other resellers. Some sales-force members, including missionary salesmen, spend little time, if any, pursuing orders. Yet they are counted as sales-force members.

Periodically, many salesmen are required to spend considerable in-person or telephone time attempting to get their home office to fill orders. Often merchandise is not available, and salesmen must return to their customers to apologize for nondeliveries, delays, etc., and to develop replacement orders or persuade disgruntled customers not to go to competitive suppliers. Frequently a customer will place a blanket order for so many dollars, and the salesman has the lengthy chore of writing up the order with the proper assortment of styles, sizes, colors, etc.

Hasbro Industries, a producer of toys and school supplies, instructs its salesmen to write up a suggested order in advance of the sales call. Although the technique is time consuming, it is a buying aid for the customer and a sales tool as well, in that the buyer talks about what might come off the order rather than what should go on.[10]

Salesmen must frequently leave the field to meet customers in the company's showroom or attend trade shows, exhibitions, and conventions. Although these activities contribute to long-run volume and profit objectives, they interrupt the salesman's daily routine of customer contact.

QUOTAS

Salespeople dream of achieving sales potential, expect to match forecasts, and hope to fulfill quotas. Goodman's definitions reflect similar ideals: "potential is a measure of opportunity, forecast is a measure of expectation, and quota is a statement of objective." [11]

As indicated earlier in this chapter, quotas are motivational targets that are assigned to field units such as regions, districts, and salesmen's territories. They help management produce incentives for salesmen, control salesmen's efforts, and evaluate salesmen's performance.[12]

Although Figure 5.1 suggests that the territorial sales quota can equal the forecast, the quota can also be larger or smaller than the forecast. As managing salesmen by objectives (MBO) increases in importance,[13] sales-force members are playing a larger part in setting their own quotas. Since salesmen are usually quite optimistic in submitting forecasting information, some companies accept the salesman's "guestimate" of his quota and secretly lower it to develop the forecast. Thus, quotas are frequently higher than forecasts for individual salesmen as well as for branches and districts.

Incentives for Salesmen

The quota is a way of letting the salesman know where he stands in terms of measurable standards. In many ways it is similar to a handicap for a golfer. A 14-handicap golfer is expected to shoot about 86 to 88 each round. If, on a given day, he shoots 95, he knows at once that he had a bad round. Similarly, a salesperson should be guided by standards which automatically tell him whether management approves of his performance during a given period.

Often the salesman's compensation plan is tied to his assigned quota. Management's thought is that if significant financial rewards are tied to high achievement, a salesman can narrow the gap between his potential and his habitual performance. Thus, a salesman often works on a straight salary plus a bonus that reflects his accomplishments in excess of his quota. A salesman on straight commission could also be rewarded with an increase in commission rate for sales over his quota.

Controlling Salesmen's Efforts

Quotas can be used to encourage salesmen to emphasize high profit items, balance sales among items in the product line, open new accounts, introduce new products and engage in other profitable activities. Such incentive programs, unless carefully monitored, may cause the salesman to concentrate on his company's interests and neglect his customers' interests. Clearly, a salesman who is strongly motivated to open new accounts at a given point in time may be compelled to reduce the time and energy spent servicing the needs of present customers. Similarly, if a salesperson's quota and attendant earnings require him to push slow-movers, high-profit items, and new offerings, he may be tempted to substitute these requirements.

Product sales quotas have been shown to be quite effective from both the salesmen's and the company's viewpoints. For example, Leon Winer [14] describes an industrial firm that tied its salesmen's compensation to both a total quota and a product quota for two of its twelve products. Many of the firm's salesmen complained that fulfilling the quota for product A consumed inordinate amounts of customer-contact time. A majority of the sales-force members said they would be willing to accept a higher total quota in exchange for a lower quota for product A. This suggested trade-off experiment was conducted within a typical district operation, and the results in the test and control groups were compared. The group that was allowed to trade-off performed worse than before in terms of both their earnings and company profits. Thus, salesmen of the company under study were considered to be "quota achievers" rather than "income maximizers."

Performance Evaluation

It has already been indicated that the quota serves as a sales standard to which results may be compared. One unanswered question is whether new or weaker salesmen should be given lower quotas than those given to high producers. This would seem appropriate. As in the analogous golf handicap, more is expected of the stronger performer. However, top salesmen do not wish to be penalized for being strong. Thus they often argue that quotas should be based on market measurements with little regard for individual differences among salesmen. [15] This is especially true in organizations where compensation is tied to quotas.

Quotas may serve as standards for guiding efforts as well results. Salesmen can control efforts better than they can control results. For example, one's quota may be to deliver fifty complete sales presentations per month. In cases where sales presentations did not result in sales, the prospect may be asked to fill out a brief rejection card, indicating reactions to the company's products, reasons for not buying, and future buying plans. Such information helps management evaluate the salesman's performance, pinpoint his weaknesses, and propose corrective measures. A salesman's effort quota may also be based on activities such as prospecting by telephone, contacting new prospects, submitting competitive bids, and making courtesy visits to customers after orders have been delivered.

Effort quotas are particularly helpful when sales-force members are expected to perform nonselling duties such as contacting physicians, training resellers' salesmen, performing service calls, arranging displays, recruiting college students, etc.

Finally, quotas may be assigned which are cost and profit oriented. This is particularly helpful when top management seeks to evaluate a territorial manager's propensity to pursue sales volume rather than profits. Territorial managers are often given quotas for costs that are subject to their control, such as travel and entertainment, district-office administrative costs, prospecting costs, etc. Field sales managers will often pass cost-control quotas down to individual sales-force members.

SUMMARY AND CONCLUSIONS

A firm's total market may be divided into territories, or segments, that are made up of prospective customers who share certain common characteristics relevant to buying behavior. Territories may be compared in terms of sales opportunity (potential), sales expectations (forecast), or motivational sales targets (quotas).

Territorial size or boundaries will normally be determined by the number and accessibility of prospective customers and the anticipated customer-service requirements. Thus, customers require service, sales employees crave sufficient territory, and the company strives for territorial profits. The simultaneous satisfaction of these three goals is downright difficult, but nevertheless the goals guide the firm's allocation decision.

Product-specialization decisions consider product complexity, the need for customer information and service, frequency of calls, number of company products sold to a given customer, and the relative costs of sales-force specialization. Specialization is almost always more costly. Yet increased revenues do not always go hand in hand with specialization.

Decisions involving sales-force size normally follow the same profit-oriented logic as territory decisions follow. However, sales managers frequently use sales-volume objectives as surrogates for profit goals. When markets are unsatiated, sales volume increases linearly with the number of salespeople. Thus many companies are always seeking to add another good salesman.

Quotas are sales, profit, and activity goals assigned to field units, including field sales managers, and salesmen. They assist management in providing sales incentives, in controlling sales efforts, and in evaluating sales performance.

NOTES

1. Charles G. Goodman, *Management of the Personal Selling Function* (New York: Holt, Rinehart, and Winston, 1971), p. 130.

2. Thomas R. Wotruba, *Sales Management: Planning, Accomplishment, and Evaluation* (New York: Holt, Rinehart, and Winston, 1971), p. 153.

3. Thayer C. Taylor, "Throwing More Light on Hard-to-See Profit Sources," *Sales Management* 114 (May 19, 1975):43–44.

4. Leonard M. Lodish, "Vaguely Right Approach to Sales Force Allocations," *Harvard Business Review* 52 (January–February 1974):120.

5. Thomas Reuschling, "Black and White in Personal Selling," *Akron Business and Economic Review* 4 (Fall 1973):9–13.

6. Walter J. Semlow, "How Many Salesmen Do You Need?", *Harvard Business Review* 37 (May–June 1959):126.

7. This list appears in Marvin A. Jolson, "How Important Is Sales Force Size?" *Business Studies* 10 (Spring 1971):32.

8. Ibid., 31–40.

9. Semlow, *How Many Salesmen*, 130–31.

10. "Hasbro Plays to Win," *Sales Management* 114 (May 5, 1975):23.

11. Goodman, *Management*, p. 329.

12. Wotruba, *Sales Management*, pp. 196–98.

13. Donald W. Jackson, Jr., and Ramon J. Aldag, "Managing the Sales Force by Objectives," *M.S.U. Business Topics* 22 (Spring 1974):53–59.

14. Leon Winer, "The Effect of Product Sales Quotas on Sales Force Productivity," *Journal of Marketing Research* 10 (May 1973):180–83.

15. Wotruba, *Sales Management*, p. 199.

QUESTIONS FOR DISCUSSION AND REVIEW

1. A frequently heard gripe of salesmen is "I've got a lousy territory." What constitutes a lousy territory? Offer some examples. How should such gripes be handled by management?

2. Under what sets of circumstances would a firm see fit to reduce the size of a district sales manager's territory? Of a salesman's territory? How can such a task be performed while minimizing the risks of losing the employee or reducing his enthusiasm and morale?

3. The vice-president of sales for a producer of ladies' ready-to-wear clothing seeks to set appropriate sales quotas for each of his three regional sales managers for 1977. The following information is available.

	Unit sales (000's)			
	Company	Region A	Region B	Region C
1977 sales potential	80	20	10	50
1977 sales forecast	60	18	10	40
1976 sales (market share, 15%)	50	14	8	28
1975 sales (market share, 18%)	35	6	8	21

4. Table 5.1 indicates that sales productivity per representative is a decreasing function of the number of representatives. How do you explain such a phenomenon? In what types of sales organizations is this likely to occur? Does this condition require remedial action by sales management?

5. Should management consider variations in salesmen's abilities when setting territorial size and boundaries and establishing quotas?

6. Support or oppose the use of salesmen's quotas when the following conditions exist:
   a. Salesmen sell directly to consumers on a straight commission basis.
   b. Salesmen sell to retailers, and the company "back orders," or is unable to fill, about 30 percent of the orders received.
   c. Sales of capital goods are made to industrial customers.
   d. Most sales are made to the government for delivery eight to ten months in the future.
   e. Sales are made over the counter in a retail store.

Case 5.1 Beldon Company

Reducing Territorial Size in the Face of Declining Sales

Before her marriage, Emily Madden had spent four years as a housewares buyer for a major Philadelphia department store. After she married Paul Madden, her only interests were tied to her roles as a wife and a mother of two fine children. After both children were in high school, Emily found herself with considerable free time and decided to accept a part-time job helping the Beldon Company to investigate the salability of a new line of decorative candles specialty gift shops in Philadelphia. Beldon Company handled some 150 houseware and gift items including glassware, pottery, ceramics, table service. When Beldon decided to experiment with decorative candles for the first time, Emily was recommended by the general merchandise manager of a Philadelphia department store.

The candle experiment was highly successful due to Emily's

outstanding sales results. Emily hired two housewives to deal with specialty-shop accounts while she directed her own efforts to department stores. Within a year she was working full time for Beldon. She had five salespeople working for her and was responsible for the entire state of Pennsylvania. Beldon had hired three women as representatives in other parts of the country, and these reps had been sent to Philadelphia for field training under Emily.

As sales volume increased, Beldon began to offer more varieties of candles in terms of functions, styles, colors, sizes, and prices. The company was most appreciative of Emily's selling, management, and training results. Emily, in turn, was delighted with her new career. She requested and was granted the addition of the Delaware, southern New Jersey, and Maryland territories. Concurrently, sales of the candle line were growing in other parts of the country such that national candle sales had grown to $2.5 million by January 1975.

Emily had eight representatives under her supervision; all were women and six were housewives who worked part time.

During the summer of 1975, sales dropped considerably in Emily's territory. Emily and Paul had enjoyed a thirty-day trip to Europe in May 1975, and when they returned the children were home from school for the summer. Emily felt that she had somewhat neglected the children due to the demands of her work, and she spent considerable time with them during the summer. Emily's assigned representatives had made similar adjustments in their work schedules. At the same time, candle buyers were requiring increased merchandising assistance in the form of inventory counts, display recommendations, exchanges for slow-moving items. Several stores complained to Beldon's home office that they were seldom visited by, and frequently unable to make contact with,Beldon salespeople.

Emily made several trips in attempts to regenerate the enthusiasm of her sales employees. She found that competitive firms had installed their lines in several stores. Three of Emily's salespeople resigned, reasoning that candles had become more difficult to sell. Moreover, they complained that they had less time than before to devote to selling. Emily had little success in hiring replacements. By October 1975, sales in Emily's territory had dropped to 50 percent of their peak level. Emily's usual sweet disposition had changed. She and Paul argued frequently. The children complained to their Dad, "What's the matter with Mother? She sure has changed."

In November 1975 Emily was requested to visit the Beldon home office. The national sales manager felt that the territorial alignment should be rearranged and that Emily should restrict her efforts to the city of Philadelphia. He reasoned that she would then be able to provide adequate service to her accounts, avoid the chores of recruiting and supervising salespeople in remote areas, spend more time with her family, avoid travel costs, increase local sales volume, and thus earn a more stable income.

Emily countered, "You people seem to forget that it was I who really got the candle operation under way. I've put a great deal of time and effort into the outside territories. I expect you to be patient and to give me some help in hiring new salespeople and servicing accounts. There is no way I will give up any territory."

QUESTIONS

1. What recommendations would you make to management?
2. Did Beldon err in its previous territorial allocations?
3. If Emily called upon you for advice, what would you suggest?

6

Designing the
Sales Message

In contrast to the many behind-the-scenes activities discussed in previous chapters, this chapter centers on face-to-face interactions between salesmen and prospects. In the broadest sense, the sales presentation is everything that happens in front of the prospect. It is viewed as the "message segment" of the communication process. An effective presentation must arouse in the prospect the need for improving his present situation. The presentation must diplomatically suggest remedial action in terms of the seller's product offering. The presentation should anticipate and hopefully eliminate all potential objections. It should be persuasive, factual, believable, and ethical. It should be complete, brief, and pegged to the needs, experience, and semantic level of the prospect.

The seller's response-goal sequence may be summarized by the prospect's propensity to understand, believe, and act upon the presentation. If the response is unfavorable at any single stage in the selling sequence, the positive effects of previous steps may be nullified and the opportunity for advancement to subsequent steps may be cancelled. Thus, the steps that precede and follow the main presentation may be as important as the main presentation itself.

STEPS IN THE SALES PRESENTATION

Chapter 1 indicated that many firms depend upon personal selling to accomplish the five sequential tasks of promotion. The sales presentation can be considered to include three of these tasks—

making contact with prospects, stimulating desire for the firm's offerings, and closing the sale. Thus the sales presentation includes everything the salesperson does and says while in the presence of the prospect.

Almost every sales presentation will require the salesperson to perform each of the following steps in the specified sequence.

1. Contact the prospect
2. Gain an audience
3. Sit down
4. Neutralize
5. Prime the prospect
6. Qualify the prospect
7. Deliver the main presentation
8. Check the prospect's "pulse"
9. Close the sale
10. Wrap up

The purpose of these ten steps is to anticipate and prepare for resistance by the prospect at three separate levels—before, during, and after the product message or demonstration. Put another way, the prospect has three decisions to make during the salesman's visit: (1) Will I admit this salesperson to my office or home? (2) Will I listen to his complete story? (3) Will I buy his product or service?

Approach

The approach consists of steps 1 through 6. The contact may be made by mail, by telephone, or in person. It consists of the salesman's introduction to the sales target or his secretary, assistant, wife, maid, or other intermediary. This introduction may be very simple: "My name is George Brown with the X-Y-Z Corporation. Can you put my name on your calendar for 1:00 P.M. on October 15?" After making contact, the salesman may have to convince a tough secretary or other buffer that he should be granted an audience with the decision maker.

If the salesman rather than the prospect is to take control of the interview, the salesman must anticipate the possibility that the busy or disinterested prospect may say, "Look, Mr. Brown, I'm quite busy today. What is it that you're selling?" To avoid being put on the defensive, the salesman might say, "May I sit *here* or would you prefer that I sit on the sofa?"

Neutralizing is the process of warming up the atmosphere immediately after the salesman has been seated. In fact, the best neutralizers consist of a patter that begins as soon as the salesman steps across the threshold, so as to establish immediate rapport and to put the prospect at ease. Neutralizing should consist of not more than a minute or two of chatter about the weather, traffic conditions, or last night's baseball game.

The salesman should then turn businesslike and move into his *primer talk:* "Well, you are probably wondering why I'm here, Mr. Foster." The priming step is an interest-generating talk designed to set the stage for the main presentation. It's a mind opener and as such is the first in a series of preplanned steps by which the prospect is led into the buying decision. The primer may consist of questions that invite the prospect to state the business conditions, inadequacies, or needs which call for the seller's remedial suggestions. The primer phase quite often ends with an attempt to qualify the prospect. Qualification takes on many meanings depending on the product being marketed. In essence, it consists of the salesman's attempt to assure himself that this is a prospect with whom it is worth spending time. A typical question in the sale of commercial antishoplifting devices would be "And so, Mr. Foster, if our company was able to suggest a system that has historically reduced shoplifting losses by over 60 percent, would such information be of value to you?"

Main Presentation

Following the primer talk and the qualification, comes the heart of the selling process—the main presentation. Everything the salesman has done, up to this point, has prepared for it. At key points in the presentation, the salesman checks the prospect's "pulse" to make sure the prospect is attentive and responsive. He might ask, for example, "Is that clear to you, Mr. Foster?" or "Would you care to comment about that product design?"

Despite the unique role of the ten presentation phases, the bulk of the salesman's time is spent in delivering the main sales presentation. Accordingly, the majority of the material in this chapter will focus on this step (number 7). However, the vital contribution of the other 9 steps is emphasized by sales managers who insist that, "The sale is *made* in the first five minutes in front of the prospect and *lost* in the last five."

Closing Sequence

Most salesmen use the term *close* to designate the act of actually getting the prospect's assent to the sales contract. Closing a sale is simply the logical conclusion to a satisfactory completion of each step of the selling plan. As one sales manager puts it, "the purpose of the close is to make thirsty prospects drink."

A major portion of the closing sequence is devoted to the quotation of prices. If the sale is completed, the wrap-up consists of a statement of delivery and/or installation schedules, an indication of the seller's pledged posttransactional services, and the collection of credit information. In some cases, an order cannot be obtained on the first sales call. Written quotations may have to be sent and additional interviews or demonstrations may have to be arranged at the convenience of the prospective buyer or his associates.

Coping with Sales Resistance

Most selling strategists agree that there are only three main reasons that a salesman will ever deliver a presentation and then leave the prospect without making a sale. (1) The prospect is not fully sold on the product. (2) The prospect cannot afford the purchase. (3) The prospect is unable or unwilling to make a decision. The ten steps in the sales presentation sequence are designed to anticipate and cope with these three sources of sales resistance.

OBJECTIVES OF THE SALES PRESENTATION

At one time, the sole purpose of the sales presentation was to persuade the prospect. However, the evolution and acceptance of the marketing concept has triggered the need for extensive, wiser, and more frequent reviews of the sales message, lest it become obsolescent as measured by market, sales force, and company needs.

Prospects expect salespeople to inform them of the availability, characteristics, and capabilities of need-satisfying products and services. The firm expects sales-force members to generate buying decisions and actual purchases within the constraints of competitive activities, societal demands, and ethical considerations. Yet it is management's responsibility to create and maintain the motivational climate in which the salesperson works.[1] The steps to this end include training, compensating, and supervising the salesperson so as to satisfy his hierarchy of needs. The appropriately structured sales presentation is a relevant variable in the process of developing a healthy sales-force climate. Thus the ideal sales-presentation design will simultaneously optimize the interests of the prospect, the sales force, and the company.

One recent research project included a detailed analysis of the sales-presentation objectives of numerous firms of different sizes selling various products and services to dissimilar target markets. Based on the above framework which combines prospect, sales force,

1. Conserve the prospect's time
2. Tell the complete story
3. Deliver an accurate, authoritative, and ethical message
4. Persuade the prospect
5. Anticipate objections before they occur
6. Facilitate training of salespeople
7. Increase salesperson's self-confidence
8. Facilitate supervision of salespeople

TYPES OF SALES PRESENTATIONS [3]

Although there is considerable debate among sales managers concerning types of sales presentations, the best presentation for a given firm is the one that most effectively achieves that firm's selling objectives. Thus, before the firm's sales presentation is designed, specific selling objectives should be formulated and ordered. Unfortunately, this step is often missing, and either the sales presentation is created on the spur of the moment or the planning process is based on a weak foundation.

The sales presentation may be prepared by the company, by the salesperson, or by both. In the early twenties, John H. Patterson, then president of the National Cash Register Company, introduced the first company-prepared sales presentation. The sales talks of the leading NCR salesmen were typewritten, analyzed, and composited to produce a standard company message which all salesmen were required to memorize and use. Following sizeable sales increases by NCR, numerous other sales organizations followed the example. Company input as a replacement for or supplement to the salesman's own message grew in popularity, and as it did, an attendant dialogue of controversy about the effectiveness of the canned presentation developed among salespeople, sales managers, and various other critics of the selling function.

What's a Canned Presentation?

Much of the argument centers on the meaning of *canned*. To those whose feathers ruffle at the mention of the word, it conjures up the image of a salesperson, not unlike a puppet, whose every word and gesture have been masterminded by a slick armchair marketer in his Madison Avenue ivory tower. Opponents of such a definition object violently to the use of the word *"canned"* but instead claim that structured, company-prepared, and planned presentations are nothing more than a track to run on, not a groove to confine the salesperson. To the latter group, an unstructured ad-lib presentation is a meandering stream of verbosity, devoid of plan and often devoid of logic or persuasiveness.[4]

Degrees of Structure

Almost always, the canned/uncanned, or structured/unstructured, dichotomy is presented as constituting opposite sides of a coin. More realistically, a given presentation design may be viewed as occupying some point on a continuum, from a complete absence of company input to total automation, with at least five perceivable degrees:

Fully automated. Sound movies, slides, or film strips dominate the presentation. The salesman's participation consists of setting up the projector, answering simple questions, and/or writing up the order. Many audiovisual systems are available.

Semiautomated. The salesman reads the presentation from copy printed on flip charts, read-off binders, promotional broadsides, or brochures. He adds his own comments when necessary.

Memorized. The salesman delivers a company-prepared message that he has memorized. Supplementary visual aides may or may not be used.

Organized. The salesman is allowed complete flexibility of wording; however, he does follow a company pattern, checklist, or outline. Visual aides are optional.

Unstructured. The salesman is on his own to describe his product any way he sees fit. Generally, the presentation varies from prospect to prospect and is therefore customer-specific.

The first three types may be designated as highly structured by the company. The last contains no structure by the company, although it may be well planned and well developed by the salesperson. The organized presentation draws heavily from both the salesperson and the firm.

CURRENT PRACTICES

Research findings indicate [5] that nearly 80 percent of the selling firms studied used more than a single type of sales presentation. Over 40 percent used two modes, over 25 percent used three modes; more than 12 percent used four modes. Of course, many firms that use multimodes sell several unrelated products and/or cater to several unrelated market segments or buying levels.

The same study indicates that the organized and customer-specific types are far more popular than the other three methods. More than 85 percent of the respondent firms used the organized talk, and 76 percent included the customer-specific (unstructured) method. One-third of the firms used semiautomated programs (flip charts, easels, read-off binders). Twenty-four percent of the firms used memorized sales presentations, while less than 10 percent used fully automated (primarily audiovisual) methods.

Multimodal Presentations

There are a number of explanations for the use of various forms of presentations by the same firm. A firm may sell several products which differ from each other in terms of price, complexity, type of prospect, or channel level of distribution. Sales-presentation preferences may vary geographically among field sales managers and/or salespeople. Even within the same district, some salespeople may prefer canned modes while others may insist upon complete freedom in developing the sales presentation.

Within the very effective Procter and Gamble sales organization, field sales managers and representatives enjoy complete liberty to use or reject sales-promotional photographs, reprints, and write-ups supplied by the company for sales presentations. Some salesmen use this literature in flipcharts or ring binders in front of the prospect; those who use an ad-lib approach use the promotional literature to suit specific customers; some salesmen hardly ever use pre-printed write-ups or illustrations. In 1972, Procter and Gamble was especially interested in promoting the T-mod combination package and display of deodorant products. A movie was developed to introduce T-mod to retailers. Some salesmen used it and others did not. It may be seen that within this organization, almost all types of presentation designs on the continuum of structure are used.

Preferred Modes

Sales managers are often queried about why they use various presentation methods in their own firm. In particular, it is interesting to investigate why customer-specific methods are substantially more popular than modes that are more highly structured by the company.

Typical replies are as follows: "It's the only way we've ever sold"; "I'm sure there's a better way"; "We'd like to introduce more company structure, but we don't know how." In general, many firms have had little experience with well-designed canned modes. Moreover, one might conclude that in many firms, methods currently employed are traditionally convenient, intuitive, or forced, but they are seldom coordinated with explicit sales or marketing objectives.

PERCEPTIONS OF SALES-PRESENTATION EFFECTIVENESS

Table 6.1 shows the approximate rankings by a group of sales executives of the various sales-presentation modes, in terms of perceived effectiveness in accomplishing the sales objectives listed above.[6]

Customer Requirements

As shown in Table 6.1, sales executives perceive the organized presentation as most effective in conserving the prospect's time and telling the complete story. This method combines the advantages of company control and situational flexibility. Company input in terms of format or sequencing helps to compensate for loss of memory by the salesperson. Moreover, the salesperson is free to adapt his message to the mood, thinking, questioning, and special needs of his audience and to surround what he sells with his personality. To a lesser degree, the semiautomated approach also combines completeness with an opportunity for salespeople to adjust their behavior when necessary.

Sales executives rank the fully automated presentation as most effective in delivering an accurate, authoritative, and ethical message. These data support the proposition that management perceives substantial structure as programming against inaccurate or unethical statements by sales-force members. A highly structured approach is also effective when the seller wishes to deliver a one-way standard interruptions, out-of-sequence inquiries, and requested shortcuts.

Company Requirements

The principal tasks during the sales presentation are to influence, to persuade, and to deal with the prospect's objections. The organized and unstructured methods in Table 6.1 are ranked first and second in terms of persuasive power. Apparently, sales executives feel that when the experienced salesman is not subjected to substantial constraints imposed by the company, he can draw from his reservoir of product knowledge, offer rebuttals, and use various other elements of persuasion as the interview progresses.

In general, sales executives believe that some company input is more persuasive than none. But memorization and full automation are perceived as detrimental to persuasive effectiveness. Those with limited experience in using substantial company input are concerned about the absence of fire and life in the message. They feel that selling cannot be both standardized and persuasive and that no two buyers can be handled alike because conditions are never the same twice. Furthermore, with memorized and audiovisual presentations,

Table 6.1 Perceived level of sales-presentation effectiveness in accomplishing selling objectives

Objective	Fully automated	Semi-automated	Memorized	Organized	Unstructured
1. Conserve prospect's time	moderate	moderate	low	very high	low
2. Tell complete story	high	high	moderate	high	low
3. Deliver accurate, authoritative, ethical message	very high	high	low	moderate	very low
4. Persuade prospect	low	moderate	low	very high	high
5. Anticipate objections before they occur	moderate	high	low	very high	moderate
6. Facilitate training of salespeople	high	high	very low	very high	low
7. Increase salesperson's self-confidence	low	high	low	very high	moderate
8. Facilitate supervision of salespeople	moderate	high	moderate	very high	low

SOURCE: Simplified version of a table which appeared in Marvin A. Jolson, "Should the Sales Presentation be Fresh or Canned?" *Business Horizons* 16 (October 1973), p. 85.

it is difficult to handle questions and objections so as to elicit feedback from the prospect.

The high rate of sales-force turnover confirms the difficulty of attracting and/or developing top salespeople, especially those who can react instantaneously to new situations, overcome resistance, and "plug in" the ideal answer to each objection. Seemingly, the experienced firm with seasoned sales managers can classify and catalog most of the objections and negative reactions of prospects for each phase of the sales presentation. The structured sales message which anticipates and overcomes objections before they occur essentially compensates for certain weaknesses of sales personnel. This stimulus–response type of selling is the rationale for the use of memorized talks, flip charts, audiovisuals, and in fact, all forms of structured presentations. It is interesting, therefore, to observe in Table 6.1 that the organized presentation is rated most effective and the memorized method least effective in anticipating objections.

Essentially, respondents may be questioning the policy of treating all sales prospects as one homogeneous group. Krech and Crutchfield argue that the shotgun approach, which treats all prospects alike, hits most prospects to some extent but hits few perfectly: "If we were to allow for the finest shading and nuance of motives among different people, we would find the number of separate human motives running well into the billions." [7]

Sales-Force Requirements

Objectives 6, 7, and 8 in Table 6.1 are concerned with training salespeople (initially and continuously), supervising their field activities, and improving their self-confidence. The appropriate choice of a sales presentation can assist the salesperson in all three areas, with attendant benefits to the firm and the prospect.

The organized, semiautomated, and fully automated presentations are rated in that order in terms of both training and supervision effectiveness. The memorized talk is perceived as least effective in terms of training and the unstructured method least effective in terms of supervision. Although subsequent chapters will again refer to the sales presentation in connection with training and supervision, a very brief discussion is in order at this point.

The level of the new salesman's confidence would appear to be related to the ease and speed of the method by which he was trained. New salespeople, especially those who are compensated on a commission basis, strive to be productive as soon as possible. Moreover, the inexperienced salesman thinks of himself as being in conflict with experienced buyers and sales-force members. Seemingly, the highly structured presentation would arm him with professionalism, tested methods, and other forms of fail-safe mechanisms that prevent loss of sales and prolonged sales slumps. However, the findings shown in Table 6.1 do not support this hypothesis. Sales managers rank the organized presentation as significantly more effective than all other methods in increasing the salesperson's self-confidence. The semiautomated and unstructured methods follow in order. These results are fairly consistent throughout all categories.

One possible explanation for these findings is that the role of the salesman is abased when a presentation contains substantial company input. One summary statement reads, "Any idiot can plug in a projector, read off a flip chart or memorize a bunch of words." Such salesmen are perceived as subordinated to some centralized, mechanized form of presentation. This conflicts with the experienced salesman's quest for wide latitude in his behavior, for example, in choosing the prospect to contact, in timing the call, and in deciding what is to be said to the prospect. A number of sales managers feel that the prospect will not hold still for any automatic method of delivery. However, several proponents of the memorized presentation and other structured forms report that even veteran salespeople welcome the support of a proven company message and other aids which can be supplemented by well-placed ad libs by the salesperson. A number of managers inserted comments to the effect that structure is readily acceptable by trainees but is hastily abandoned by the more seasoned salesperson. The resultant presentation can be termed organized since certain forms of company input remain.

Sales supervision is viewed as the company backstop system to prevent and/or correct sales-force errors or failures in the field. In an unstructured presentation, management is not sure of the content of the sales message or the sequence of its parts. Therefore, troubleshooting the poor-producing salesperson is difficult, and the lowly rating of the unstructured presentation is understandable. One can only speculate as to why the organized presentation, with its limited company structure, ranks so high for the supervision objective. One possible explanation is the observed lack of experience with more structured methods. Another is that the quest for sales is more important than supervision as an objective, and the organized presentation is a more effective sales producer even if a less effective tool for supervising salespeople; this is a conflict of objectives. Finally, the meaning of supervision varies considerably between sales managers and between authors.

PERSUASIVE PRESENTATIONS

It was shown in Table 6.1 that the unstructured sales presentation is rated low to moderate in effectiveness for all objectives except persuasiveness. Why then is this method used by 76 percent of the sampled firms? Seemingly, a focus on consumer interests is still being dwarfed by an overwhelming drive for sales.

However, the more structured modes may be more persuasive than some sales managers think. One experiment attempted to subject two matched sets of prospective purchasers to different sales presentations of the same product.[8] Although few of the prospects had ever heard of the product prior to the sales presentation, the semiautomated version of the sales presentation was significantly more persuasive than the customer-specific presentation in that 42 percent of the former group expressed definite buying intentions.

Very few salespeople or sales managers have read about this experiment. Even fewer firms have conducted their own research to compare the persuasiveness of the several types of sales presentations. Although the author has no personal preferences or hangups relating to any of the presentation methods, his experiences as a salesman, sales manager, and sales consultant confirm the fact that canned presentations are often equal or superior in persuasiveness to ad-lib presentations.

Since people are normally afraid of foods they haven't eaten or actions they haven't tried, sales managers are somewhat reluctant to depend on the memorized or automated presentation when persuasion is required. One sales manager for a very large seller to retail food accounts said, "We don't use canned talks or audiovisuals because we have many top salesmen." First of all, an overabundance of top salespeople is rare. Second, guidelines, material to be memorized, visual aids, films, etc., may, in many instances, help to improve *any* salesperson's effectiveness.

Many consumer and organizational buyers are visually oriented and actually lack the power to form clear images from the spoken word.[9] When the product is too large or fragile to be carried around by the salesperson, photographs or films are effective tools in the sales-presentation kit.

Early in this chapter, the reader was introduced to ten steps in the sales-presentation sequence. Any or all of these steps may be structured or canned by management. There are excellent standardized methods for getting through protective secretaries and wives, for qualifying and priming prospects, and for checking the prospect's "pulse." In numerous creative selling situations, a memorized closing sequence including automatic rebuttals may spell the difference between the salesperson's success or failure. In many businesses there are standard answers to frequently heard objections or excuses such as "I want to think it over," "I'd like to talk it over with my partner," "the price is too high," or "I want to look at your competitor's product."

SELLING AIDS AND TECHNIQUES

Dramatization in the sales presentation is not restricted to the fully automated or semiautomated methods. If the reader will review the degrees of structure on the continuum of sales presentations, he will note that the unstructured or organized presentation allows the salesman complete flexibility such that he is free to use photographs, pictures, reprints, charts, graphs, diagrams, slides and movies, whenever and wherever he wishes to do so.

Flip Charts and Read-off Portfolios

Many salespeople are unwilling or unable to memorize lengthy sales presentations. One company alternative is to reproduce the desired sales talk, word for word, on standard ring-binder pages or flip charts. The salesperson may read the presentation to the prospect, word for word, or he may refer to the printed material to emphasize key points. The "read-off" sales talk is often a professionally done promotional piece with laminated pages, color, tables, diagrams, photographs, cartoons, and other helpful materials.

The flip chart may be constructed in easel form so that it stands by itself on the prospect's desk. Sometimes the material viewed by the prospect will consist of few words and many pictures or diagrams. The sales talk may be written on the reverse side of each page so that it is seen by the salesperson and not the prospect.

Many salespeople ignore these aids which are provided by the company because they assume that prospects will not allow a sales talk to be read or that prospects will be bored or that reading a talk is ineffective. Such general assumptions are completely false and merely indicate that the firm has done a poor job in indoctrinating and training its sales-force members in the effective use of read-off sales talks.

Audiovisuals (AV)

Table 6.1 discloses the perceived effectiveness of the fully automated and semiautomated methods in delivering an accurate, authoritative, and ethical message. The forces of consumerism are compelling sellers to accept new standards and to reconsider their hierarchy of sales objectives, particularly relating to control of the sales message. If the salesperson has confidence that the company-prepared message is impressive and effective, his temptation to improvise his sales talk, insert untrue statements, and generally misrepresent the facts will be minimized.

For these reasons, and others to be shown, movies, color slides, and filmstrips are playing an increasingly important role in delivering the sales message. New audiovisual equipment is lighter, easier to operate, and capable of better sound and picture quality than ever before.

Films are particularly useful for educating distributors, dealers, and their salespeople. For example, in the spring of 1975, the John Deere Company introduced its 1976 snowmobile line by subjecting four thousand dealers to a professionally staged, multimedia, multiscreen program featuring intensive use of AV equipment. Ten slide projectors and a sound movie projector beamed the images onto a 140-foot snowbank of screens and, at the climax, when the screens were lifted to show four new snowmobiles, the dealers came roaring to their feet.[10] Amway uses flexible records that can be mailed and played on a standard phonograph to send monthly training and instructional messages to its distributors.[11] In addition to the training benefit of AV materials, these and examples to follow illustrate the fully automated sales presentation in action.

AV equipment is an indispensable input to third-party selling. This approach involves the use of a well-known and/or unusually capable person to deliver all or part of the sales presentation. For example, during the fall of 1975, Dow Chemical's salesmen faced the very difficult selling task of telling recession-pinched customers that chemical prices were about to rise. The firm made up a video program that explained the factors behind the increase so that customers could understand historical price patterns in the industry along with forecasted prices for the near future. The message was recorded by company officials on Sony U-matic videocassettes and shipped to salespeople in various parts of the world.[12]

The medical and dental fields are particularly inviting for AV sales presentations.[13] Salesmen representing Chayes Virginia, a manufacturer of dental chairs and instruments, use a thirteen-minute film that shows dentists how to eliminate backaches. Squibb's salespeople also use AV equipment to tell physicians about the company's product line, as does Warner-Lambert, in demonstrating its soft contact lens.

AV use is increasing at an accelerating rate in selling to industrial buyers, retail stores, business offices, and consumers. Salespeople are using AV equipment to deliver in-home presentations, and AV use is becoming increasingly popular in retail stores. For example, Wallpapers, Inc. used portable projectors made by MPO Videotronics to demonstrate its theme of a "room in a box" in J. C. Penney stores.[14]

AV equipment is expensive but since the equipment can be used for selling, training, recruiting, and other purposes, the cost may be justified. Some sales managers may prefer to rent the equipment. Rental and purchase costs are readily available for comparison.[15]

Finally, elaborate or expensive audiovisuals and other props seem to suggest company bigness, success, and quality. They also suggest products with broad consumption patterns because the prospect is aware that costly techniques used in sales presentations are designed for use with a large number of prospects over time.[16]

Nonpersonal Personal Selling

AV can sometimes take the place of a salesperson's call. The Datavision Division of 3M mails videocassettes to prospective customers, thus sparing the salesman from legging around a heavy piece of equipment while freeing him for more intensive selling. Similarly, Alza Pharmaceuticals mailed a film and a viewer to ophthalmologists to promote its new Ocusert Glaucoma-treatment system.[17]

Nonpersonal sales presentations using AV equipment are featured at trade shows, airports, railroad stations, convention centers, and other locations. These displays demonstrate products, answer anticipated questions, and sometimes persuade prospects to deposit orders and appointment requests in nearby receptacles.

More recently, telephone selling has entered a new phase of sophistication with the use of personal messages on tape. With the aid of telephone tapes, authors have helped to sell textbook adoptions, a magazine publisher has called thousands of prospects, Golda Meir has engaged in house-to-house fund raising, and Mickey Mantle has sold exercise apparatus. Murray Roman of Campaign Communications Institute of America, a leader in the area of taped phone messages, personalizes the communications by using a live operator to introduce the tape and to answer questions and take orders following the tape.

RESPONSE TO OBJECTIONS OF PROSPECTS

Sales resistance and objections by prospects are quite normal, and they occur whenever the salesman delivers his sales presentation. It has been observed earlier in this chapter that a major goal of the sales presentation is to anticipate objections before they occur. However, the finest sales presentation will seldom anticipate all objections, nor will it deal effectively with all objections that do arise. The salesperson must be prepared before he makes the sales call to respond to the huge array of potential objections by prospects.

Many textbooks and articles attempt to provide a set of general methods and techniques to be used in handling objections. Although some methods are interchangeable among salespeople, companies, and products, most techniques for overcoming objections are tied as closely to a given company as is the sales presentation itself. Since the company exists in perpetuity, management is in a position to assemble and catalog objections received over time and to develop an appropriate set of responses for the use of the sales force. Transmitting these techniques to sales-force members constitutes a sizeable proportion of management's training and supervision functions.

What D'ya Do When . . . ?

Typically, after he's encountered an objection, the new salesman will ask his manager, "What do you say when the prospect says he has no use for our product?" The ideal answer is "Make sure the prospect doesn't say that." This response assumes that the sales presentation has already anticipated the objection and has built in the rebuttal.

For example, when selling the thirty-volume set of the *Encyclopaedia Britannica* to military families, the anticipated objection is

> We move so frequently that we prefer not to carry around
> a heavy set of books. It would probably be better if we
> used the public or post libraries.

Rather than wait for this expected objection to arise, the salesperson is instructed to say:

> We do realize that you are subject to frequent relocation.
> Therefore, we suggest that you don't discard the three
> convenient shipment containers. When you move, just
> slip ten volumes in each carton and seal them up. Also

remember that the *Britannica* is part of your household belongings, which the government pays to transport. Frankly, one of my associates was speaking to another military person who mentioned that his children attend so many different schools over the years that the *Britannica* is the only permanent part of their education.

Verbal-Proof Story (VPS)

The above rebuttal used by the *Britannica* salesman is canned (structured by the company) such that it is recommended for use whenever a military family is contacted. It will be noted that the salesperson does not claim that the *Britannica* is the only permanent part of the child's education. Instead, he refers to a third person who made such a claim. It is to be emphasized that statements attributed to third parties must be those *actually* made by such parties and not statements invented by sales personnel. This technique of using a third party's statement (VPS) is effective because the prospect cannot doubt or argue with a statement made by a person who is not present.

Although the VPS can be used by any sales organization to anticipate or respond to specific objections, the specific stories can be developed by management only after years of exposure to the experiences of many salespeople.

Canned Responses to Objections

Once the objection appears, different salespeople will respond in different ways. There are a number of possible reactions in addition to the VPS, such as, arguing with the prospect, using the "yes—but" approach, trying to destroy competitors, turning objections into sales points. There is no such thing as the right way or even the best way to react to objections. However, there may be a company way—the way management would like sales-force members to respond.

For example, the company may prepare a small file of rebuttals which is indexed by the nature of the objection. If the prospect should say, "We really cannot afford your product," the salesman can flip, almost unnoticed, to the price-objection rebuttal.

This collection by the company of standard responses to objections or "rebuttal files" is essentially *canned* or *company structured* and is considerably more effective than putting the new salesman "on his own" to instinctively dream up an instantaneous response to an objection he's never heard before.

One author offers examples of how objections are handled by

such well-known firms as Remington Rand, Bendix, Mutual Benefit Life Insurance Co., Westinghouse Electric, Royal Typewriter Co., Lily-Tulip Cup Corp., and the Frigidaire Division of General Motors Corp.[18] For the most part, these companies offer standard procedures, rules, routines, and sequential methods of handling objections.

SUMMARY AND CONCLUSIONS

There is a willingness for firms to condone concurrent use of several diverse and often discordant sales-presentation modes. As tendencies continue toward conglomeration, market segmentation, organizational decentralization, and consumerism, and as sales personnel become scarcer, multiple-presentation policies will undoubtedly continue.

Clearly, many sales managers are inexperienced with memorized presentations, flip charts, and audiovisuals. Consequently, they are unaware of the potential effectiveness of these methods in achieving many of the firm's selling objectives.

Although current practices indicate a limited amount of company input, there are signs that the use of audiovisuals and other techniques structured by the company are appearing more frequently. Such input is not restricted to the main sales message and can be used during the approach, the close, as rebuttals to objections, or at any place in the selling sequence.

Major reasons for the relative avoidance of high levels of structure in presentations are the dominance of persuasion as an objective and the perceived ability of customer-specific methods to develop needed collaboration and interdependence between salespeople and prospects. However, the forces of consumerism are compelling sellers to accept new standards and to reconsider their hierarchy of sales objectives. In a sense, consumerists are calling for both more personalized contacts and more company-controlled sales messages.

When company input is very high, control over the sales message is quite complete in that the design of the sales message resembles the method of developing an advertising message. In both cases there is little likelihood of discrepancy between company policy and the content of the message.[19] This reason alone is sufficient to suggest an increasing use of more automated sales-presentation modes.

The quandary of the sales manager in choosing the most effective sales-presentation mode stems from the existence within the firm of multiple sales objectives occupying different dimensions. As customer and sales-force needs grow in importance, management may be required to determine the relative weight of each sales objective. This across-the-board approach will allow for selection of presentation modes that will maximize total sales effectiveness rather than effectiveness in accomplishing any single sales goal.

NOTES

1. Robert M. Olsen, "The Liberating Motivational Climate—An Essential for Sales Effectiveness" in Thomas R. Wotruba and Robert M. Olsen, eds., *Readings in Sales Management* (New York: Holt, Rinehart, and Winston, 1971), pp. 245–56.

2. Marvin A. Jolson, "Should the Sales Presentation be Fresh or Canned?" *Business Horizons* 16 (October 1973):82.

3. Ibid., pp. 81–88. Parts of this section were borrowed directly with permission of the publisher.

4. "Is the Canned Talk Death on Sales?" *American Salesman* 3 (June 1958):87–88.

5. Jolson, *Sales Presentation*, 83–84.

6. Ibid., 81–88.

7. David Krech and Richard S. Crutchfield, *Elements of Psychology* (New York: Knopf, 1961), p. 265.

8. Marvin A. Jolson, "The Underestimated Potential of the Canned Sales Presentation," *Journal of Marketing* 39 (January 1975):75–78.

9. Carlton A. Pederson and Milburn O. Wright, *Salesmanship: Principles and Methods* (Homewood, Ill.: Richard D. Irwin, 1971), p. 373.

10. "Marketing Turns to Sight and Sound," *Sales Management* 115 (4 August 1975):53–54.

11. "AV Plays a Leading Role," ibid., p. 55.

12. "AV Tells it Like it Should Be," ibid., p. 64.

13. "AV Helps to Show and Sell," ibid., p. 68.

14. Ibid., p. 71.

15. See "AV Plays a Leading Role," op. cit., p. 56, for comparison of costs of buying versus renting AV equipment.

16. Sidney J. Levy, in *Managerial Analysis in Marketing*, ed. Frederick D. Sturdivant, et al. (Glenview, Ill.: Scott, Foresman, 1970), pp. 398–99; and Jolson, "The Underestimated Potential," p. 77.

17. "AV Helps to Show and Sell," op. cit., p. 68.

18. Pederson and Wright, *Salesmanship*, p. 425.

19. Harold C. Cash and W. J. E. Crissy, "Comparison of Advertising and Selling," in Eugene J. Kelley and William Lazer, eds., *Managerial Mar-*

keting—Policies, Strategies, and Decisions (Homewood, Ill.: R. D. Irwin, 1973), 439–43.

QUESTIONS FOR DISCUSSION AND REVIEW

1. Chapter 3 stated that "a powerful sales presentation is like the Green Bay Packers playing against a high school team." What is the role of company structure in creating this offensive power? Does this power refer only to the main presentation or to everything the salesperson does in front of the prospect? Discuss.

2. Sidney Land accepted a position as a salesman for a business machine distributor. The first day on the job he was handed an eighteen-page sales presentation and told to go home and memorize it word for word. After two hours of the exercise in memorization, Land became disgusted, mailed the presentation back to the company, and resigned. Support or oppose his action.

3. Order and weigh the eight sales-presentation objectives used in this chapter for two companies of your choice. In your opinion, do the companies explicitly consider these objectives when designing the sales message?

4. Is it possible for the salesperson to develop a highly structured sales presentation on his own with little or no input from the company? Discuss.

5. Select two similar audiences of classmates or colleagues. Deliver a persuasive message to one group using ear appeals. Deliver a persuasive message about the same subject or product to the second group using both eye appeals and ear appeals. Measure the effectiveness of adding eye appeals.

6. One of your newer salesmen delivers an effective "read-off" presentation using a ring binder. He tells you (his sales manager) that prospects frequently refuse to sit still for the full presentation. How would you advise him?

7. Discuss the use of a highly structured sales presentation as a technique for reducing irregularities, misrepresentations, and misleading statements by the salesperson.

8. The sales presentation is occasionally referred to as the "pitch." Is this a degrading term?

Case 6.1 Business Seminars, Inc.

A company-controlled sales presentation is suggested in an effort to reduce sales irregularities and facilitate training and field supervision.

Ralph Tiant is the national sales manager for Business Seminars, Inc., a marketer of customized seminars, workshops, and business-education programs for management. The company designs these programs for specific client needs, and supplies hardware, software, and personnel to deliver lectures and to lead conferences, seminars, and workshops.

The company now has 27 district sales offices and a total of 104 sales people. The company has consistently increased its annual sales volume and profits. Field sales managers and sales representatives are reasonably high spirited since their offerings are well received and their commissions are rising steadily.

However, during recent months, Tiant and his home office sales colleagues have observed some very unfavorable trends:

Customer complaints have almost doubled during the first six months of 1976 in comparison with a similar period in 1975. Almost all the incidents concern discrepancies between the programs and prices agreed upon with salesmen and those actually delivered or billed. For example, in one case, the customer's copy of the contract called for a three-day seminar at a price of $2,700 whereas the company's copy of the same contract called for only a two-day seminar. The salesman claimed it was an honest mistake on his part. In another case, the customer claimed that the saleswoman promised textbooks supplied by the company for seminar participants at no extra charge, whereas the standard company plan was to charge an additional $10.00 for each textbook. Although the contract showed this additional cost, the customer claimed that the salesperson told him the charge would be cancelled if fifty or more employees attended the seminar. The saleswoman denied that she made such a statement.

As a result of these claimed irregularities and misrepresentations, the involved salespeople and customers were at odds with each other and Tiant was cast in the role of a referee. The company was compelled to develop more explicit, detailed, and lengthy contracts which contained a great deal of red tape. Finally, a verification system was developed whereby Tiant's staff telephoned every new customer to double-check every detail of the sales agreement. This process was costly and time consuming for all parties.

The sales-training period, according to Ralph Tiant, was excessively lengthy. Sales recruits spent ten days in class, participated in a minimum of three actual conferences or seminars, and traveled with a field manager or senior salesman for a full week. During the training period, the salesman was denied the opportunity to contact prospects or to earn commissions. The increasing rate of sales irregularities compounded the training period.

As the size of the sales force increased and supervision requirements intensified, district managers complained that troubleshooting slumping salespeople was becoming more difficult. Since there was no standard company sales presentation, each salesperson delivered the sales message as he or she saw fit. The company supplied sales-force members with literature describing completed sessions and suggesting outlines for manpower-development programs. However, the representatives were at liberty to use or not to use these materials in their presentations.

Despite the firm's success, the turnover rate had risen to 100 percent, and Tiant felt that company control of the sales presentation would do much to prevent serious company problems. Moreover, Tiant and his staff were so engaged in putting out fires that drastic action was called for.

Tiant's plan was to invest approximately $30 thousand to produce a thirty-minute color-slide presentation describing all company offerings. Each person on the sales force would be supplied with a slide projector and all salespeople would be encouraged to use the AV presentation with every prospect. The presentation would include written details on all offerings, including types and prices of programs, and extras.

In addition, the salesperson would be provided with a portfolio which included promotional literature on previous programs, biographies and photographs of program leaders, current pricing details, etc.

Salespeople would introduce themselves, make arrangements for the slide presentation, plug in the projector, and let the audiovisuals do the selling job. They would then answer questions with the aid of their portfolios. It would be the representative's responsibility to see that misunderstandings did not occur. Moreover, misrepresentations would result in the dismissal of the offender.

Tiant argued that he couldn't care less if the company did not have a single supersalesman. All he wanted was a substantial staff of honest men and woman who could locate prospects, call on them, plug in a projector, and make sure that prospective customers received straight answers to their questions. Salespeople would carry a standard written series of rebuttals which they would be required to memorize.

Home-office officials would not compel any representative to switch to the new method. However, it was felt that if all new representatives were trained in using the automated system, their success would persuade incumbent sales-force members to accept and, in fact, request the transition.

ASSIGNMENT

Defend or oppose Tiant's plan.

Section III

Establishing the Sales Organization

7

Compensating
Sales Personnel

The author's review of several popular sales-management texts indicated that the question of sales-force compensation is almost always discussed after the reader has been exposed to chapters covering the recruitment, selection, training, supervision, and evaluation of sales personnel. Such an approach neglects the interdependency of the firm's compensation plan and all the above sales-management functions.

For example, unless a prospective sales recruit is satisfied by the firm's level and method of compensation, he or she may reject the job offer, thus nullifying the need for his training, supervision, and evaluation. Similarly, the intensity, length, and format of the training program is highly dependent on the way a salesperson is paid. Finally, since financial outlays to salespeople represent major sales costs, the firm's supervision and evaluation systems are strongly tied to the methods by which money flows from the firm to the sales employee.

This chapter examines sales-compensation plans as they relate to the dual purpose of generating productive selling results while controlling company sales costs. Since the salesperson may be considered to be an "internal consumer" [1] who consumes management's offering of the job package, the firm's trade-off between profits and sales-force satisfaction is analogous to the trade-offs encountered when dealing with buyers in the marketplace.

OBJECTIVES OF THE SALES-
COMPENSATION PLAN

Sales compensation may be properly presented as having a series of broad company objectives. This text will concentrate mainly on financial forms of compensation, including direct payments of earnings, expense allowances, and financial fringe benefits. Little will be said about nonfinancial rewards, such as recognition, time off, job security, attractive office space, etc.

The firm is concerned with how much to pay salespeople (compensation level) and how salespeople reach their level of income (method or mode of compensation). The sales-compensation scheme can help fulfill at least five major company functions: (1) attracting sufficient and desirable salespeople, (2) rewarding sales employees for productivity, (3) retaining desirable salespeople, (4) correlating sales costs with sales results, and (5) controlling selling activities.

Attracting Sufficient and
Desirable Salespeople

Financial reward is a major consideration for any job seeker, particularly for individuals switching to different sales jobs or entering selling for the first time. Although most sales recruits will indicate that compensation level is far more important than compensation mode, many will reject any plan that includes considerable variability of income. These security-minded applicants prefer a salary base or drawing account so that they will enjoy some steadiness of income on a weekly or bimonthly basis. This argument is particularly valid when a salesperson requires a regular income to pay basic living expenses, when sales are normally infrequent, and when selling results are seasonal.

Straight commission plans feature incentive rather than security and ordinarily result in a higher earning level than salary-based compensation plans for similar employees. Why is it then that potentially unlimited earnings do not appeal to all job seekers who want to improve their levels of income? One answer is that the applicant does not have sufficient confidence that the purported high earnings potential exists in the given company. Another applicant may be convinced of the earnings opportunity, but he may not have the confidence that he is capable of performing well enough to earn the available rewards. Finally, there is the applicant who believes in both the existence of the earnings opportunity and his own ability to funds in a proven person such as himself.

The level of salary, draw, commission rate, and fringe-benefit package has much to do with whether a desirable applicant can be hired. Yet a sound compensation program is but one of a number of attractions that assist the firm in its recruiting program.

Rewarding Sales Employees
for Productivity

Ideally, the most productive salespeople will receive the largest earnings. Seemingly, the productivity of salespeople is more easily measured than the productivity of other employees, such as foremen or executive secretaries. Productive salespeople usually write orders; nonproductive salespeople do not.

This generalization is true, up to a point. For example, salespeople often have other assignments which prevent them from writing orders. These assignments include setting up customer displays or performing inventory counts, training customers' salesmen, filling out call reports, offering technical or engineering advice, and so on. Many salespeople are never required to write orders.

Often productivity is more properly measured by effort than by results. In some selling situations, orders are not forthcoming until after the salesperson has spent weeks or months training, observing, or preparing for acquiring orders. When territorial sales potentials differ within the same company, similar selling efforts may result in varying levels of sales volume. Some observers believe that a salesman has been productive when he has delivered numerous sales presentations, even though he has received very few orders, because he has exposed the company's offerings to many potential buyers. Others argue that salespeople with low conversion rates (orders as a percentage of sales presentations) may have permanently turned off potential buyers when sales could have been made by better salespeople. The latter approach views prospects and territories as scarce resources which, once they are destroyed by an inept salesperson, are lost to the company forever.

Retaining Desirable
Sales Employees

If the unproductive salesperson is compensated by straight commissions, resignation may be imminent. If, on the other hand, the poor producer is receiving a substantial guaranteed income, termination would appear to be a viable company alternative. Many will argue that since poor producers are not desirable sales employees their leaving represents no great loss. Others point out that the firm's better salespeople may also have been poor producers at one time, and that a salesperson's strength may lie in his ability to overcome sales slumps and periods of poor production.

Companies and industries with low average pay scales tend to have high turnover rates.[2] However, the relationship between the turnover rate and the percentage of total compensation that is fixed or guaranteed is not as clear-cut. For example, one study indicated that for members of trade, missionary, or technical sales forces, turnover rates rise as the proportion of fixed income increases. The opposite was found true for creative or new-business sales forces, where organizations which used a nonsalaried form of compensation were found to have high turnover rates despite higher than average compensation levels.[3]

Often resignations will take place when management refuses to modify the firm's compensation policy to accommodate a current need or an emergency faced by a salesperson. For example, a commissioned salesman may request an advance or loan, say of two hundred dollars, to enable him to meet a pressing obligation. A rejection of his request may hasten his departure.

The problem of requests for advances was so prevalent in one company that several of the firm's district sales managers had signs put on their desks which read "No orders, no money." One sales manager of a home-improvement company had a humorous method of rejecting requests for advances: "I'd be glad to lend you the money except that I have a special arrangement with the branch manager of the First National Bank. I promised him that if he won't sell any home improvements, I won't lend any money."

Some companies have developed supplemental compensation programs especially designed to retain sales-force members. One health- and accident-insurance company awards stock options in proportion to the salesperson's productivity. If the price of the firm's common stock rises, sales-force members are reluctant to leave without exercising their options. With continued employment and productivity, more options are granted and the company's power to retain employees increases.

Several years ago, Encyclopaedia Britannica, Inc., introduced its salesman's annual incentive fund to retain members of the firm's vast sales organization. Under SAIF, the salesperson contributed one dollar for each order he sold; the company contributed much more for each order. The salesman's equity proportion increased each year that he remained with the company. If a salesperson left, his own contributions were returned but his equity in the fund was lost. An average producer who remained with the company for three years could earn an annual bonus that approximated one-third of his annual income. In addition to its retention power, SAIF added a security dimension to a basic straight-commission system.

Correlating Sales Costs
with Sales Results

A major rationale for straight-commission plans is that compensation costs are proportional to selling results. Thus, many companies will hire people on commissions only, provide little training and field supervision, tolerate high turnover rates, and operate under the illusion that the selling operation is quite cost efficient. Yet this sink-or-swim approach neglects the fact that high turnover rates result in the need for continuous hiring and training activity; an indifference to sales-force quality; the need for additional supervision, which puts an added strain on management; and an image and selling climate which is not conducive to the attraction and retention of desirable sales employees. Moreover, intangible costs from lost sales, lost customers, and other forms of poor sales productivity may exceed the measurable out-of-pocket costs.

For example, one study of the life-insurance industry measured the business obtained from orphan policyholders (customers whose original salesmen were no longer employed by the company). It was found that the business obtained from such customers was significantly less than that received from policyholders whose original agent was still employed by the company.[4] The insurance industry is but one of a number of examples of the need for a continuing relationship between customer and salesperson. Often, the purchaser, as in the case of the department-store buyer, is more loyal to the salesperson than to the firm or the product. In these cases, termination of a salesman's employment may mean the company's loss of a valuable account.

Proponents of compensation guarantees favor a level of earnings that is fair, reasonable, and commensurate with effort expended and services rendered, without regard for sales results. Under these conditions, employers are responsive to the novice or slumping salesperson who may call on prospects for days or even weeks, make few or no sales, and earn very little. Salesmen on straight commissions are abused under certain conditions. Territories may be withdrawn as commissions build. A company's failure to ship orders and provide quality products and customer services can result in orders being returned and the loss of commissions by salesmen. The company may fail to provide literature, samples, and other sales aids;

may fail to pay commissions promptly, or at all; and may fail to compensate salesmen when customers are delinquent in payments.

The payment of salaries and the granting of guarantees to novices and marginal producers introduces the risk of increasing sales costs without an associated rise in revenues. However, it is argued that more selective hiring and more intensive supervision or subsidized salespeople will result in lower turnover rates and decreased sales costs.[5]

Controlling Selling Activities

Many outside salespeople work wholly without supervision, receive no specified routes or territories, and have no regular work or reporting schedules. They may combine casual or intermittent selling efforts with social calls or other forms of communication. They may have other jobs and may represent other companies. Perhaps in no other line of endeavor are employees given as much freedom to work and to progress at their own pace. A firm often cannot control or even meaningfully define such an employee's input. The supervisor may have no practical way of distinguishing diligence and skills from actual sales; no way of knowing or regulating the number of contacts and presentations made by salesmen.

It is the flexibility of the work schedule of the outside salesman that is inherent to the problems of control. Since the employer is often compelled to accept the salesman's self-serving allegations of hours worked, salaries or guarantees are often paid for time that is not spent at work.

Historically, the commissioned salesman has been viewed as an independent contractor earning commissions from his results rather than wages for his efforts. This feeling of independence manifests itself in the saleman's reluctance to respond to customers and company needs, to fill out call reports, to assist other salespeople, and to attend company functions, such as sales meetings and clinics. This indifference on the part of top-producing commissioned salespeople discourages nonselling duties and team spirit, while encouraging price cutting, padding of expense accounts, concentration on fast-selling items in the line, and the use of questionable selling presentations and techniques.

On the other hand, the salesperson who is salaried or has a guaranteed minimum income is subject to the same company constraints, regulation, control, and whims as conventional nonselling employees. Seemingly, when the company is willing to disassociate sales compensation from selling results, it earns the right to control the salesman's working hours, travel schedule, nonselling responsibilities, product-line emphasis, territories, and the content and mode of his sales presentation. In such cases, the security-minded sales representative must either conform to company needs or face the implicit threat of termination. This helps explain why the salaried salesperson, such as the in-store or route salesman, is often regarded with less respect than the salesperson on a straight commission.

BASIC SALES-COMPENSATION PLANS

The simplest types of compensation plans call for either straight salary or straight commission. In between are various plans that combine incentive and security. The number of combinations seems endless, considering the wide variety of expense-reimbursement practices and long-term financial fringe benefits.

The Straight Salary

The salesperson working on a straight salary receives a predetermined fixed sum of money at regular intervals (usually weekly, monthly, or bimonthly). The salary level is usually set after a consideration of the employee's needs, his expected productivity, and the company's existing wage scale and policy. The chief feature of this plan is that the salesperson's earnings for the period are independent of sales, profits, customer contacts, sales presentations, and any other measure of field productivity.

This plan alleviates the salesman's concern about financial uncertainties and fluctuations of earnings, a concern which may be present when plans tie earnings to sales performance. However, when there is a ceiling on earnings, salesmen may not be motivated to perform in keeping with their highest potential. Nevertheless, many salesmen insist that the certainty of a regular income overshadows all the advantages of other plans; a salary permits them to devote themselves wholeheartedly to work.

From management's point of view, the primary advantages of the straight-salary plan are that the salesperson's activities can be controlled and directed toward satisfying company and customer needs. The company is also in a position to modify or redirect salesmen's efforts to accommodate changing environmental conditions and evolving customer and company demands. High production over a period of time can always be rewarded by salary increases, while subpar performance can be dealt with through salary decreases or termination. Salary is tangible, a sure thing in the eyes of the newcomer. It is therefore highly effective for attracting beginners and for inducing people to work in pioneering or highly competitive industries and territories.

It is difficult, however, to reduce the salesman's income when his poor production is the result of economic conditions, industry downturns, or inefficiencies on the part of the company. Yet, the economic slump of the mid-seventies and the threats of bankruptcy resulted in numerous layoffs of salaried salespeople, who then found it difficult to relocate, especially to new opportunities which were "commission intensive."

Another problem in administering a straight-salary program is the difficulty of rationalizing salary variances among employees. Whereas productive foremen, researchers, secretaries, and assistant professors may not object to a smaller salary than their less productive but more experienced colleagues, a highly productive salesman is quick to criticize a plan that offers more compensation to a person who has more seniority but turns in inferior sales results. This management dilemma receives more attention in Chapter 12 where the appraisal of sales personnel is discussed.

Straight Commission

The basic assumptions of the straight-commission plan are that salespeople should be paid only for productivity and that sales volume is the best measure of productivity. Accordingly, straight commissions resemble the built-in risks and rewards of independent entrepreneurship.[6]

Depending on the type of product sold and the company doing the selling, the salesman may receive his commission when the order is written and accepted, when the order is shipped, or when the order is paid for. This plan is based on incentive, in that it offers unlimited rewards for productivity, and thus inspires selling efforts which are seldom appealed to under salary plans. It is ideally suited to the superstar performer, since income is determined by productivity.

There is little doubt that the tremendous incentives inherent in the straight-commission plan are advantageous to the firm. One study compared the annual productivity of 1,500 salesmen of heavy equipment and found that those on straight salary produced an average of $135,000 while those working on commissions produced an average of $262,000.[7] As previously mentioned, another benefit is the low risk of compensation costs in the absence of productivity. Straight commission is also an ideal plan when part-time salespeople are employed; when hours and scheduling are not supervised; when nonselling duties are few and unimportant; when getting the order is the most important selling requirement; and when company financial resources are limited such that the subsidy of nonproductive people is unfeasible.

The above advantages are often sufficient to overcome the following disadvantages of straight-commission plans:

1. Straight-commission plans instill uncertainty and insecurity in many sales employees.[8] This increases turnover probabilities and intensifies the need for recruitment and supervision.
2. Little employee loyalty is developed because of the "If I don't sell, they won't pay me" attitude.
3. A push for orders may be stimulated, and a lack of concern for customer needs may result. This is especially true when repeat sales are not involved.
4. Salespeople are difficult to control, especially when no systematic management exists.
5. When high turnover is present, it is desirable to avoid the additional costs for such things as federal social security taxes, unemployment taxes, withholding income taxes, and associated record keeping. In such cases, it is advantageous to have salespeople qualify as independent agents rather than company employees. Although legal interpretations vary, the primary distinction is that an independent agent is not subject to detailed direction from the company and must be free to work when, where, and how he chooses. Therefore, the degree of control the company can legally exercise is limited largely to making suggestions.
6. Flexibility to split territory or transfer salespeople is sharply reduced.
7. Paradoxically, in spite of the greater volume produced, the cost of sales may be somewhat greater. This is because the salesperson on straight commission tends to earn disproportionately more than his equally productive peer who is salaried.
8. The straight-commission plan will not result in increased productivity when sales-force members have low levels of aspirations.
9. A straight-commission plan often results in a lack of selectivity in recruiting because of a notion held by many sales leaders that little is lost by trying out a questionable recruit when he is paid only on the basis of his sales volume. As mentioned already, increased turnover rates result in increased recruitment, training, and supervision costs, in addition to the intangible cost of lost sales.

Straight-commission plans come in so many shapes and sizes that it is beyond the scope of this relatively brief text to elaborate upon the uses and advantages of each type. A straight commission can be based on arrangements such as the following:

1. A fixed rate of commission on all sales.
2. A fixed rate of commission plus a higher rate on sales over a given volume.
3. A multirate step-up commission plan.
4. A multirate step-down or regressive plan, to guard against windfall earnings.
5. A commission on factored sales total; for example, double credit for selling tough items and half credit on easy items.
6. Commissions tied to the profitability or gross margin of items sold.
7. Commission rates tied to total or product quotas.

Bonuses

Bonuses are financial incentives offered to sales-force members for accomplishing special sales tasks. The tasks may relate to overall sales, profitability, or sales of specific products; they may involve opening new accounts, training new salesmen, servicing accounts, delivering an assigned number of presentations, or other achievements beyond normal expectations. Bonuses may be based on individual accomplishments or on the collective accomplishments of groups of salespeople.

Bonuses are always used in combination with a basic compensation plan, such as salary or commission, and may be paid weekly, monthly, annually, or on any other periodic basis.

Drawing Account versus Commissions

One of the more popular methods of combining the incentive of a commission with the security of a fixed income is the draw vs. commission, or periodic advance, against future commissions.

Consider, as an example, a saleswoman who sells cosmetics to department stores. If her compensation arrangement is a draw of $200 per week against 10 percent commission on sales, and her account is to be settled quarterly, her earnings statement will look like that shown in Table 7.1.

It will be noted that she failed to produce any sales during the first two pay weeks. Thus at the end of week 2, she had an overdraft or indebtedness to the company of $400. Her overdraft or debit bal-

Table 7.1 Example of a weekly drawing account of $200.00 vs. 10 percent commissions—quarterly settlement

Pay week	Sales volume	Earned commissions	Weekly draw	Balance
1	0	0	$ 200	$−200
2	0	0	200	−400
3	$ 2,500	$ 250	200	−350
4	1,000	100	200	−450
5	1,000	100	200	−550
6	3,000	300	200	−450
7	4,000	400	200	−250
8	4,500	450	200	0
9	5,000	500	200	300
10	2,000	200	200	300
11	6,000	600	200	700
12	8,000	800	200	1,300
13	0	0	200	1,100
Total	$37,000	$3,700	$2,600	$1,100

ance continued to rise through week 5. She then became reasonably productive so that at settlement time, end of week 13, the company owed her a settlement of $1,100.

The salesperson in the example enjoyed the stability of an income of $200 per week during the first five weeks while she was learning the business. At the same time, she had the incentive to strive for high sales volume and a substantial quarterly settlement.

Suppose management became disenchanted with her at the end of week 5. The alternatives available are reducing the amount of her weekly draw or removing her draw and placing her on straight commission. Suppose she was unwilling to accept either of these alternatives and resigned from the company at the end of week 5?

The company might attempt to recover the amount of the overdraft. The representative might be quite willing to return the $550, either because of a promise to repay or because she had signed a contract or note agreeing to repay any debit balances at the time of termination. Historically, there have been very few legal decisions requiring a terminated sales employee to repay overdrafts to the company, despite the existence of contractual agreements calling for such repayment. If the employee showed a "red" figure at settlement time, all of the previous strategies would be available or the firm could also let the overdraft ride until the next settlement period.

In the example in Table 7.1, the saleswoman, after receiving her $1,100 settlement, could request that her draw be increased to $250 or more per week for the forthcoming quarter, or she might suggest that she be switched to straight commission so that her earnings would not be held by the company until the settlement period. The company might be willing to grant her wishes, with the understanding that she would remain on straight commissions and not request reactivation of the drawing account in the event of diminished future sales and earnings.

Many variations of the draw are available. For example, the firm could use a guaranteed drawing account, whereby the employee would not be required to pay back overdraft balances. It is also possible for the employee to be allowed to choose between a weekly draw or commissions, whichever is greater. The danger of such a plan is the possibility that the salesperson will "sandbag" orders, that is carry orders over to the following pay week, while drawing the guarantee during the current week. The key is for management to set the amount of the draw high enough so as to offer the employee the needed security, and low enough so as to prevent excessive overdrafts. Another possibility would allow management to set a top overdraft limit so that the employee would work on straight commissions temporarily until his account balance was in line with the overdraft limit.

Other Combination Plans

In lieu of the drawing account, the salesperson may be compensated by combinations of salary, commission, and bonus, which would provide incentive plus security plus the obvious benefits of salary and commission plans.

Suppose the company can afford to pay out sales costs of 10 percent of sales and assumes that a given sales recruit is capable of acquiring an average of $2,000 per week in sales. Whereas the firm would be willing to pay a straight commission rate of 10 percent, salary plus commission might call for a salary of $100 per week plus 3 or 4 percent commission. The lowering of the commission rate to less than half of the standard rate is to compensate the firm for excessive sales-compensation costs when salaried salespeople fail to produce sales compatible with their salaries.

Linkage to Marketing Goals

It was indicated earlier in this chapter that company control of the salesperson's activities and behavior is directly related to the degree of disassociation of sales compensation from actual sales results. For example, even though the straight salary plan may not directly reward a salesman for results, it does buy his commitment of time, energy, and services to the company. Management may choose to have the salesperson devote himself, permanently or temporarily, to achieving something other than overall sales volume, for example, to selling designated items in the product line, rendering special service to a customer, assisting a new sales recruit, investigating the feasibility of tapping a new market or creating a new product, or scrutinizing the literature of competitors. The commissioned representative may view these marketing needs as incompatible with his or her earning goals. Conversely, the employee on fixed or guaranteed income, being less independent, may be more obliged to accede to the wishes of management.

Mixed compensation plans, especially those including some form of salary, offer management some opportunity to direct and control at least a portion of the sales employee's schedule, work load, and activity mix. As will be shown in the section to follow, sales personnel have seemingly become more willing to give up some freedom of action in exhange for more security in the compensation mix. As expressed by consultant Barry K. Moffitt, "sales compensation programs aren't merely the burrs under a salesman's saddle. They can be the reins as well, to move him in the direction of management's wants."

TRENDS IN SALES-COMPENSATION PLANS

Incentive-Security Mix

Between 1950 and 1965, salespeople became increasingly less willing to take compensation gambles. By examining a composite of the research of several compensation studies, it can be seen that the number of firms using straight-commission programs declined almost linearly from over 23 percent in 1950 to only 5 percent in 1965. While straight-salary plans were used by 20 percent of the firms in 1950, there was a dramatic increase to more than 45 percent in 1955. However, from 1955 to 1965, firms using straight salary backed off in straight-line fashion to about 17 percent in 1965. In 1965, about 78 percent of all the sales forces were participating in one of the mixed plans which combined security and incentives.

A study by the Research Institute of America in 1975 disclosed that 24 percent of the responding companies had changed their pay plans during the preceding two years.[9] Of this 24 percent, about one-third reported that they had moved toward more salary, less incentive, while 42 percent had introduced more incentive, less salary. The latter move toward incentives represented the largest move in that direction since the RIA surveys of compensation began in 1965. It is apparent that fewer are paying straight salaries although there is no evidence that more firms are using straight commissions. It is safe to presume, however, that more firms than ever before are using drawing accounts or other combination plans.

Earnings of Sales Managers [10]

It has been previously emphasized that a major attraction of selling as an occupation is the salesperson's early opportunity to move into management. Few occupations or professions offer the earnings opportunities available to sales managers and executives.

A 1974 survey of the eighty top sales executives, as measured by annual earnings, indicated that the average earner in this group received $91,000 in 1974 as compared with $73,000 in 1971. Examples of top sales executives who are managing to keep ahead of most Americans in outrunning increases in the cost of living are the executive vice-president of sales for Russ Togs, who received $240,000 in aggregate direct remuneration in 1974; Firestone's executive vice-president of sales, who received $123,000; and the senior vice-president of sales for Fieldcrest Mills, who earned $122,000. Top sales executives were also rewarded handsomely in the area of fringe benefits.

In addition to their pension benefits and life, hospitalization, and major-medical insurance coverage, many of these sales executives also collected long-term disability protection. Some enjoyed longer vacations, freer use of company cars, and company-sponsored social club memberships and physical examinations. Of the eighty executives in the survey, all but a handful received stock options, twenty-two enjoyed profit sharing, and twelve received various forms of deferred compensation.

All executives in the survey worked for larger firms whose annual sales volume ranged from $24 million to $18 billion. Surprisingly, many sales executives employed by smaller firms earn more than their counterparts who work for giant corporations. In addition, it is often field sales managers, not home-office executives, whose earnings are highest. This is because the earnings of home-office executives are normally salary based while field sales managers often enjoy the windfall earnings that frequently accompany commission plans. Yet, many highly successful field sales managers are willing to sacrifice up to 50 percent of their direct compensation in exchange for promotion to a position as vice-president of sales in the home office.

Stock-Option Plans

The author, in his interaction with students and field sales personnel, has discovered that the least understood financial fringe benefit is the stock option, a major compensation technique, especially in hiring and retaining key sales leaders.

To describe how this plan works, let us say that Henry Brendel, a successful regional sales manager for a privately held paper-products firm, has earnings, including salary and bonus, of approximately $70,000 per year. A major publicly held competitive firm, let us call it the Morse Williams Corporation, seeks to acquire Brendel's services but cannot exceed his current front-end income. However, they are in a position to offer him a stock option of 5,000 shares of common stock at the market price of $14.

Assuming the offer is accepted, Brendel will receive a certificate which indicates that he has the right to buy 5,000 shares of Morse Williams stock at a price of $14 at some time in the future. The waiting time is clearly specified in the firm's published stock-option plan for employees on Brendel's level. Normally, the waiting time will be two or three years so that management can observe Brendel's progress on the job before granting him what could turn out a substantial financial benefit.

Brendel has studied the progress of the firm's operations and stock in the recent past and he sees himself as making a substantial contribution to future sales and profits. Accordingly, he feels that the price of the stock will enjoy a substantial rise over the next several years.

He accepts the position and the firm progresses in accordance with his expectations. Three years after his employment the stock is selling for $37. Brendel decides to exercise his option. He makes the following calculation for 5,000 shares of stock: the purchase price at $14 a share will be $70,000; the market value at $37 a share will be $185,000.

On paper, Brendel will realize a profit of $115,000. If Brendel does not have the $70,000 he can offer to put up the stock as collateral, which should be sufficient to obtain the required loan. He may agree to repay the loan over a period of time, or he may elect to sell enough shares at some later date to pay off the balance of his loan. His tax liability on the $115,000 is subject to lower rates since the earnings are capital gains, and the interest on his loan is completely deductible.

Obviously, if the stock price does not rise as expected, Brendel will not exercise his option. In such an event, he will be disappointed that this anticipated part of his compensation will not be forthcoming and the firm may elect to offer Brendel new options at or slightly below the current market price.

The sales executive who is attracted by stock options should be familiar with his firm's option plan and should be careful to observe the required waiting time for exercising his option. Unfortunately, during a period of rising stock prices, firms have been known to terminate a person's employment prior to expiration of the waiting time, thus automatically canceling the options. This makes good business sense when the sales employee is not performing satisfactorily but is highly unethical when a good producer's employment is terminated because the company decides not to sell a highly inflated stock at the lower option price. It is for this reason that sought-after selling leaders insist on an employment contract to cover the waiting period.

THE COST-PROFIT IMPLICATIONS OF SALES-COMPENSATION PLANS

Over the years, a number of ill-founded generalizations have related sales-compensation plans to company costs and profits. To mention a few:

Straight commission plans are less costly than other plans.

Rising sales volume and market share are automatically accompanied by higher profits.

Cost and output standards belong in the factory rather than in the sales organization.

While one or all of these suppositions may be valid in a given situation, they are not true for all sales organizations, especially in the face of market changes, product proliferation, shorter product life cycles, fierce competition, and sales-cost escalation. This section suggests a framework for relating sales compensation practices to the specific cost and profit conditions.

Compensation-Cost Ratios

Salesmen's compensation is by far the biggest element of direct sales costs, and accounts for roughly 79 percent of the total mix.[11] Travel and entertainment contribute 11 percent and auto expenses the remaining 10 percent. However, compensation's share depends on the selling environment, management's policies, and the type of salesperson required in a given firm. For example, sales-force compensation expenses are less than 2 percent of sales volume in the food industry but often more than 20 percent in the encyclopedia industry.

To evaluate the impact of a sales-compensation method on the compensation-cost ratio (compensation costs as a percentage of sales), hereafter expressed as CCR, consider the example of three salesmen on three different pay plans within the same firm. Salesman A works on a straight commission of 10 percent; salesman B earns a straight salary of $1,000 per month; salesman C is paid a salary of $500 per month plus a 5 percent commission.

Table 7.2 shows the compensation costs and CCR equations for all three salespeople, along with calculations of each for various sales volumes. Figure 7.1 indicates that even though the straight-commission plan is considered a variable expense from an accounting point of view, it can be considered as just the opposite from a CCR standpoint since the ratio of compensation costs to sales remains fixed at all sales levels. The reverse is true for the salary plan.[12]

Table 7.2 Relationship of sales volume to compensation cost

	Compensation-cost function	CCR
Salesman A (straight commission)	$C = .10S$	$C/S = .10$
Salesman B (straight salary)	$C = 1,000$	$C/S = 1000/S$
Salesman C (salary + commission)	$C = 500 + .05S$	$C/S = 500/S + .05$

Assumed sales volume	Compensation cost		CCR (%)
$ 5,000	Salesman A	$ 500	10.0
	B	1,000	20.0
	C	750	15.0
10,000	Salesman A	$1,000	10.0
	B	1,000	10.0
	C	1,000	10.0
15,000	Salesman A	$1,500	10.0
	B	1,000	6.7
	C	1,250	8.3
20,000	Salesman A	$2,000	10.0
	B	1,000	5.0
	C	1,500	7.5

C = compensation costs
S = sales volume
CCR = C/S × 100

7. Compensating Sales Personnel

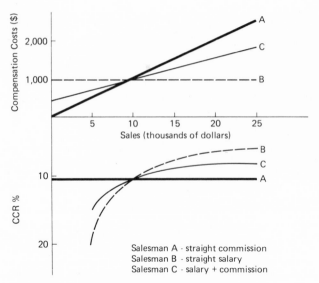

Figure 7.1 Comparison of relationships between sales volume and compensation cost

From a cost-ratio reduction approach, it becomes apparent that the straight-commission plan is preferred at lower levels of sales volume (in this example below $10,000 per month), with the straight-salary plan becoming more efficient at higher levels. This preference is frequently exercised when a firm replaces a commissioned sales agent with a salaried captive sales force once the organization has elevated sales volume beyond the indifference point. Management may also view combination plans, that is, salary plus commission, as attractive trade-offs with straight commission or salary plans since they allow for ratio improvement while providing sales-force members with both security and incentive.[13]

Profit Emphasis by the Salesman

It should be reemphasized that cost control is but one part of the profit equation. Sales-force members must be motivated to concentrate on sales volume and cost considerations simultaneously. One investigation of companies which were using profitability as the criterion of selling effectiveness disclosed that the factors affecting profit are too complex to permit precise evaluation of the contribution made by focusing salesmen's efforts on company priority objectives.[14] Two major approaches predominated in these companies: (1) salespeople should be trained to make profit-oriented decisions and

(2) salespeople should be compensated for profit rather than simply
for sales results.

The study reported that many firms were reluctant to provide salespeople with detailed information about the profitability of specific products because of potential leaks to customers or competitors. Moreover, most companies found it difficult to develop an information system that was capable of providing these data to salespeople promptly and economically.

In addition to being provided with profit data, the salesperson who emphasizes profit must often be granted the managerial rights to adjust prices, discuss advertising contributions with customers, authorize returns and allowances for markdowns, entertain when necessary, and make some credit decisions.

If commissions are to be based on profits, the relevant cost information must be available, understandable, and controllable. For example, salesmen cannot be concerned with or constrained by costs for such things as executives' salaries or rental of corporate office space. Accordingly, many firms base commissions on the gross margin of each product, as in the case of the automobile salesman.

A profit-based compensation plan is of particular value when the firm seeks to avoid unbalanced efforts by salesmen. A salesperson who is responsive to an incentive system based mainly on sales volume will concentrate on the products, customers, and territories that generate the easiest type and greatest number of sales. When commissions are based on gross margin or profits, salesmen are automatically encouraged to push high-margin items.

MONEY AS A MOTIVATOR

It is fashionable to argue that money is somewhat passé as a sales incentive. Clarence Francis, former chairman of General Foods, said it this way: "You can buy a man's time or his physical presence. You can even buy a measured number of skilled muscular motions per hour, day, or week, but you can't buy enthusiasm or loyalty or devotion of heart, mind, and soul." Dr. Karl Menninger, speaking before the American Association of Advertising Agencies, said: "Money in any form—salaries, pensions, trusts, or profit-sharing—won't bring in or buy the loyalty or high morale we strive toward."

The literature abounds with assumptions about the responses of salesmen to compensation offerings. René Darmon recently tested, with mixed conclusions, the impact of various compensation plans on company profits.[15] There are four major theories concerning a salesperson's motivation, some of which were confirmed by Darmon's study.

> *The salesman strives for a predetermined earnings target.* This person works hard enough to keep the wolf away from the door or to enjoy a constant living standard. He produces just enough to keep favor with his superiors. Consequently, there is a substantial gap between his performance and his potential. This is the type of salesman who consistently earns $400 per week on a 10 percent commission rate, and maintains the same earnings level when inflation drives up the price of his product line. In other words, he can still earn $400 per week by putting in less effort and selling fewer units.

> *The salesman is interested in acquiring sales, not earnings.* Such a salesman seeks recognition as an achiever, with limited regard for earnings. He seeks to gratify his higher-level needs, to reach and exceed his quotas, and to be recognized as a producer by his superiors and his peers.

> *The salesman is a maximizer of his utility function.* This salesman allocates his time between work and leisure on a programmed basis. He is reluctant to travel, work nights and weekends, and otherwise deprive himself of the good life. The prospect of earning more will not motivate him to alter his work and pleasure mix.

> *The salesman is interested in increasing his expected monetary gains.* This person wants money and is willing to do whatever is necessary to maximize his income. He will work whenever and wherever potential financial rewards dictate. He will forgo pleasures, family obligations, and even health precautions when money beckons. Some people in this category may be persuaded to employ questionable sales techniques or behave in ways which may be damaging to customers, company, competitors; and society.

Hopefully, the reader will recognize that the selling profession includes all four types, distributed in accordance with the selling needs of their respective employers. Different companies appeal in varying degrees to salesmen's money needs, competitive spirit, and desires for recognition, advancement, promotion, and job satisfaction. However, the author concludes that while money may not make salesmen entirely happy, it certainly allows them to choose the kind of unhappiness they want.

SUMMARY AND CONCLUSIONS

Since sales-compensation packages are designed by the firm rather than by the employee, they generally embody combinations of characteristics that are not exactly what the salesperson would dictate if he were customizing the compensation plan to his own taste. Both fixed and variable earnings have attractive and unattractive features, to both the employee and firm.

The causes of dysfunctional sales-compensation plans group themselves into three categories: (1) some originate with the salesman, through illness, laziness, or failure to apply himself to the task at hand. (2) Some seem to be the responsibility of management, including poor recruitment, selection, training, direction, and development of salesmen and myopic cost-control approaches. (3) Some are outside of the control of either, such as changing environmental conditions, competitive strategies, consumer actions, and channel reorganization. Most of these problems are tightly related to the faultiness of the measures of performance and the inconsistencies among company goals, task assignments, and salesmen's behavioral patterns.

Most changes in sales compensation over recent years involve the proportions of security versus incentive. Many sales employees prefer a heavy dose of time wages because these are not correlated with output. Simultaneously, employees are uncovering many sales duties which may not produce immediate orders. These duties include prospecting, missionary work, servicing accounts, counseling customers and channel-facilitating organizations, and internal sales reporting to assist company sales and cost controls and forecasting.

As the trend toward mixed compensation plans continues, firms are attempting to tie payments to specific marketing goals rather than having compensation vary directly with dollar sales volume. Finally, it appears that management and sales representatives alike are caught in a conflict of values, such as the conflict between the old standbys of initiative, risk, and reward and the fashionable new notions of security and controlled costs. The classical assumptions about the effects of pay on sales productivity may require a bit of fresh rethinking.

NOTES

1. Robert W. Sweitzer and Dev S. Pathak, "The Self-Actualizing Salesman," *Southern Journal of Business* 7 (November 1972):1–8.
2. Turnover rate is the number of exits divided by the average sales force

size. Thus, if a firm begins the year with 65 salespeople, hires 30 new people during the year, while losing 20, the turnover rate will be 20/70, or 28.6 percent.

3. Derek A. Newton, *Sales Force Performance and Turnover* (Cambridge, Mass.: Marketing Science Institute, 1973), pp. 57–58.

4. David J. English, "The Effects of Agent Turnover on the Orphan Policyholder" (doctoral dissertation, College of Business and Management, University of Maryland, 1974).

5. Marvin A. Jolson, "Minimum Wage Laws: A New Challenge for Sales Administrators," *Personnel Journal* 52 (April 1973):284–85.

6. Gerhard W. Ditz, "Status Problems of the Salesman," *MSU Business Topics* 15 (Winter 1967):72–73.

7. Robert N. McMurry, *How to Recruit, Select, and Place Salesmen* (Chicago: Dartnell Corp., 1964), p. 19.

8. Marvin A. Jolson, "Managing the Salesman's Wife," *Sales Management* (1 July 1971):36–37; and Marvin A. Jolson and Martin Gannon, "Wives: A Critical Element in Career Decisions," *Business Horizons* (February 1972):83–88.

9. "What Salesmen Earn," *Sales Management* 115 (6 October 1975):55–56.

10. Much of the compensation data reported in this section were given in "What Top Sales and Marketing Executives Earn," *Sales Management* 115 (6 October 1975):50–54.

11. "Selling Costs Index Soars 14 Percent in 1974," *Sales Management* 114 (6 January 1975):10.

12. William P. Hall, "Improving Sales Force Productivity," *Business Horizons* 18 (August 1975):36–37.

13. Ibid.

14. Charles W. Smith, "Gearing Salesmen's Efforts to Corporate Profit Objectives," *Harvard Business Review* 53 (July–August 1975):12.

15. René Y. Darmon, "Salesmen's Response to Financial Incentives: An Empirical Study," *Journal of Marketing Research* 11 (November 1974):418–26. Parts of these theories emerged from this study.

QUESTIONS FOR DISCUSSION AND REVIEW

1. Should salespeople be paid for their time, their efforts, or their results?

2. Should travel entertainment expenses be paid on a fixed or variable basis?

3. A furniture wholesaler is experiencing difficulties in hiring salespeople because the firm's compensation plan is based on commissions only. Write the section of the newspaper recruitment ad that relates to the compensation method. Discuss the likely results of your approach, including the necessary follow-up procedures during the hiring interview.

4. Discuss the following statement: Compensation incentives are vector not scalar in character.

5. Defend or oppose these examples of discretionary earnings adjustment: (1) The commission rate of a Denver salesman was raised because the tremendous distances between customers reduced effective selling time. (2) A typewriter salesman in Manhattan received an under-the-table bonus because competition had become quite fierce. (3) When a top salesman threatened to quit because he was passed up for a promotion, he was pacified by being offered a 15 percent salary increase.

6. Criticize the following statement: The sales manager must attempt to structure a pay plan that will not produce excessive earnings at a future date.

7. Describe a situation which would call for each one of the following sales-compensation plans:
   a. A straight-salary plan plus a quarterly bonus based on activities rather than sales results.
   b. A straight salary during a sixty-day training program. Thereafter, a weekly draw against earned commissions with a settlement at the end of the year. Overdrafts not recoverable.
   c. A straight-commission plan tied to both an overall quota and individual quotas on each of several products.
   d. A small salary plus a regressive commission rate as follows: 6 percent on all sales up to $60,000, 5 percent on all sales between $60,000 and $80,000, and 4 percent on all sales above $80,000.
   e. A straight commission on sales, plus quarterly stock options based on sales volume.

Case 7.1 Leonard Lipman

A Successful Salesman's Concern about Compensation Methods

Leonard Lipman was one of three salesmen in the Southern California Division of the Clearwater Swimming Pool Company. He had been with the company for nearly three years, had earned $18,400 in 1972 and $26,700 in 1973, and had already earned over $30,000 by November 1, 1974. Len was one of the most respected salespeople in the national organization and had won the national man-of-the-month honors three times during his employment with Clearwater.

All salespeople in the firm worked on straight commissions, and sales were not seasonal, especially in the state of California. Leonard had a wife and three children, owned two relatively new automobiles, and had recently purchased a nice home in the Van Nuys area. He was a valuable aid to district manager Barry Townsend, and often trained new salespeople in the field and assisted others who were experiencing sales slumps. Lipman was an excellent prospect finder, delivered "professional" sales presentations, and converted one out of every three presentations into a sale. He expressed his interest in relocating to San Francisco, Las Vegas, or any other warm climate as soon as a district manager's position became available.

On November 4, 1974, he came into Barry Townsend's office with the following request:

> Barry, I've done quite well with the company and I appreciate everything you've done to help me. My wife Shirley and I had a long talk last night, and it is my wish that you put me on a $500 per week draw with a settlement every ninety days. I realize that every salesman in the company works on straight commissions, but I just can't work that way any more. This might sound crazy since I've never really had one bad month since I've been with the company. If a person earns good money, it shouldn't matter how he gets paid.
>
> Shirley and I recognize that good times can't continue forever and sooner or later, I'm going to have some bad months. I'm really committed in terms of obligations and expenses, and a couple of bad months could knock me on my butt. A draw arrangement would give me peace of mind. To be honest, Barry, I've been scared to death lately.

QUESTIONS

1. What you think brought about Leonard's sudden request?
2. Assuming that no salesman in the company has ever been paid on any plan except by a straight commission, how should Townsend respond?

Case 7.2 Hollywood-at-Home, Inc.

Unique Compensation Package for Sales Managers

Hollywood-at-Home, Inc., contracts with film studios to rent 35 mm. films that are transcribed into video tape and then transmitted in scrambled form by microwave from a ministudio in each major city to receiving antennas erected by HAH on the roofs of apartment buildings and hotels. The coded signal is then fed into the building's master TV antenna system. The decoding is done at the TV receiver in the room by a small black box called a decoder. Operating costs consist primarily of film rental, transmitter time rental, approximately $1,000 for each building antenna, $20 for each decoder box, plus marketing and general administrative overhead. These costs are minimal in contrast to the huge investment required for cable TV.

The company has found that there is substantial demand for the showing of current movies in homes and hotel rooms since these movies are uninterrupted by commercials and are in the same unedited form shown in theaters. HAH has installed this system in several New York high-rise buildings. Building owners are happy to offer this service, and a large proportion of the tenants have subscribed by paying a $22 installation fee and signing a one-year contract at $10 per month for the service. HAH is experimenting with the appropriate fee arrangement for hotels, but at the present time is charging 30 cents per rented room per day.

HAH proposes to open company-owned offices in each major city, each office to be headed by a regional manager. The regional manager will be credited with 50 percent of all sales volume, out of which all expenses will be charged. This will include all of the previously mentioned expenses in addition to commissions paid to part-time salespeople who call on tenants and overrides to field supervisors. It is proposed that the regional managers will do all of the field selling to hotels while controlling the operations in high-rise buildings.

The regional manager will have no out-of-pocket costs. All sales and costs will be posted on his monthly statement and all authorized commissions, salaries, and bills will be paid by the HAH home office and charged against the regional manager's statement. The regional manager will be granted a draw of $2,000 per month against his profit statement, with a quarterly settlement.

A one-year experiment in the New York area has been quite profitable for HAH and the regional manager running the pilot operation has earned about $4,000 per month after expenses.

QUESTIONS

1. Why would HAH choose this method of compensating field sales managers? Compare this approach with (1) the salary plus bonus method and (b) a draw against commission on sales volume.
2. If you were a prospective regional manager, would you prefer the HAH method of compensation to the other methods?

8

Recruitment and Selection of Salespeople

Quite often, the terms *recruitment* and *selection* are used interchangeably. Instead, they should be considered two distinct sequential processes. Recruitment is the act of inducing qualified personnel to apply for employment. As indicated in Chapter 2, recruitment of salespeople is a communication process whereby the sales manager attempts to encourage desirable people to apply for an available sales position. Prospective job applicants must be located, contacted, and stimulated to submit a job application. Once the application has been received by the firm, the selection task takes over, in that management attempts to match the applicant's set of qualifications and attributes with the requirements of the sales position to be filled. When the number of recruits exceeds the number of job openings, management attempts to select and hire those recruits who demonstrate the highest probability of success on the job.

In selecting salesmen, as in selecting an office, a gardener, a college, a manuscript for a new textbook, or a wife or husband, one stands a better chance of getting exactly what he is looking for if he considers several possible choices instead of only one or two.

RECRUITMENT PHILOSOPHIES AND PREREQUISITES

Managers are consistently disappointed with the quality of newly hired salespeople because the selection criteria and instruments were not applied to a sufficiently large number of candidates.[1] In essence, the best of a bad lot are often hired. The primary reasons for a lack of candidates are (1) qualified and willing candidates are difficult to find, (2) recruitment is costly and time consuming, and (3) the sales manager's ego convinces him that a large number of applicants is not necessary because he "can pick the right man at ten paces."

Recruiting Difficulties

The potential applicant formulates his own selection approach well in advance of the firm's selection strategies. The job seeker first decides that he wants a selling job and then decides what types of sales jobs appeal to him. To determine whether the job is worth applying for, he must coordinate the various forms of information about job openings (newspaper ads, university bulletin boards, word-of-mouth messages, direct contact by recruiters, etc.) with his employment interests.

Assuming the real or imagined job features are attractive (or not unattractive) to job seekers, numerous applications will result. On the other hand, many sales positions may carry the stigmas of straight commission, excessive travel, difficult-to-sell products, and other perceived negatives that result in a minimal number of applicants in response to a recruitment communication.

Often the stigma-producing stimuli are not explicit in the description of the job opening. However, the reader, in his cursory scanning of the employment ad or message affixes certain negative characteristics to a job. Among these perceived mythologies are: blind ads are run by low-prestige organizations, consumer goods manufacturers are looking for traveling salesmen, home improvement companies are seeking high-pressure door-to-door people, department stores are looking for retail clerks, industrial marketers seek technically trained salespeople. Often the reader's assumptions are invalid. More often, the job seeker rejects jobs with "undesirable features" which he is not qualified to judge as being "undesirable." For example, if he has had no experience with unknown companies or with in-store or direct-to-home selling, or with a job requiring substantial travel, how does he know he will not enjoy the job or that the positive features of the job will not overshadow the perceived negatives?

To avoid these unfounded preconceptions of undesirable job features, many messages describing job offers omit the mention of explicit job negatives or implicit hints of undesirable conditions of employment. One approach is the use of the blind ad which may omit the company name, product, compensation mode, and specific job requirements, and duties. This subject receives special attention later in the chapter.

Frequency of Recruiting

It should be clear that the importance and the difficulties of the recruiting task vary from firm to firm. Some large low-turnover firms hire less than twenty new salespeople a year. However, these same companies may be recruiting continuously, that is, management may be accumulating the names of prospective sales employees so that a reservoir of applicants will be available to fill future needs. Alert managers recruit at social gatherings, on the golf course, on the college campus, or through continuous relationships with employment agencies. Well-known firms, including Bethlehem Steel Company and Procter & Gamble, always have key executives available to make guest appearances in college classrooms whether or not job openings are currently available. The effective development of a prospect list eases the firm's hiring task, even though many people on the list are happily employed elsewhere when the job opening occurs.

Conversely, a great many firms with high turnover rates recruit vigorously on a weekly and even daily basis because of the need to hire as many people as possible, as soon as possible. In-store and direct-to-home retailers have more sales openings than there are available recruits. Prestige firms such as Avon, Electrolux, World Book, and many of the major insurance and brokerage houses advertise for and interview prospective new salespeople almost every day of the year. Accordingly, their sales managers spend a huge proportion of their time performing the recruitment function.

Improper Recruitment and Selection

It was established in an earlier chapter that when a salesman fails management is at fault—either because the wrong person was hired or because the person hired was improperly trained, supervised, or motivated. One Australian management consultant has found that the major cause of sales-force turnover is improper recruitment and selection.[2]

What is meant by improper recruitment and selection? Generally this boils down to the hiring of salespeople who have a low probability of success on the job. Why does management hire such people? The answer is that sales managers are either unwilling (do not care) or unable (do not know how) to take precautions that will prevent the hiring of unqualified people.

Why would a firm be unwilling to devote substantial care and attention to something as important as recruiting? A primary answer is that some managers believe that all the care and attention in the world will not improve the recruiter's ability to predict which hirees will be successful salespeople. The overwhelming attitude of these sales managers is "This is a turnover business so let's run more ads for salesmen and spend more time recruiting." In these cases, recruiting is dominant and research on the cause of turnovers is virtually nonexistent. Since "good men are not available," careful screening of applicants is rare; company recruiters are often top salesmen, who sell the job harder than they sell the firm's products.

Recruiting Part-time Salespeople

Because their primary obligations lie elsewhere, part-time salespeople are often difficult to interview, train, control, and supervise. Yet many sales organizations are highly dependent on part-timers. For example, one highly respected quality-shoe producer, the Hanover Shoe Company, advertises almost continuously for part-time sales recruits in newspapers, magazines, and specialty publications. Almost all those who reply are sent a sales kit by mail. Despite the fact that the company's selection ratio is nearly 100 percent, and that over one-half of those receiving kits never sell a single order, Hanover Shoe Company is considered to be a successful recruiter of salespeople.

Establishing Job Specifications

What are some examples of a recruiter's inability to attract qualified people? The variety of selling jobs was emphasized in Chapter 2. Each type of selling job requires a different type of salesperson, and many recruiters search for, interview, and select new salespeople without a clear-cut idea of the unique type of salesperson who would be best for the job. According to Carl Maier of the United States Rubber Company, recruiting efforts fail because the recruiter fails to describe in specific detail the type of person that is desired.[3] Too many field sales managers, when asked by recruitment sources to describe their need, respond with a vigorous and heartfelt "What I need is a good, hard-hitting salesman who can get out there and bring in some business." Not only is such a request vague and meaningless, but the recruiter would not recognize such an applicant if he bumped heads with him.

Prior to launching the recruiting effort, the sales manager should construct a well-thought-out picture of (1) what is the job to be done and (2) what kind of person is required to do the job? These two needs refer to the *job description* and the *job qualifications*, respectively. Ideally, both should be precisely prepared in writing and circulated to recruitment sources and managers who will participate in the recruiting functions. At the least, the contents of each should be firmly fixed in the recruiter's mind and written down somewhere, even on a calendar pad or on the back of an envelope.

The job description should describe the requirements of the job in considerable detail, including what products will be sold, to whom will they be sold, what kind of selling will be required (creative, missionary, trade)? What other promotional work or non-selling activities will be required? What is the nature and extent of responsibility, supervision, and accountability? The job description should also include travel requirements for contacting prospects, assisting resellers, and attending meetings and conventions. Finally, the assigned territory should be defined, along with such factors as working hours and relocation expectations, if any.

The job description is prepared by management, usually with considerable input from sales-force members. It serves as the basis for identifying the job qualifications, that is, skills, knowledge, abilities, experiences, and attitudes necessary for success on the job. Although the job description may be perfectly and precisely defined, qualified applicants come in all sizes and shapes and are anything but a homogeneous lot. This is equally true for all employees including secretaries, professors, quarterbacks, third basemen, and salesmen. Despite the fact that there is no known formula for matching the job description and the job qualifications, the recruiter must know enough about what he is looking for to describe the desired applicant in the recruitment message. Some skill requirements logically ensue from the job description. Others do not.

For example, a salesman selling radio altimeter systems that open parachutes might require a degree in electrical engineering, a background in the air force, a pilot's license, and considerable experience in selling to military arms of the government. On the other hand, a more abstract set of attributes has been associated with the job of the successful, creative specialty salesperson. These are: a high level of energy, abounding self-confidence, a chronic hunger for money, a well-established habit of industry, and a state of mind which regards each objection, resistance, or obstacle as a challenge.[4]

SOURCES OF SALES RECRUITS

The type of individual required will logically suggest where management should begin its search for sales recruits. A young, unspoiled, technical type who could sell to industrial buyers might be found in the college of engineering of the state university. A specialized superstar who could take over a lucrative territory might be recruited from the competitor's sales force. An experienced saleswoman who could take on a supplementary line to sell to department stores might best be found through a small ad in *Women's Wear Daily*, the industry trade journal.

It would not be difficult to devote a full chapter or two to the sources of sales recruits. Since succinctness is a major objective of this text, the present discussion is restricted to a few major sources. Although the ultimate criterion in selecting sources is, in most cases, based on the total cost of recruitment and selection per successful recruit, a number of other factors are often considered. These include the urgency of the manpower need, turnover constraints, corporate-image restrictions, and relevant quality/quantity/cost needs. Some notes on the more important and more interesting recruitment sources follow.

Advertisements

One glance at the classified help-wanted section of the morning paper or at the display ad section of the Sunday paper or *The Wall Street Journal* will convince the reader that firms spend more money on advertising for sales recruits than on any other recruitment source. Similar ads for sales personnel appear in trade journals, specialized magazines, association and company house organs, and professional and consumer magazines and journals. Moreover, for many firms, printed ads generate more recruits than any other source. Since the quantity of responses is so large, many low-quality applicants are among those who respond.

Often the local newspaper ad is the only source available to the recruiter because of its perpetual availability, rapid turnover time, and at a relatively low cost. Moreover, the local sales manager is in a position to exercise some control over the quantity and quality of applicants and over the costs of the ad and the subsequent selection process. The key to such control is the adjustment of the ad in terms of size, and spacing, content, originality, caption, level of disclosure, and suggested method of contact with the employer.

An examination of Figure 8.1 will allow the reader to compare several ads by competing burglar-alarm companies in the same large city. Some of the ads use larger center captions. Others use side headings or none at all. Some ads offer phone numbers; others require the applicant to reply by mail. Ad 5 is a full-disclosure type in that the precise type of selling, the pay plan, and even the name of the company are given. Ad 6 is completely blind in that it discloses nothing, not even the fact that selling is involved. Because of the latter omission, most newpapers will not permit it to appear in its present form. Similarly, alert newspapers may require advertisers to specify the precise type of selling to be done, the type of sales-compensation plan, and in some cases, the name of the company.

A number of sales managers have suggested that open ads which disclose the company name, product to be sold, compensation plan and level, and specific job duties generate higher-quality applicants, decreased turnover rates, and lower recruitment and selection costs than blind ads. However, in one selling organization with a high turnover rate, the effects of blind and full-disclosure ads on turnover rates were compared, but no significant difference in rates was found.[5] Blind ads produced three times as many applicants per ad and over twice as many reportees (those who reported for work). However, a higher percentage of the open-ad applicants were hired.

As shown in Table 8.1, the average blind ad is about one-third more expensive (because it has more lines); but because of the higher response rate, the ad cost per reportee is much lower. Similarly, the average selection cost per reportee is substantially higher for blind than for open ads. This is because blind ads delay the applicant's possible rejection of perceived negatives (cold canvassing, straight commission, night work, excessive travel, etc.) until he is face-to-face with the recruiter. At that time, the recruiter is in a better position to compose a persuasive presentation that will inform the applicant of job requirements in a logical and psychological sequence, which is more likely to achieve the desired effect. In other words, when the blind ad is the source of referral, a more creative, more detailed, more lengthy, and thus more costly employment interview is often required.

The combined average costs of recruitment and selection per applicant are approximately equal for the two advertising modes.

Since blind ads produce more employees per ad and since sales volume has been found to be a linearly increasing function of the number of active salespeople,[6] this method may be advantageous in an unsatiated sales market when sales-force turnover is high and terminated salesmen are difficult to replace. This is particularly true

Figure 8.1 Ads for burglar-alarm salespeople

when a job has advantages comparable or superior to other job opportunities though not readily apparent without detailed explanations. Blind ads also help the firm to avoid the "high turnover" image that may be attached to the firm that advertises continuously for new employees.

8. Recruitment and Selection of Salespeople

Table 8.1 A comparison of costs and personnel data by type of newspaper ad

| | Type of ad | | |
	Blind	Open	Total
Number of ads	210	118	328
Ad cost [a]	$9748	$4170	$13918
Cost/ad	$46.42	$35.34	$42.43
Number of applicants [b]	818	142	960
Applicants/ad	3.90	1.20	2.93
Selection cost [c]	$16360	$2840	$19200
Selection cost/ad	$77.90	$24.07	$58.54
Total costs (ads + selection)	$26108	$7010	$33118
Number of applicants hired [d]	377	94	471
Number reporting for work [e]	267	73	340
Reportees/ad [f]	1.27	0.62	1.03
Reportee/applicant ratio	.326	.514	.354
Ad cost/reportee	$36.50	$57.13	$40.94
Selection cost/reportee	$61.28	$38.90	$56.47
Total cost/reportee	$97.78	$96.03	$97.40
Reportee/hiree ratio	.707	.776	.721
Number of successful salesman [g]	53	12	65
Success/applicant ratio	.065	.085	.068
Total cost/successful man	$492.60	$584.17	$509.51
Hiree/applicant ratio	.461	.662	.490
Successful men/ad	.253	.103	.198

[a] Consists of payments to newspaper

[b] Number of applicants appearing at company office in response to ads

[c] Since interviewing constitutes bulk of the selection process, these costs consist of hours spent interviewing times average hourly salary rate of interviewers.

[d] Number of applicants who were offered and accepted a position following the personal interview.

[e] It is observed that many of those who accepted a job failed to report for work at the designated time.

[f] A reportee is a hiree who actually reported for work.

[g] A salesman who is still a sales producer one year from the date he first reported to work.

SOURCE: Marvin A. Jolson, "A Comparison of Blind vs. Full-Disclosure Ads for Sales Personnel," *Akron Business and Economic Review* 5 (Winter 1974), p. 17.

Employment Agencies

Employment agencies collect their fees either from the employee or from the employing firm. Usually, for less prestigious jobs such as in-store and direct-to-home selling the fee is paid by the employee.

A given agency will ordinarily adhere to an established fee plan, i.e., *no* fees will be paid by the employee or *all* fees will be paid by the employee. Similarly, agencies will frequently specialize in spe-

cific types of salespeople, such as executive salesmen rather than retail clerks or canvassers. A very few agencies specialize in recruiting
salespeople. For example, *Sales Consultants,* a division of Management Recruiters (Cleveland based), has over sixty offices throughout
the country, and is one of the rare national sales-recruiting specialists.

It has been hypothesized that job seekers go to employment
agencies only after all other employment efforts have failed.[7] Larger
employment agencies frequently employ their own sales forces to
contact employers and persuade them to place job orders. When a
firm decides to use an agency as a recruitment source, job descrip-
tions and required job qualifications should be submitted in written
form to discourage the fee-seeking agency from recommending obviously unqualified candidates.

Internal Sources

The company's selling and nonselling employees often serve as
outstanding sources for obtaining new salespeople. Since birds of a
feather often flock together, successful salespeople are often in a position to select certain of their friends and associates and convince
them to join the sales force. A potential employee is more likely to be
convinced of an excellent job opportunity by talking to a happily and
successfully employed friend than by submitting himself to the more
impersonal recruiting messages of the recruiter or the employment
agency.

Firms with high turnover rates who require a large number of
full- and part-time salespeople often offer attractive cash and other
incentives to sales-force members who bring in new sales recruits.
One organization that uses a large number of housewives and
teachers for part-time work encourages their salespeople to "hire
them if they can't sell them." The rationale is that if the prospect
doesn't buy the product because she can't afford it, she probably can
use the extra income of a part-time job.

It was indicated in Chapter 3 that nonselling employees are
often delighted to move up to a selling position. These people are familiar with the company, its products, its customers, and the high
earnings of the better salespeople. Yet the sales manager must recognize that these forms of knowledge only partially qualify a person for
saleswork. Selling requires skills and attitudes that are different from
those of other jobs. Selling may look easy when viewed from the factory or the lab or from behind a desk. Once in the field, the converted
engineer or administrator may adopt a different viewpoint. It is illogical to assume that the engineer who designs the stereo set or the

editor who helps develop the encyclopedia will necessarily be successful in selling their respective products.

Outside Companies

Many companies consider it standard practice to hire their supplier's salespeople. For example, client firms frequently hire an ad-agency account executive who has spent considerable time learning their business. In certain cases, people wish to become agency account executives in order to get the opportunity to be exposed to a large number of clients who, in turn, may offer improved job opportunities. No violation of ethics is involved since the client normally requests and is granted permission to enter into employment discussions.

Sellers often receive recruiting assistance from their customers. For example, department-store buyers and merchandise managers may inform vendors about sales reps from other firms who are seeking to add lines. If the store already buys from the recommended rep, the chances are that he is a well-qualified recruit.

The matter of recruiting a customer's employee is a bit more touchy in that the vendor would be reluctant to lose a worthwhile account by proselytizing a key employee. However, few customers would prevent an employee from advancing himself if the job switch is handled diplomatically by both the employee and the recruiting firm. A case in point is the situation where a retail clerk is capable of improving his employment situation by joining a vendor's sales force.

The question of proselytizing key salespeople from rival firms is a complex matter with far-reaching implications. Obviously, a competitor's top salesman would bring with him knowledge, skills, and attitudes that would minimize training and supervision requirements by the receiving company. Furthermore, the pirated salesman may be in a position to transfer a substantial number of active customers to his new company.

Yet, the acquiring firm must be concerned with the reason that a top salesman could be lured away, for fear that the person would be susceptible to further proselytism in the future. Aside from the consequences of an employee-stealing war within an industry, proselytism is often considered an unethical or predatory practice, and in some industries is taboo. The key ethical issue often hinges on whether the suggested job change was initiated by the employee or the firm.

The stealing of sales employees is not restricted to an interfirm level. Often multibranch companies are troubled by intrafirm transfer attempts initiated by field sales managers to attract successful company salesmen into their territories. Top management is often hard pressed to resolve the dramatic conflicts that can result from such practices. (Case 10.1 deals with such a situation.)

Schools

Due to the differing philosophies and requirements of each selling organization, many recruiters are reluctant to seek experienced salespeople who were trained elsewhere. Many sales managers regard experienced salespeople as "used," that is, having been tampered with and ruined by others. They prefer fresh, unspoiled young people who have no previous sales experience and who can be molded in accordance with the company's ideas, ways, and needs.

Herein lies the reason for emphasis on college recruiting. For some time, college students were uninformed about the selling profession and what a salesman does. This resulted in a lack of respect for and interest in careers in selling. More recently, universities have been increasing the number of courses in salesmanship and sales management. With few job offerings in other areas, these courses and numerous work-study cooperative programs have been instrumental in generating more student interest in selling. Accordingly, many firms make regular recruiting visits to campuses to interview placement personnel, professors, and graduating students. In addition, numerous firms, including Exxon, FMC Corporation, and many well-known banks, address recruiting messages to college graduates through elaborate advertisements in magazines with high student readership.

Other Recruiting Sources

One of the most desirable applicants is the one who makes a voluntary inquiry, that is, takes it upon himself to approach the sales manager and ask for a job. This person shows a desire to work for the company and, moreover, demonstrates at least one characteristic of a good salesman—the drive to pursue something that he really wants.

Alert recruiters read the situations-wanted or business-opportunity sections of newspapers and other publications to learn of job seekers who are inclined toward selling. They also contact other recruiters who may have an overabundance of applicants. Finally, in keeping with the definition of recruiting as given on the first page of this chapter, many of the methods used in prospecting for customers can be used in prospecting for employees. An interesting direct-mail piece used by the Metropolitan Life Insurance Company is shown in

Figure 8.2. The company's message focuses on the advantages of commissioned earnings and the long term nature of earnings on each sale, which is a unique feature in the life-insurance industry.

WHO SHOULD BE HIRED?

Selecting salespeople is somewhat analogous to forecasting sales (Chapter 4) in that both attempt to predict future events. When a sales manager selects an applicant from a group of recruits, he is es-

Figure 8.2 Direct mail recruitment by the Metropolitan Life Insurance Company

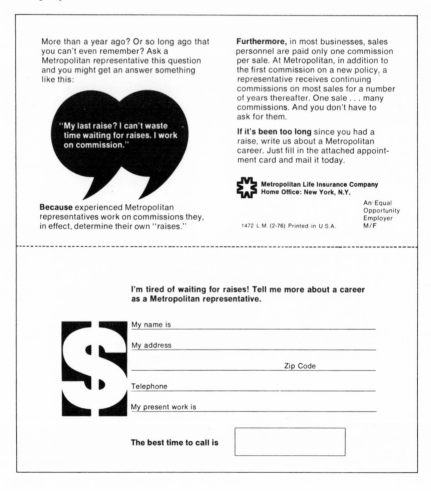

Selling the Job

In most situations, the job seeker appears at the hiring interview eager to make a favorable impression, particularly if he is a graduating student seeking his first job or a person desperately seeking to make a new job connection. Other recruits are persuaded to visit the company offices by an enticing blind ad or heavy-handed recruiting, or because more attractive job opportunities have not been made available. Such an applicant is desirous of looking over the job, judging the interviewer, or generally allowing the sales manager to try to sell him on the idea of going to work.

In either case, a personal selling situation exists. Either the applicant will attempt to sell the employer on the idea of hiring him or the sales manager will attempt to sell the recruit on the idea of going to work.

Both parties will attempt to move into the driver's seat by diplomatically taking control of the situation. The following dialogue is an example of how the interviewer can attempt to get the ad-answering recruit to reach for the job at the outset of the interview.

MANAGER: I see you're answering our ad in the *Times*. There are lots of ads in the *Times;* how is it you chose ours to answer?

RECRUIT: Well . . . uh, uh . . . I've been wanting to get into sales for some time and your ad looked interesting.

MANAGER: Yes, but there are many different types of sales jobs. Have you given any thought to the specific kind of selling you would be most comfortable with?

RECRUIT: Well . . . no, not exactly.

MANAGER: Let me ask you this. Do you know enough about what you're looking for to recognize it if you saw it?

There are numerous cases where the recruit indicates at the outset of the employment interview that his major employment objective is money and that he is willing to make all sacrifices necessary to realize high earnings. Why is it, then, that highly talented interviewing personnel using superb procedures may be ineffective in convincing such a person to accept a straight-commission job, even though it may offer legitimate opportunities for earning $400 to $500 per week and his previous earnings may never have exceeded $7,500 a year? This happens because the recruit does not believe the opportunity exists or because he does not believe he is capable enough.

Selection Criteria

It has been inferred that a person with both "can-do" and "will-do" characteristics will be successful in selling. In listing the "can do" factors, McMurry includes appearance, health, overt conduct, and personality, education, intelligence, and experience.[8] For the most part, these characteristics can normally be observed by studying the completed application blank and interviewing the job candidate.

What an applicant will do is considerably more difficult to predict and requires probing in the interview and investigations beyond face-to-face contact with the applicant. One version of "will-do" factors is shown below: [9]

Character traits and basic habits

Stability: maintaining same jobs and interests
Industry: willingness to work
Perseverance: finishing what he starts
Ability to get along with others
Loyalty: identifying with employer
Self-reliance: standing on own feet, making own decisions
Leadership

Job motivations (not already satisfied off the job)

Need for income or desire for money
Need for security, status, power
Need to investigate
Need to excel and compete
Need for perfection
Need to serve

Basic energy level

Vigor, initiative, drive, enthusiasm

Negative factors against which to measure emotional maturity

Dependence
Disregard for consequences
Incapacity for self-discipline
Selfishness
Show-off tendencies
Pleasure-mindedness
Destructive tendencies
Wishful thinking
Unwillingness to accept responsibility

It is reasonable to say that the hiring firm uses selection techniques to investigate the applicant's abilities, desire, and capacity for human relationships.[10] Abilities consist of one's experience with or aptitude for the sales job at hand. A recent graduate who is bright but has no previous selling experience may nevertheless possess enough ability to succeed. Desire refers to the salesman's dynamic inner drives, his capacity to overcome obstacles, his willingness to do whatever is required for success, such as working long or odd hours, traveling, or giving up personal pleasures to meet the demands of the job. Human relations refers to the ability to get along with one's customers, peers, and supervisors and one's empathic perception of the roles, needs, and reactions of business associates. A salesman should have empathy, not sympathy, such that he understands the prospect's point of view but tries for the sale anyway.

SELECTION TOOLS AND TECHNIQUES

The primary objective of the selection process is to ascertain the extent to which the recruits measure up to the "can-do" and "will-do" job criteria, that is, it should measure ability, desire, and human relations characteristics. As has been suggested, there are some situations where selection tools are also used to sell the recruit on the idea of applying for the job.

The major selection tools are application blanks, interviews, reference checks, tests, field observations, and physical examinations. Some writers have attempted to rank these tools and others in terms of the best sequence, the most effectiveness, and the lowest costs, but the findings have not been consistent. In general, application blanks and interviews are almost always used as the first two steps in the sequence. The popularity of the other tools is related to size and level of sophistication of the employing firm, sales-selection ratio (hirees as percentage of applicants), number of salespeople employed, sales-force turnover rate, and compensation level of the sales employee. Tools that can be used quickly and are least costly should be used first.

Application Blanks

A properly structured application form allows the prospective employer to take a good look at the applicant in black and white, before he is seen in the flesh. As a written record of the recruit's background and experience, it lists many of his can-do traits, or emphasizes their absence, while providing the backdrop for the personal interview. Under certain circumstances, the application blank will suggest an early knockout if the applicant is too old, too young, too inexperienced, lacking in education, etc. Recent charges of employment discrimination have resulted in widespread elimination of information relating to race, religion, sex, and age.

Often the application blank is weighted with scores assigned to answers such that each applicant's form can be quantified. Applicants with scores below a predetermined level can be eliminated, while high scorers can be granted priority interview times. Finally, a detailed application blank is desirable for hard-to-fill sales jobs where the selection ratio is high. The purpose is to convince the applicant that the job is harder to get than it really is.

Interviews

The employment interview is analogous to the sales presentation in that it consists of an oral exchange of information between the applicant and members of the employing organization. Many firms will use a preliminary interview, in advance of the main interview, to screen applicants and eliminate those who are obviously disinterested or undesirable. This procedure saves time for both applicants and company executives.

When the main interview is conducted in several stages by one or several members of the sales-management staff, several types of interviews can be used with the same applicant. A background-information interview determines the experience, education, interests, and goals of the applicant. A job-facts interview informs the applicant about the company, its products, its employees, its customers, and company expectations of new sales-force members. The applicant is permitted to ask questions about the job and an informal question-and-answer session usually follows. A situation-analysis interview places the applicant in a hypothetical selling situation to which he is asked to react. Stress interviews are deliberate attempts to create pressure through interruptions, criticism, silence, etc., in order to predict how well a candidate will perform when subjected to similar treatment by a prospective customer.

The interview serves purposes which are not served by other selection techniques. First, the interview puts the recruit in the spotlight, in that he must perform by asking and answering questions. It is a test of the applicant's instinctiveness, warmth, tact, forcefulness, and general ability to communicate orally. Second, the interview clarifies facts and fills in the gaps on the application blank. Third, information is delivered about the sales position in both an appetizing and truthful manner. Despite the need for romancing certain new job candidates, interviewers should stress "telling it like it is," explaining job and company limitations and weaknesses when they exist. Exaggerations or important omissions may lead to unrealized expectancies on the part of the salesman which in turn may generate a state of dissonance with attendant decreased productivity, and job switching.[11]

Finally, the interview can provide the sales manager with information which, if properly developed, can provide valuable insights relating to the applicant's will-do characteristics. This is particularly true when stress or situational-analysis interviews are used or when the applicant's spouse is present at the interview. The interviewer is often misled by the applicant's appearance or ability to sell himself at the interview. It is one thing to perform well in a plush, air-conditioned executive suite, and another to pursue elusive prospects in mid-July, in warehouses, up escalators, and in third-floor walk-up apartments.

The interviewer seeks to learn about the applicant's basic habits and character makeup, including his stability, industry, congeniality, perseverance, loyalty, integrity, and self-reliance. Does he possess leadership traits? What really motivates him? What levels of energy, drive, and initiative does he possess?

Certain questions posed by the interviewer can elicit difficult-to-obtain answers. It has been found that the applicant's responses to the following questions are indicative of his present job aspirations. Accordingly, the interviewer is assisted in forecasting the applicant's confidence, intellect, entrepreneurship, leadership, need for power and superiority, and propensity to be lazy, lethargic, or irresponsible.

> Suppose you were suddenly financially independent. Would you still be here talking about our job? Would you start your own business? Would you spend your time traveling, reading, swimming in your pool, or dating beautiful girls?

Another key question has proven to be effective in uncovering the applicant's bad habits and trouble-proneness. It is almost magical in eliciting information about alcoholism, narcotics, broken marriages, criminal records, and clashes with past employers.

> Let me ask you this, Mr. Applicant. Suppose I were to conduct a very thorough investigation of your past activities, on and off the job. What unfavorable findings would I uncover, if any? In other words, have you any skeletons in the closet? If so, I'd like you to tell me about them.

It is apparent that some interviewers and certain interviewing techniques are more successful than others. It is also true that some job candidates are more capable than others of concealing information, transmitting false information, providing support for inadequacies, or in generally taking control of the interviewing session. As in the case of the sales presentation, most firms have developed time-proven interviewing material and techniques, which are highly effective in selling the job and selecting the better candidates. These have substantial company input in terms of what questions to ask, when to ask them, how to interpret the answers, how to deal with capable but elusive and domineering applicants, and how to present the company story in the most favorable light without distorting the conditions of employment.

Thus, the continuum of structure that prevails for the sales presentation also pertains for the employment interview. The interviewing process may include films or stand-up easels with key phrases, guidelines, or word-for-word copy on the interviewer's side of the across-the-desk easel. McMurry developed the "patterned interview" more than twenty years ago. The content and structured sequence of the patterned interview is especially effective for the novice interviewer since the prepared interviewing form anticipates almost all the informational needs of the firm and provides an interpretation of the applicant's responses.

The informal, nondirected, unstructured interview is applicant-specific and thus recognizes that all applicants are different. Although it is more flexible and versatile, it lacks the standardized ratings that are possible with the patterned interview. Moreover, the nondirected interview often introduces much irrelevant conversation about meaningless experiences, mutual friends, and last night's baseball game.

Standardized ratings are particularly helpful when the applicant is passed from one interviewer to another. Multiple interviews allow for a comparison of notes and ratings, which minimizes individual biases and omissions and allows the sales management staff to detect contradictions in the applicant's dialogue. This procedure is also effective in making the candidate reach for the job. For example, the unit manager may conclude his preliminary interview, as follows:

> Mr. Graham, it appears that you have many of the qualities we're looking for. However, I'm not the one you're going to have to sell. I'm going to send you in to visit with Ron McCall, our sales manager.

McCall, in beginning his interview might glance at the rating
sheets submitted by his unit manager, and say:

> Mr. Graham, it seems that you've done a pretty good job
> selling Ted Brown, our unit manager, on your qualifica-
> tions. Apparently you've convinced him that you have
> quite a few selling strengths. Tell me a little bit about your
> weaknesses. Do you have any?

Ideally, the firm's preliminary interviewing goal would be accomplished when the applicant says, "I'd like to be considered for
the job." Sometimes this statement is not forthcoming and it must be
forced by the interviewer. One effective closing question is

> Now that we know a little bit about each other, tell me,
> what is there in your background or experience that leads
> you to believe you could be successful in the work we've
> described?

The interview could be concluded by informing the applicant of
the company's follow-up appraisal procedures, including internal
discussions, future interviews, tests, and intentions to investigate
his references.

Reference Checks

If one were to review systematically the names of those who
failed in selling jobs, a large proportion would be found heavy in
"can-do" and light in "will-do" characteristics. In other words, there
was a substantial gap between the potential and the achievement of
the failures. Therefore, most sales managers agree that the salesperson's desire is more important than his ability.

A telephone conversation with an applicant's former employers
and working associates (peers, customers, etc.) will alert the investigator to past occupational drive, work habits, and overall accomplishments. Since the best basis for predicting what a person
will do in the future is to ascertain in some detail what he has done in
the past, the reference check is the primary means of predicting
"will-do" qualities in candidates.[12] Past employers may be contacted
by mail or in person. These methods are slow, costly, and time consuming. The difficulty with written inquiries is that they generate a
low response rate. In addition employers are reluctant to place negative comments in writing.

Although some authorities will argue that references should be
checked before the main interview, it must be remembered that

while second or third interviews can be scheduled with the applicant, more than one contact with a former employer is not recommended. Therefore, it is wise to become thoroughly acquainted with the candidate, and his suspected strengths and weaknesses, before formulating the sequence of investigative questions to be directed to former employers. Certain questions are not productive, such as, "Were you satisfied with Al Graham's performance?" Questions such as the following will elicit the necessary information: "Can we assume that Graham was salesman of the Year in 1974?" "Did he travel three out of every four weeks?" "Did he spend about 30 percent of his time performing in-store inventory and merchandising functions for customers?" "Did he train one or two new salespeople each month?" If inconsistencies are discovered in information from application blanks, personal interviews, and reference checks, the seriousness of these discrepancies can be determined in a subsequent interview.

It is extremely important to convince former employers and peers of the confidentiality of your inquiry so as to get them to speak openly about the applicant's positive and negative characteristics. The vital closing question should relate to the former employer's willingness to rehire the applicant.

In many cases, the investigator will seek to check with former supervisors other than those named by candidates on their application forms or during interviews. Some applicants are experienced and proficient in covering up unfavorable experiences, distorting their background in a favorable direction, and submitting the names of friendly former associates who are willing to support undeserving job candidates.

Psychological Testing

As valid predictors of a person's sales success, intelligence, aptitude, and personality tests are not very effective. More often, testing for sales selection is done for other reasons: to justify selections arrived at by other methods; to impress top management, employees, candidates, and customers with the sophistication of the sales department's methods; to keep up with the fashionableness of using management-science techniques; or to find uses for the acquired skills of isolated members of sales management.

Hopefully, as the reader visualizes the endless number of sales activities which are demanded of the infinite variety of salespeople, he will understand that a test which may predict success in one type of selling may be useless in forecasting selling proficiency in another type of endeavor. "Can-do" traits are readily predictable by other selection tools, but no standardized tests have been able to measure the sought-after "will-do" characteristics.

Field Observation

All selection techniques are artificial in that they are in-office processes that lack the realism of face-to-face contact with live prospects. With this in mind, one successful sales executive for a large insurance company terminates his interview with impressive job applicants, as follows:

> To be frank, Mr. Applicant, I'm really the wrong person to give you objective information about the job opening. This company has been very good to me and I've been fortunate to enjoy the rewards that come with selling success—a nice income, a nice home, two cars, benefits for my family. Truthfully, I'm so favorably biased that it's difficult for me to point out the difficulties and disappointments of the work.
>
> Therefore, before we go further, I'd like to invite you to spend a day in the field with one of our representatives. I'd like you to observe his successes and failures, the way he is welcomed and resisted by prospects. This experience will tell you more than I could, even if I took all day to explain our business to you. After your day in the field, let's meet once again to see if you have any additional questions and to make sure you're just as enthusiastic then as you are now.

The field-observation method is likely to "burn off" inexperienced applicants if they see a substantial amount of sales resistance. However, it is preferred that discouragement take place during the selection process rather than after considerable time and money has been spent in training the new salesperson.

Conversely, a highly successful field-observation experience may convince the naive recruit that selling is easier than he thought. Unless he is reminded that one day in the field is not indicative of what the future holds, he may be highly disappointed when he meets the resounding resistance of his first set of live prospects.

Physical Examinations

Most firms do not require medical examinations unless there is some question concerning a highly desirable candidate's physical capacity to do the work. The company may ask an applicant to authorize his personal physician to submit a copy of his most recent medical report. If frequent illnesses or inability to cope with the stresses of sales work is suggested during the interview, this may be a pertinent subject of inquiry during the reference check with former employers.

EMPLOYMENT DISCRIMINATION

Perceived manpower shortages in concert with activities of organizations such as the Equal Employment Opportunity Commission and the National Alliance of Businessmen have accelerated the hiring of females, blacks, senior citizens and members of minority religious groups for sales work. Most of the attempts to determine the level of employment discrimination have introduced considerable artificiality by using data based on historical hiring practices or self-serving attitudes of recruiters or applicants. Moreover, few studies have focused exclusively on employment barriers in the selling profession.

In one recent experiment designed to determine how employers would react to an applicant's race or religion, identical resumes, except for race or religion, were submitted to firms who had advertised for high-level sales employees.[13] Even though a previously reported religious bias was not evident, the data suggested that race remains a barrier to employment in sales and sales management. Seemingly, there is a significant reluctance by firms to place blacks in positions of continuous exposure to the firm's customers and sales-force members. Even firms who have opened the door to some black salespeople contend that there is still a risk in terms of customer acceptance.

Direct-to-consumer selling organizations are more receptive to blacks due to high turnover rates and relaxed screening policies. Yet, because of reported collection problems with black installment buyers and the reluctance of housewives to admit black salesmen to their homes,[14] some employment barriers prevail even in this area of distribution.

As more women graduates from business schools are entering business careers, there is reason to believe that the pool of female salespeople is increasing. Moreover, there is considerable feedback attesting to the fact that, in some selling situations, women are superior to men. Opposition to the employment of saleswomen focuses largely upon problems in connection with physical constraints, marriage, pregnancy, family relocations, and romantic involvements with customers and fellow salespeople.

SUMMARY AND CONCLUSIONS

Sales jobs differ in many ways including skill and experience requirements, degree of difficulty, and degree of attractiveness to the applicant. Consequently, it is more difficult to find job candidates for some job openings than for others.

An effective recruiting program will supply a sufficient number of applicants so that the firm can be truly selective in hiring applicants with the highest probability of success on the job. In many respects, the recruitment function requires a selling effort in that the recruiter uses techniques which encourage likely prospects to apply to his firm. This is particularly true when the job has undesirable features or when desirable people are not actively seeking new jobs.

Often the selling position is coveted by many applicants, each attempting to sell company officials on the idea that he is the most desirable candidate. The applicant's "can-do" characteristics are relatively easy to uncover with selection tools such as application blanks, interviews, tests and physical examinations. However, since these techniques fail to simulate actual field selling conditions, they are relatively ineffective in measuring intangible but important factors such as the applicant's inner drives, attitudes, stability, empathy, and ability to relate with customers and other business associates. Accordingly, the elusive "will-do" traits are more realistically determined by systematic discussions with the applicant's past employers or by having the applicant observe a company salesperson in the field.

Recruiting and selection techniques vary depending on the company structure. For example, employment ads will differ in content, format, frequency, and degree of disclosure, and various media can be used. Personal interviews may differ in the number of stages and interviewers and in interpretive procedure. Reference-checking procedures also vary by sequence, choice of respondents, and types and wording of questions.

NOTES

1. Carl W. Maier, "Recruiting Salesmen" in Albert Newgarden, ed., *The Field Sales Manager* (New York: American Management Association, Inc., 1960), p. 282.

2. Wilbert J. Miller, "Why Salesmen Change Jobs," *Sales and Marketing in Australia* (February 1974):2–3.

3. Maier, "Recruiting Salesmen," p. 283.

4. Robert N. McMurry, "The Mystique of Super-Salesmanship," *Harvard Business Review* 39 (March–April 1961):118–19.

5. Much of this material was borrowed from Marvin A. Jolson, "A Comparison of Blind vs. Full-Disclosure Newspaper Ads for Sales Personnel," *Akron Business and Economic Review* 5 (Winter 1974):16–18.

6. Marvin A. Jolson, "How Important Is Sales Force Size?" *Business Studies* (Spring 1971):31–40.

7. Thomas R. Wotruba, *Sales Management—Planning, Accomplishment, and Evaluation* (New York: Holt, Rinehart, and Winston, 1971), p. 312.

8. Robert N. McMurry, *How to Recruit, Select, and Place Salesmen* (Chicago: The Dartnell Corporation, 1964), p. 61.

9. Ibid., pp. 149–81. This author shows how to measure "will-do" qualifications by use of the personal interview.

10. These are treated in detail by William J. Reilly, *The Law of Intelligent Action* (New York: Harper & Row, 1945).

11. Marvin A. Jolson, "The Salesman's Career Cycle," *Journal of Marketing* 38 (July 1974):45.

12. McMurry, *How to Recruit,* pp. 68–69.

13. Marvin A. Jolson, "Employment Barriers in Marketing," *Journal of Marketing* 38 (April 1974):67–69.

14. Thomas Reuschling, "Black and White in Personal Selling," *Akron Business and Economic Review* 4 (Fall 1973):9–13.

QUESTIONS FOR DISCUSSION AND REVIEW

1. Recruitment ads for salesmen may ask applicants to apply by telephone, by mail, or in person.
   a. Under what circumstances would each approach be used?
   b. Which approach would draw the largest number of applicants?
   c. Which approach would attract applicants of the highest quality?

2. The firm whose data appear in Table 8.1 wishes to maximize its number of new sales reportees (those who actually report for work). The firm must limit its annual ad budget to $15,000 and its annual selection costs to $20,000. The company is concerned with employee turnover and will not be satisfied unless at least 60 of the new employees remain with the company for a minimum of one year. Since firms in this industry are affected by the forces of consumerism, management insists that the ad mix include at least 65 full-disclosure ads and no more than 250 blind ads. What is the optimal ad mix? (ans: 138 blind ads and 242 open ads.)

3. Type each one of the six ads of Figure 8.1 on a separate sheet of paper and insert the following scale at the bottom of each sheet:

Following graduation

_____ I would definitely inquire about this position.

_____ I would probably inquire about this position.

_____ I would probably not inquire about this position.

_____ I would definitely not inquire about this position.

_____ I'm not sure whether I would inquire or not.

The reason for my above response is as follows: _____

With the assistance of several fellow researchers, distribute at least 30 copies of each of the six ads to a random sample of students. The total sample will consist of at least 180 students. Test the significance of your findings using chi-square analysis. Discuss your findings in terms of the ad designs. Speculate as to the probable results if these ads appeared in the local newspaper.

4. Design a test whose purpose it is to measure a sales applicant's "will-do" traits.

5. Tell what circumstances would encourage a firm to recruit the following types of salespeople: women, part-timers, blacks, senior citizens, students.

6. Would a given company recruit and select field sales managers in the same way it seeks to hire salespeople?

7. Compare the *patterned* interview to the *canned* sales presentation. Are the advantages and disadvantages of each analogous?

8. Different firms give different amounts of emphasis to the various recruitment and selection tools. Compare these activities for companies seeking to hire the following types of salespeople:
   a. Full-time in-store furniture salespeople
   b. Saleswomen for an exclusive dress shop
   c. Sellers of materials-handling equipment to industrial accounts
   d. Sellers of electric typewriters to commercial accounts
   e. Sellers of health and accident insurance to farmers
   f. Women to sell cosmetic products to households
   g. Sellers of expensive leather goods to stores

Case 8.1 Butler's Dilemma

The Recruiter's Attempt to Minimize Perceived Job Negatives

Wayne Butler is Oregon sales manager for an organization that employs salespeople on a straight commission basis to sell directly to consumers in their homes. Since the unit sale is in excess of $600, both husband and wife must be present at the time of the sales presentation. Thus, evening and weekend calls are essential. Moreover, the company has found that the best method of prospecting is the cold canvass.

Turnover has been 400 percent during the past year, and because of perceived negative job conditions, recruitment of qualified people has been next to impossible. The firm has used a large number of well-written blind ads, which have elicited numerous phone responses and/or personal contacts by desirable applicants. However, it seems that the better people have rejected employment, so that the majority of the hirees have been marginally qualified.

The product is an outstanding one, and the company training and supervision program is superb. Therefore, the qualified newcomers who give the job half a chance are quickly convinced that the job hours and method of prospecting are really not bad at all. Furthermore, the commission-compensation plan is quite generous; salespeople who have been with the company a year or more are earning in excess of $500 per week.

Seemingly, newspaper advertising is the only recruiting approach that has generated a sufficient number of applicants. The firm has tried a few full-disclosure ads. These ads, which cost over $250 each, yielded a negligible number of applicants.

Butler is convinced that the solution lies in the development of an innovative interviewing technique that will convey the job requirements to the recruit without destroying his desire for employment.

QUESTIONS AND ASSIGNMENTS

1. If you agree with Butler, describe what the highlights should be in the format, content, sequence, and general procedures of the interview. If not, suggest an alternative solution.

2. What other recruiting and selection recommendations can you offer?

9

Training
Sales Personnel

The sales manager and his firm have invested considerable money, time, and effort to recruit and select a new salesperson. The effectiveness with which the manager uses indoctrination and training does much to determine whether a good investment was made or whether money and effort were thrown down the drain.

Frequently the manager assumes that he has hired a winner—a proven, experienced salesman, who needs only to be handed a sales kit and pointed in the direction of prospects—and that before long, the orders will begin to flow in. Such an assumption is one of the greatest misconceptions in sales management.

Salesmen are people, not counters or pawns with dollar signs on them. They may have considerable knowledge and selling skills, but being people first and producers second, they need security, acceptance, recognition, encouragement, and sometimes a kick in the pants.

They produce because they have a desire to work with and for their leaders, a confidence in their ability to do the work, a belief that management will help them, and a faith in their superiors that will carry them through inevitable disappointments and discouragements. These inner resources, without which no salesman can succeed, are fostered largely by the sales manager and his staff. It is the sales manager who equips salesmen for success. The manager who thinks and acts in terms of what he can do for his salespeople normally finds that the more he gives, the more he gets.

The new salesman can be compared to a market opportunity that is ready to be tapped and cultivated. Both must be developed carefully before their possibilities become actualities.[1] The sales recruit has been influenced by parents, teachers, and former employers. Management has not hired him because he has the knowledge, skills, experience, and desire to be successful on his own, but because it is confident of its ability to convert a newcomer with appropriate "can-do" and "will-do" characteristics into an effective producer for his new company.

The initial step in this conversion program is sales training—the process of imparting knowledge, developing skills, and shaping attitudes and work habits for the purpose of maximizing the salesperson's effectiveness.

SHAPING ATTITUDES AND WORK HABITS

Indoctrination

The new salesman reports to work with stars in his eyes. He has been wooed by the recruiter. He has survived the successive hurdles of the selection process. He may have been wined and dined and given every attention during the hiring sequence. The recruit feels wanted, valued, and enthusiastic.

At this point, many sales managers are guilty of a glaring error. They ignore the newcomer, shifting their attention to other functions, such as putting out "fires," hiring other people, doing paperwork. A relocated employee may be left on his own to locate a new residence, find a school for his children, initiate family social contacts, meet his fellow workers, and generally establish himself and his family in a new and possibly strange community. As described by one authority:

> It comes as a blow to the new worker to encounter such apparent disinterest, since during the previous period in which he was being interviewed for a job he was given the utmost care. Then suddenly the honeymoon is over; he now knows it was just sales talk. The administrator has forgotten that many people allow their social and psychological needs to overrule their economic requirements.[2]

Often the indoctrination process is limited to getting the new salesman souped-up enough to get out and knock on doors:

> You convince him there's nothing to it. Here's the presentation and there are the prospects. All you do is go out and show the product to the prospects and the money comes rolling in. Being a good salesman yourself, you can tell this story so persuasively that the new man is convinced.

Of course, he hasn't learned anything, but you've got him wound up enough to go out and make contact with prospects. The law of averages will take care of him. If he hits enough doors, he'll find an order somewhere. Maybe he'll make it and maybe he won't. When he finally falls by the wayside, you can hire another poor slob to do the same thing. Hire enough people and you'll probably make your district quota.

Strangely, the foregoing procedure frequently follows a meticulous recruiting and selection sequence. Ideally, indoctrination should be a process of laying the foundation for building the confidence, faith, and determination which the newcomer will need to become a skilled, enthusiastic performer that management is seeking.

The new sales recruit may be lonely, uncertain of what he is getting into, a bit frightened, maybe even desperate. He may be down on his luck or discouraged. The Horatio Alger dream may not be coming true. Perhaps he has experienced the taste of failure. Perhaps a new sales position is his gamble that it can be different and he is experiencing the feeling of a man putting his few remaining chips on this turn of the wheel. He needs to be encouraged and to feel a strong, sure, helping hand.

Indoctrination should build understanding and convictions that will last, not wear off the way a quick shot in the arm does. Indoctrination is a necessary preliminary function, separate from training. Plunging headlong into training frequently results in instant terminations.

Indoctrination should be a positive process—welcoming the recruit to his new work environment, introducing him to fellow workers, informing him of job details and company philosophies, policies, and expectations, and generally preparing the recruit for his subsequent training and his subsequent life with the new company.

The Right Mental Attitude (RMA)

Many salesmen tend to resist training, especially if they are not convinced of its value to them.[3] The trainee must respect the company, its products, its selling methods, and its policies toward solving customers' problems. Above all, the recruit must be convinced of his sales manager's willingness and ability to tell him, show him, and teach him how to be productive. Trainees need more than a warm and friendly leader. Research has shown that nice guys often make bum bosses.[4] The power-driven manager has been found to be the most successful sales manager because of his basic desire to influence and lead others by creating a good climate. His subordinates have both a sense of responsibility and a clear knowledge of the organization. They adhere to the work rules, not because they are hit over the head, but because they become loyal to the institution.

The power-driven manager will quickly convince the recruit that the RMA and solid work habits will develop the salesman's ability to manage himself, which is a prerequisite for managing prospects and closing sales. Such a manager will do what he requires his salesmen to do. His attitude will be "Let's go into the field together; when it rains on you, it will rain on me."

He will demonstrate that classroom-taught selling methods *work* in the field. Numerous cases have been cited where a sales trainee is trained in the classroom to use a given sales technique but when he is field-trained, the trainer uses an entirely different method. For example, the trainee is taught to use a semi-automated sales presentation but his field trainer uses a completely different, unstructured form during the initial field training.

WHAT KNOWLEDGE DOES A SALESMAN NEED?

A salesperson comes to his firm with a certain level of education, experience, and knowledge. However, there is always a gap between what the trainee already knows and what he needs to know. The size of this gap depends on whether the recruit is new to his present firm, new to the product he will sell, or new to the occupation of selling. The sales trainee must first be made aware of his own role with respect to both prospective buyers and his own organization. He must clearly understand the functions he is to perform and the environment in which he is to perform them.

Knowledge needs will vary widely with the type of sales position. Usually, where the salesperson's primary function is in-store or route selling, the required knowledge is quite simple and can be obtained by reading descriptive literature and manuals, attending brief classroom sessions, and observing an experienced salesperson. The knowledge-gathering process may be considerably more complex and time consuming for many other sales-force members. For example, the aspiring salesperson in life insurance or real estate may be required to take in-house or outside courses, do considerable studying at home, or use programmed learning materials in order to prepare for license-granting examinations. Industrial selling will often require extensive exposure to formalized training media including audiovisual materials, literature, lectures, case histories and field trips. Because trainees have had different levels of preparation, some firms will divide the training program into segments so that a trainee can attend only the sessions which he requires.

In general, the salesperson must acquire knowledge about four broad areas of the company: its offerings, its environment, its history and policies, and its operations and procedures.[5]

Offerings

It should be reassuring to even the most inexperienced salesperson that he knows more about the product than any prospect he will ever encounter. Thus, he should be intimately familiar with every feature of every product he sells and with how it is designed and manufactured. In addition, he must be aware of why the product incorporates these features and of what benefits the features give to the ultimate purchaser. He must be prepared to discuss limitations in usage as well as causes and frequency of failures. He must understand the foundation of his firm's pricing programs, discount prices, and advertising allowances.

Environment

The salesman should be familiar with his competitors, their relative sales and profit volume, and their methods of operation. He must understand the advantages and disadvantages of his competitors' products, prices, and selling programs, as compared with his own. Moreover, he must be aware of the extent to which competitive offerings are being accepted by the marketplace.

He should be able to determine customer needs and whether or not these needs are currently being satisfied. He should understand the dynamic influences in the general environment, including changing life styles, social pressures, technological advances, regulatory activities, and business trends, as they affect present and emerging new markets. Finally, he must attempt to understand why his customers, and his customers' customers, do or do not buy.

Company History and Policies

The salesman should understand why his company uses its current channel structure and distribution methods. He should understand and be able to support his company's policies concerning returns, allowances, billings, cancellations, and markup-granting policies. He must also know the company's history, philosophy, objectives, and standing in the trade. He must be aware of policies concerning personnel and compensation. He should be familiar with the background of the firm's executives.

Company Operations and Procedures

The salesperson should be able to discuss his company's plan of organization and the relationship of the sales function to other functional areas. He should be particularly familiar with the areas of the company which closely support the selling operation (marketing research, advertising, sales promotion, and customer service). He should have a thorough understanding of the company's sales-control techniques and systems, including the format and need for call reports, sales meetings and clinics, quota systems, and profit-sharing plans.

He should be well versed in the principles behind the company's selling techniques as they apply to stimulating purchases, solving customer problems, and upholding the highest standards of ethical selling practice.

DEVELOPING SELLING SKILLS

After a sales trainee has obtained the required knowledge, he must acquire the necessary skills to use that knowledge effectively and productively. In contrast to the acquisition of knowledge, developing skills requires practice, either in front of prospects or under conditions that closely simulate such situations.

The following golf poem by Dick Emmons emphasizes the gap between knowledge and execution: [6]

> My golf swing is a joy to see
> I keep my head down on the tee
> I always hold my left arm straight
> I'm flawless when I shift my weight
> My backswing, never hurried, jerky
> Is praised from here to Albuquerque
> The same is very largely true
> About the way I follow through
> My pro, not known for thinking small,
> Predicts that soon I'll hit the ball.

The mastery of selling, not unlike the mastery of golf, requires continuous practice of the fundamental techniques, under the watchful eye of the sales manager, the selling pro. However, the golfer, including the weekend duffer, views golf as a pleasurable recreational activity, an opportunity to enjoy himself with his friends, an

athletic function which has no major impact on his financial resources or family happiness (unless he's a heavy bettor or his wife is
a golf widow). Thus, he can enjoy the game despite his inability to
develop golfing skills.

Early Failures

Unlike the weekend athlete, however, the salesperson is not
psychologically armored to withstand repeated failure. Rejection is
particularly distasteful when earnings are tied to sales volume. Paradoxically, the salesman who needs money the most may be the least
willing to prospect, make calls, deliver sales presentations, or otherwise display good work habits.

Poor work habits evolve from a poor mental attitude, which, in
turn, often results from recollections of recent failures. Therefore, the
training sequence must be structured to maximize the number of
successful experiences. An ill-timed negative experience early in the
training process can be an early knockout blow.

The intense pressures on the sales trainer are apparent in the
following dialogue between a sales trainee and his wife. They are
discussing his first day of field observation:

WIFE: Golly, you did put in a long day today. You left home at 8 A.M.
and you didn't get back until 11 P.M. What did you do today?

TRAINEE: I went out in the field with the company's branch manager,
Harry Moore. I watched Harry contact prospects and deliver
sales presentations.

WIFE: Is Mr. Moore a good salesman?

TRAINEE: Good? Harry is the very best there is. For five years in a
row, he has been the top salesman in the southwestern region.

WIFE: How many sales did he make today?

TRAINEE: Well . . . er . . . he didn't make any sales. But he did
deliver six full sales presentations—six excellent sales presentations.

WIFE: How much is he paid for giving a sales presentation?

TRAINEE: You don't get paid for giving a sales presentation, silly. But
on the average, Harry sells one out of every four presentations.

WIFE: George, I've been worried sick all day about your taking a
straight commission job. Now I'm sure I'm right. If an experienced and successful man like Harry Moore couldn't make any
sales, a new person like you can expect many bad days. To be
very honest, George, I don't think this is the job for you.

George's early termination could be most frustrating to management, especially if considerable time and money has been spent on recruiting, selecting, and inside-training him. Perhaps George should not have been hired, since he cannot be expected to sell prospects if he cannot sell his own wife. Perhaps the wife should have been informed about the law of averages sometime during the recruiting or indoctrination process or following the day in the field. Perhaps the field trainer was ineffective. Maybe George was not quite ready for field training. Perhaps field training was not an appropriate method.

Needed Skills

In broad terms, the successful sales trainee must learn to apply the principles of the company's selling techniques. Applied to the basic promotional functions introduced in earlier chapters, he must learn how to find prospects, call on them, stimulate desire for possession, close orders, and retain customers.

He must develop an instinct in selling situations for perceiving and diagnosing prospects' problems and needs, for probing and finding clues which will enable him to uncover latent desires, and for providing a desirable remedy at the right moment. Especially vital in developing communications skills is learning how to listen, absorb, and react when prospects, managers, and peers are expressing their needs. Salesmen must learn how to plan and use their time systematically and how to analyze their successes and failures so that each experience serves as a building block for future self-confidence and success.

Skill-Training Methods

The trainer must foster instinctiveness in communication by compelling the trainee to actually perform selling activities. Reading, hearing, and thinking, as previously indicated, are not enough. Skill training calls for more than telling the new person what to do and how to do it. It calls for showing and teaching him how, and then reviewing and critically analyzing the trainee's performance.

Skills can be developed in the training classroom through role playing, relevant sales casework, analysis of salesmen's call reports, business games, and other methods.

A unique skill-development method was devised by the Seminar Film Company, which customizes "films that talk back" for larger firms. This method employs movies showing typical company prospects in various situations, and calls for instinctive sales responses. For example, the movie might show a protective receptionist being approached by a salesman and saying, "Yes, may I help you?" Immediately a vanishing white line appears on the screen and the sales trainee must learn to respond before the line disappears. After the trainee has delivered his response, the receptionist might say, "I don't believe Mr. Big will have time to see you today." Again, a gradually vanishing white line appears and the trainee practices delivering his response during the limited time frame. Similar practice films have been developed to permit trainees to perfect their skills in reacting to interruptions, objections, prospect requests, and other typical selling situations.

Field Training

Despite the helpfulness of simulated situations, true interaction with prospects can only take place in the field. Ideally, as the trainee observes the field trainer in action, he will be convinced that what he was taught really works. The trainee observes the field trainer's selling plan, prospecting, setting of appointments, approaches in business offices and at residential doors, sales presentations, closes, use of rebuttals—all the consecutive detailed steps of selling under live conditions.

The astute trainer will confer with the trainee after each call or series of calls to answer questions, to associate what happened with material covered in classroom training sessions, to highlight critical incidents that took place during the call, to explicitly recall the reasons for the success or failure of the call, and to allow the trainee to take notes where needed.

After field observation by the trainee has shown him how, the trainee does it himself while the field trainer observes. Often the trainer and trainee will alternate in making calls and also have "curbstone conferences" between calls. The trainer can use a prepared checklist to quickly locate a trainee's weak points. The alternate-calling system is particularly useful when the trainer uses his own presentation to demonstrate the method of correcting weaknesses in the trainee's presentation. The trainee's next presentation should include the improvements that have been recommended by the trainer.

Any system that requires a sales manager or experienced salesman to observe the trainee is costly since the trainer's personal production will normally be reduced. Moreover, a trainee is often reluctant to perform in front of experienced salesmen or managers for fear he may do poorly and be subjected to considerable negative criticism. Therefore, if the curbstone conference or end-of-the-day critique is to be welcomed by and constructive to the trainee, the trainer must focus on showing the newcomer how to improve his strengths rather than on emphasizing his weaknesses. Many firms will compensate trainees by paying them full or partial commissions on sales made by the trainer. These earnings are deserved when the trainee has been active in setting up prospects for the trainer.

Training Sequence

As mentioned earlier, the realities of the firm's specific selling situation may not be obvious to the trainee until he has observed in the field. If prospects are hostile, if his trainer meets with many rejections, if the work looks too demanding, the trainee may become disenchanted and either leave at once or continue his training with tongue in cheek.

For this reason, some sales managers schedule field observation as the first item on the training agenda—even before indoctrination and inside training. Of course, this may not be necessary if field observation is part of the selection process. Although early field trips may be effective in separating the men from the boys and saving the time and costs of training those who disqualify themselves, it may prematurely expose an unconditioned trainee to complex salesman-prospect interactions which would be better understood following detailed classroom training.

The primary objective of field observation is to demonstrate the application of company selling techniques and methods. If preliminary field observation is to be used at all, it should be in addition to, not instead of, the field sessions that follow inside training. Obviously the costs of additional field training and the risk of confusing the unprepared newcomer are related to the nature of the specific selling task.

STANDARDIZATION AND DISCIPLINE IN TRAINING

Sales training is a planning process in that it establishes the specific courses and methods of action that management desires the new salesman to follow. Supervision involves directing and controlling the activities of the salesperson to be sure he does not wander too far from the prescribed course of action. Any plan must be subject to a certain amount of standardization and the people who implement the plan must be disciplined to some degree. Properly applied, standardization and discipline are more for the benefit of the salesman than for his managers and company. Standardization prescribes a track for the salesman to run on (not a groove to confine him) while discipline keeps him on the track.

Many salespeople are narcissistic exhibitionists at heart, and are never happier than when in front of prospects making a pitch. They love to be the center of attention and find that an audience inspires them to surprising heights of artistry. Yet, it has been found that even better salespeople do not have the raw creativity to develop original selling techniques.[7]

Sales Presentations

It was indicated in Chapter 6 that sales presentations with high amounts of company input were perceived by sales executives as most effective in facilitating the training of sales-force members. Yet the memorized presentation was rated as least effective.

Despite the apparent ease of training a person to plug in a projector or flip the pages of an easel, flip chart, or read-off binder, this training procedure is not completely without challenge. The trainee must still be taught to gain an audience, neutralize, and prime the prospect for a captive session. One well-known, direct-selling company delivers the sales presentation by use of a three-ringed binder containing more than twenty laminated pages which the sales representative turns and reads to Mr. and Mrs. Prospect. The placement of the husband and wife is quite critical and the sales-person must memorize the following lines in order to set up the presentation:

> In order to give you the information you've requested without omitting anything, or without being too wordy, the company has prepared a rather colorful open letter which they have asked me to cover with you. So that you can see it all right, Mr. Prospect, could you sit on the sofa on my right with your wife on your right?

Sales trainees often find it difficult to memorize lengthy presentations. Therefore, training consists of pounding the material into the salesman's brain by use of repetitive drills and role-playing sessions. This process demands much of the trainer's time, patience, and energy. Moreover, as indicated in Chapter 6, salespeople often resent being servile to considerable structure in terms of what to say and how to say it.

Yet, salesmen are best compared to actors who must be fed their lines.[8] They may be articulate, but they are not necessarily good extemporaneous speakers. For example, when they are thrown off-

208   stride by some incident or interruption, many salesmen tend to return to the beginning of a sales presentation section.

A number of training procedures can develop skills in extemporaneous speaking, delivering lines, and reading with feeling, enthusiasm, and sparkle. One trainer holds impromptu speaking sessions where trainees are required to deliver spur-of-the-moment three-minute speeches on such far-out subjects as baby carriages, grandfather clocks, and mirrors. In another organization trainees are drilled in reading brief arbitrarily selected newspaper articles aloud in a sparkling and scintillating way.

Rebuttals

Even the veteran salesman often has difficulty in coping with a new objection or new form of sales resistance. When salesmen get together at sales meetings, conventions, social events, or over a cup of coffee, they exchange ideas or phrases which have worked in the past. The newcomer has not had these opportunities and is concerned with his ability to handle objections such as "I'm happy with my present supplier" or "how do I know it will sell" or "the price is too high" or "I've used up my open-to-buy." As mentioned earlier, many firms prepare a booklet of standard rebuttals and verbal-proof stories which respond to recurrent objections. Classroom drill sessions help the trainee build a reservoir of answers to meet nearly every contingency. Some trainers recommend ways that the salesman can use his rebuttal folder in the presence of the prospective customer in case of memory lapse.

Input by the Fledgling Salesperson

It would seem that the new salesman would be delighted to be guided by a structured, proven selling plan that has been designed by specialists. This is quite true during the early training stages.

But the person in selling is often quite impatient. If the company selling plan does not result in instant results, the greenest recruit may not hesitate to figure out a better way. This amateurish reconstruction is, more often than not, so ill-conceived and remote from the company plan that the product could not be given away, much less sold.

Even the intelligent trainee who experiences early successes by using his learned routine with few modifications is likely to try to improve the system. This person may want to do his own thinking and use his own knowledge. He absorbs the company method, evaluates it, masters it, and then comes to his own conclusions. Certain adjustments in the sales presentation may come quickly, but the major changes may involve matching the presentation with the salesman's personality. In due time, he is still using a structured presentation but the structure is a result of input by both the company and the salesman.

ORGANIZING FOR TRAINING EFFECTIVENESS

Who Is Responsible?

In larger organizations, the sales-training function may be a team effort. Home-office personnel may design the program, the district manager may supervise the training program, staff instructors may conduct classroom sessions, while experienced salesmen, unit field managers, branch managers, or the district manager himself may conduct the field-training activities.

When the inside training program is divided into discrete sessions or courses, outside training specialists or consultants may be called upon to conduct various segments. For example, several sales consulting firms are specialists in lead-getting or telephone selling, or servicing department stores.

In smaller firms and in the local operations of some larger firms, a single sales manager may personally perform all the training functions listed in the first paragraph of this section. In considering such a possibility, one reopens the argument (see Chapter 3) of whether the sales manager should be actively involved in personal selling and field-related activities.

In some companies, trainees are sent to universities or special schools for part of their training. Occasionally sales trainees join other newly hired people in indoctrination sessions conducted by the firm's personnel department. The lineup of training personnel will depend on the size and the unique demands of a given firm. One useful guideline is to delegate the field training to the same individual who will later be responsible for supervising the trainee. This is particularly effective when the supervising manager receives permanent overrides on the trainee's production. Money is a major motivating force for convincing field managers to develop skillful trainees.

Duration of Training Programs

Some training programs can be completed in a few hours; others last for two or more years. If the trainee is salaried, it will be to the firm's advantage to prepare him as quickly as possible for field productivity so as to avoid undue delays in generating a profit on the firm's investment in training and compensation costs. New salesmen who are compensated on a commission basis, are anxious to go out in the field as soon as possible. If there is neither money nor the promise of a paycheck in time to pay the grocery bill, the new salesman may be persuaded to search the want ads for a salaried job.

The speed of training a given individual will receive depends on the number and complexity of the knowledge, skill, and attitude requirements, the number of trainees being trained simultaneously, the availability of trainers, whether training is done individually or in classes, where the training takes place, the steps in the training process, the design of the training program, the teaching ability of the trainers, and the learning capacity of the trainees. When replacement trainees are readily recruitable, trainers may have limited patience with trainees who catch on slowly.

When one speaks of the speed of training, the question arises as to when a new salesman is no longer considered to be a trainee. Realistically, training is a continuous process, such that even the most experienced and successful salespeople should be subjected to periodic retraining and refresher courses. However, one approach suggests that the salesperson moves through a salesman's career cycle (SCC) consisting of the four stages of preparation, development, maturity, and decline.[9] This model suggests that the preparation stage is concluded when the salesman completes his initial training and is permitted to call on prospects without being accompanied by a field manager. To determine whether a given sales trainee should be advanced to the development phase, management might require an affirmative answer to each of the following questions:

1. Is he aware of his specific job requirements?
2. Does he have favorable attitudes toward the learning process?
3. Does he perceive direct and purposive relationships between customer needs, company goals, and his own behavior?
4. Has he developed an understanding of personal interaction and the barriers to making it successful?
5. Has he developed the skills to put his knowledge into action?
6. Does he appear willing and able to acquire new capacities?

Training Locales

In practice, field training takes place in the prospects' offices and residences, on curbstones, in restaurants, and enroute to and from sales calls. In larger firms, inside training may either be decentralized, and allocated to local district or branch offices, or centralized in the company's home office.

Decentralization has a number of advantages in that the trainee is trained by the same people who will ultimately supervise him and benefit from his productivity on a regular basis. Moreover, he will be indoctrinated in the same regional environment that he will have to "live with" when he advances to the development stage of his career cycle. The disadvantage is that training personnel in the local office may be part-time trainers who may not offer the trainee the required intense attention because of other managerial demands such as administrative duties, hiring, supervision, and personal selling.

In a centralized framework, a full-time staff of teachers is usually available. These specialists are totally devoted to training and are skilled in introducing newcomers to all dimensions of the company operation, including production, advertising, marketing research, and major corporate entities less visible at a local level. Elaborate home-office training programs, such as those conducted by Bethlehem Steel, Remington-Rand, Legg-Mason, and others, remove the trainee from his or her home for many weeks or months. Indeed, there are advantages, from a learning viewpoint, in being removed from the distractions and temptations of one's daily routine. Yet there is little doubt that centralized training is costly in terms of financing trainees' travel and hotel expenses and supporting large-scale training facilities and personnel.

In a number of firms part of the initial training takes place at national or regional headquarters and part in a local setting. Normally, the visit to central headquarters will come first. Promising recruits are introduced to members of top management, taken on a detailed tour of the central office, and provided with a basic introduction to company policies and philosophies and fundamental selling techniques. The detailed nitty-gritty skill-development exercises take place in the local office, where they can be reinforced by training in the field.

BEYOND INITIAL TRAINING

Retraining Experienced Salespeople

Retraining is all too often a remedial rather than a preventive process. In other words, additional training does not take place until *after* management receives such signals of ineffective performance as excessive turnover, low morale, customer complaints, and decreasing revenues or market share. Frequently, management takes fren-

212 zied steps to inject belated doses of retraining and motivation after a salesman resigns and the sales manager is trying desperately to "save him."

The preventive approach looks at sales training as an ongoing, continuous process whereby management anticipates retraining needs and actually searches for symptoms and cues which will suggest the direction of retraining programs. The recently trained salesperson will eventually encounter changing sales circumstances and environments for which his initial training program has not prepared him. For example, new products and additional applications of present products may appear in both consumer and industrial sectors; buying habits and procedures may change drastically; regulatory constraints may increase; customers may demand new types of assistance from sellers. In response to these situations, marketers modify their order-processing systems, channel structures, physical distribution strategies, credit and collection programs, and reactions to competitive promotional programs. All of this calls for an updating of company selling policies, procedures, and strategies. The firm must often alter its selling approach, customer mix, territorial alignment, and sales-force compensation package, all of which calls for the reorientation and reeducation of sales-force members.[10]

Instead of waiting for troubles to crop up, management often probes to find out what the retraining priorities are by surveying salesmen and customers for suggestions, scrutinizing salesmen's call reports, inspecting and analyzing sales records, observing salesmen in action, and compiling information from exit questionnaires.[11]

Retraining or refresher sessions may be directed to an individual salesperson or to a group. When one salesman is involved, his manager might say, "Let's ride together for a day or two" or "Come in to the office after work tonight so we can go through some role-playing sessions to sharpen-up your closing techniques." On-the-job coaching is undoubtedly the best method of maintaining a salesman's effectiveness, especially during the development stage when the employee has not as yet acquired undesirable behavior patterns.

Informal group discussions and clinics may be conducted on an ad hoc basis when management suspects that several salespeople are confronted with a common sales problem. Regularly scheduled brief clinics covering preannounced subjects are also useful to reinforce forgotten fundamentals or prevent the obsolescence and deterioration of knowledge and skills.

Often, formalized in-house refresher courses are given at central or regional headquarters, and seminars and university courses are offered. Because of the high costs of travel, tuition, and removing of the salesman from field productivity, attendees must be selected with great care.[12] Selection may be rotational and based on seniority, such that all sales-force members will eventually be included. Retraining can also serve as a reward for outstanding performance or as a punishment for below-average performance. Attendance can also be optional or granted in response to special requests by employees who seek to further their education. A recent study of the relationship between sales experience and performance in in-house formalized retraining programs suggested an inverse relationship between sales tenure and learning effectiveness.[13] These findings hint that senior salespeople may have the least desire and/or need for formal retraining. Some of the disinterest may have to do with the experienced salesman's reluctance to forgo selling activities and possible earnings to attend sessions which he perceives as only marginally helpful.

Developing Field Sales Managers

Despite the obvious complexity of the sales manager's job in contrast to that of the salesman, relatively little attention is given in the firm and in the marketing literature to the initial training and perpetual development of sales supervisors and field sales managers at all levels. As the reader reviews the various means of classifying selling jobs, as shown in Chapter 2, he will recognize that the standards established for the selection of managerial candidates and the knowledge, skill, and attitude requirements for sales managers will vary from company to company.

Most frequently, sales supervisory talent will come from the ranks of salespeople within the firm. However, the firm seeking to develop managers quickly will successfully recruit and hire sales leaders from other companies and convert them to the hiring company's methods of operation.

In many situations, sales management is largely a process of multiplying one's personal selling ability. Fundamentally, a sales manager is a proven salesman who trains, supervises, and develops another salesman. As the manager advances to the branch, district, or regional levels, the training and development program emphasizes administrative, decision-making, and leadership skills. When the new manager has previously served as a salesman, it cannot be assumed that his promotion will automatically shift his orientation from one of personal selling to that of company profits and concern for the welfare of subordinates, customers, and his company's reputation. As illustrated by Case 3.1, a certain amount of modification in attitude and behavior is required to effect a satisfactory transition.

Although there are many ways to develop sales managers, the

following five-stage procedure, used by a large consumer-goods organization, is a typical model from which other firms can extrapolate.

First, the managerial candidate must indicate that he is capable of maintaining his personal selling proficiency while being observed by trainees. His selling techniques and style must conform to company standards and they must be readily transferable to trainees who have less knowledge, skills, instinctiveness, experience, and confidence than the trainer.

Second, he must demonstrate his ability and willingness to guide new salespeople in their scheduling, programming, and selling efforts and to motivate, stimulate, and supervise them on a continuing basis. In this stage, considerable on-the-job coaching by the candidate's district manager is necessary, and there are required reading assignments in job manuals and selected management journals and texts.

Third, he must spend considerable time "hanging around" his district manager in order to observe certain techniques. He must learn how to handle complaints of customers and grievances of sales-force members, and how to perform administrative duties, including forecasting, budget and quota setting, and the analysis and interpretation of sales, costs, and profit data. He is invited to contribute toward decision making so that his deductive reasoning ability and flexibility in thinking can be developed. This stage often includes visits to other offices, meetings with home office officials and other functional supervisors, and attendance at seminars, conferences, and other executive development programs.

Fourth, if the prospective manager's growth continues, he assumes the position of assistant branch manager with an attendant broadening and integration of duties and responsibilities. Concurrent with the supervision of several assigned salesmen, he is expected to perform hiring and administrative functions including correspondence, preparing company newsletters, analyzing sales information, and preparing reports. At the same time, he is expected to maintain a specified level of personal selling activity. During this phase, the district manager is available at all times for guidance and consultation, especially on the subject of managing time and energy.

Fifth, after the above phases, the new manager's strengths and weaknesses will become apparent, such that his present state of readiness will dictate his appropriate assignment and the necessary areas of concentration in his further development.

SUMMARY AND CONCLUSIONS

Inside training and field training work hand-in-hand to develop attitudes, knowledge, skills, and work habits of both beginning and experienced salespeople and field sales managers. Although much selling knowledge is transmitted through lectures, seminars, audiovisual equipment, and other classroom techniques, the most formidable job in developing a devoted career salesperson is creating and maintaining a climate for growth within which the sales manager and the trainee work together in the field in pursuit of common goals and rewards.

Training consists of telling, showing, and teaching the trainee and then monitoring his results and making constructive corrections. New salespeople often resist excessive structure in the training program. Yet, it has been shown that unless a trainee learns a routine and uses it uncritically at the outset of his employment, supervision and control will be difficult later. Accordingly, some standardization and discipline are management necessities.

Management should search continuously for clues that suggest the direction and content of retraining or refresher programs. All too often, retraining the experienced salesman takes the form of a shot in the arm after the salesman is already in the decline stage of his career.

The salesperson who has been promoted must be trained to think and behave like a manager. Despite its relative neglect, the development of the field sales manager is much more vital to the firm than the training and development of a salesperson. The properly developed field sales manager will ultimately control a level of sales and profits that will far exceed the productivity of any single salesperson.

NOTES

1. Thomas R. Wotruba, *Sales Management: Planning, Accomplishment, and Evaluation* (New York: Holt, Rinehart, and Winston, 1971), p. 348.

2. William J. Stanton and Richard H. Buskirk, *Management of the Sales Force* (Homewood, Ill.: R. D. Irwin, 1974), pp. 284–87.

3. "To Me, Training is the Lifeblood of Any Successful Salesman," *Sales Management* (1 April 1966): 72.

4. David C. McClelland and David H. Burnham, "Good Guys Make Bum Bosses," *Psychology Today* (December 1975):69–70.

5. Charles S. Goodman, *Management of the Personal Selling Function* (New York: Holt, Rinehart, and Winston, 1971), pp. 210–12. See also Myles S.

Gaythwaite, "Motivating Salesmen: Some Ends and Means" in Albert Newgarden, ed., *The Field Sales Manager* (New York: American Management Association, Inc., 1960), pp. 161–85.

6. Although the poem was received from an indirect source, the author has been informed that the item was printed in an unknown issue of *The Wall Street Journal*.

7. Robert N. McMurry, *How to Recruit, Select, and Place Salesmen* (Chicago: Dartnell Corporation, 1964), pp. 13, 18.

8. Ibid., pp. 16–17.

9. Marvin A. Jolson, "The Salesman's Career Cycle," *Journal of Marketing* 38 (July 1974):39–46.

10. See John J. Withey, "Retraining the Experienced Salesperson," in Marvin A. Jolson, ed., *Contemporary Readings in Sales Management* (New York: Petrocelli/Charter 1977). This article makes an excellent contribution to this section.

11. Richard R. Still and Edward W. Cundiff, *Sales Management: Decisions, Policies, and Cases* (Englewood Cliffs, N.J.: Prentice-Hall, 1969), pp. 226–27.

12. Withey, "Retraining," op. cit.

13. Ibid.

QUESTIONS FOR DISCUSSION AND REVIEW

1. You are a sales-training consultant who seeks to interest organizations in your services. Respond to each of the following arguments by sales managers:
   a. "We'd like to do some sales training but we're not big enough. It would cost more than it would pay out."
   b. "We don't need sales training. We rely on the men to learn on the job. That's the way all our top people learned to sell. It must work—our company is one of the leaders in our field."
   c. "Ours is a rough, tough business. We've always had a lot of turnover and we always will. We can't hire the top people, so we hire the best we can, and when they quit, we run another ad. Why should we get frustrated trying to train mediocre people to be supersalesmen? You can't make a silk purse out of a sow's ear."

2. Defend and oppose each of the following criteria for selecting veteran salespeople for an extensive retraining program:
   a. Selection serves as a reward for superior performance.
   b. Selection serves as a punishment for below-average producers.
   c. Selection is a voluntary process which is the option of sales-force members.
   d. Selection is made on the basis of seniority.

3. How could you measure the effectiveness of your company's sales training program?

4. Contrast field training and inside training in terms of:
   a. Which should come first?
   b. What proportion of the trainee's time should be spent in each area?

5. The new sales manager is feared by the salesmen he inherits because he is unknown to them and because he represents change, which destroys security. Yet management expects him to be a superman who can correct, supposedly overnight, all the inequities, injustices, and failures of the past. He is the person who will inject new enthusiasm and confidence in a sales force that has been mismanaged by its previous leader. What kind of a training program would you use in preparing the new sales manager for the problems of such an assignment?

6. Describe what type of training program and teaching methods you would use to accomplish each of the following objectives:
   a. Teach a trainee to apply newly acquired product knowledge to a customer's problem.
   b. Teach a trainee to make telephone appointments with prospects without disclosing requested pricing information.
   c. Teach a trainee to develop skills in overcoming objections.
   d. Teach a new field sales manager (who has been recently promoted from the sales ranks) to recruit new sales people.
   e. Teach a new female field trainer to train male sales trainees.
   f. Train a Spanish-speaking New York salesman to sell in Madrid.
   g. Instruct a salesman in the art of maintaining his sales volume while satisfying the increasing service needs of his retail customers.

Case 9.1 Breakstone Advertising Agency

Training a New Manager

Please reread Case 3.1.

QUESTIONS AND ASSIGNMENTS

1. Based on the company's experience with Leroy Saine, outline a specific training and development program to prepare another of the company's top salesmen for a regional manager's assignment.

2. If you were the candidate for promotion, how would you react to the program recommended in the answer to the previous question?

Case 9.2 Durango Combustion Products, Inc.

Accompanying a Stumbling Trainee on a Sales Call

Nick Pope was a reasonably articulate salesman. For reasons unknown to himself, he had switched sales jobs three times in the past two years. At one time he had sold a line of chain saws and allied tools through distributors and dealers, but recently he had switched to selling a line of fire extinguishers, escape ladders, and smoke detectors for Durango Combustion Products, Inc.

The company's principal customers were owners of commercial, government, and industrial buildings. However, in mid-1975, it recognized a splendid opportunity to sell self-contained, battery-operated smoke detectors to high-rise apartment buildings. In several states, smoke detectors were mandatory in new residential construction. Durango had successfully tapped the apartment-building market in the East and was in the process of building a similar operation in the Midwest.

Nick had spent two weeks at Durango's home office near Philadelphia, where he met home-office officials, engineers, and administrators. The midwestern sales manager of the smoke-detector division took him out to several high-rise buildings where the company had already installed smoke detectors in each apartment. The building owners, managers, and tenants seemed delighted with the installations. For about ten days, Nick attended sales classes where he was exposed to all the features of the product and their benefits for apartment-building tenants. The company used a memorized sales presentation which was supplemented by colorful broadsides and brochures. The presentation also called for the salesman to light a cigarette and blow smoke into an actual detector.

After Nick returned to his district office in Chicago, he was up to his ears in training and was ready to go out and sell. But he was then sent to a motivational seminar for three days where he listened to lectures about self-motivation, the right mental attitude, enthusiasm, and all of the motivational subjects which Nick felt he knew all about. Nick was bursting at the britches to go out to contact prospects.

But he was required to attend two more days of district office classes where he was bored to death by training films featuring people such as Arnold Palmer, George Blanda, and Vince Lombardi who, in Nick's opinion, were lousy actors, incapable of stirring up his enthusiasm. Nick felt he was amenable to training, but he was sure Durango was overdoing a good thing. To his chagrin, he was then told he would be assigned to a field trainer for two days of field observation.

Nick was ready to explode and probably would have sounded off. What prevented this was his field trainer, Betty Barnes, a personable and attractive young woman, twenty-four years of age. She had been an outstanding Durango saleswoman in the East and had been promoted to field trainer in order to spearhead the midwestern sales program. Betty did well while Nick was observing. She delivered six full sales presentations, received one signed contract for seventy-six units ($2,500 in volume), and made an appointment to call back when all the owners in one building were present.

At the end of the first day, Nick pleaded to be sent out on his own, but Betty refused to budge. "I was told to take you out in the field for two days—and two days it will be."

After his observation period, Nick was issued a sales kit. Betty listened to his sales talk in the office, approved it, and informed Nick she would ride with him for several days, observing his presentations, holding curbstone conferences after each call, and delivering presentations in front of him, when necessary.

Nick had some difficulty in getting apartment-building owners and managers to hold still for sales presentations. However, he felt his presentations were quite good. He had emphasized the early-warning features of the unit, its ability to detect smoke as well as invisible gases of combustion, and the loud built-in horn which would warn sleeping tenants to leave their apartments before flames appeared. He indicated that the unit was attractive, the size of a dinner plate, and easily installed in just five minutes. He also emphasized that the unit was U.L. listed, and that the horn would beep every hour when the battery got low.

He delivered four presentations his first day. Three prospects asked for his card and indicated they would think it over. The fourth said it was a good idea but they would have to ask the tenants whether they wanted it, and, if so, whether a rent increase of one dollar per month would be justified. Nick reacted aggressively to this procrastination and said "the lives of tenants were at stake." In one case, a prospect said, "You're an aggressive little devil, aren't you?"

Betty and Nick had a cup of coffee at the end of the day's work. She wrote out some suggestions for Nick to read over that night and she informed Nick that she would deliver the first couple of presentations the next day to illustrate the use of rebuttals. At this point, Nick could no longer contain his feelings. "Betty, you're a very capable person and I know you're only trying to help me, but I am absolutely fed up with being treated like an infant. I'm a professional salesman who doesn't need all of this mothering. I've been sitting through this nonsense training for weeks. Now, why don't you go tend to your knitting and let me work this out for myself? Tell your bosses to save all of this attention for some kid sales trainee who is wet behind the ears."

QUESTIONS AND ASSIGNMENTS

1. Evaluate the company's sales training program.
2. Was Betty Barnes an effective field trainer?
3. What should she do now?
4. Was Nick Pope's attitude reasonable? If you were his close friend, how would you advise him?

Section IV

Maintaining and Improving the Sales Organization

10

Stimulating Sales-Force Members

> The mediocrity of salesmanship is but a part of our national pattern of being willing to settle for something less than the best. For this, in America, is the high tide of mediocrity, the era of the great goof-off, the age of the half-done job. The land has been enjoying a stampede away from responsibility. It is populated with laundrymen who won't iron shirts, waiters who won't serve, plumbers and electricians who ignore customers, executives whose minds are on the golf course, teachers who demand a single salary schedule so that achievement cannot be rewarded nor poor work punished, students who take cinch courses because the hard ones make them think, and spiritual delinquents of all kinds who have triumphantly determined to enjoy what was known until the present crisis as "the new leisure." The salesman who won't sell is only a part of this overall mess.

The above excerpt from a talk by Charles H. Brower is both true and sad, especially to the sales manager who has devoted much time, effort, and money to recruiting, selecting, and training what he presumes will be a hard-hitting, productive sales force. A careful rereading of Brower's statement will convince the reader that selling mediocrity is related to what the salesman *won't do* rather than to what he *can't do*.

If the selection process has been even mildly effective, the new salesman will have come to the firm with a certain amount of desire to do the job. A properly executed training program should develop that desire into flaming enthusiasm. However, there are times when a salesperson becomes discouraged, apathetic, disenchanted, or disinterested. In other words, his "get-up-and-go" has "got up and went."

This chapter discusses the occupational factors that reduce the salesman's ability to persist in successful sales activities and also examines the reasons for the scarcity of self-starters on most sales forces. The follow-up managerial activities required in such situations involve continued motivation, stimulation, and supervision. These are examined in this chapter and the next.

THE SELLING PENDULUM

The decay of selling proficiency and the need for external stimulation by management can be likened to the movement of a playground swing, which begins with a push by the parent (see Figure 10.1). Without additional shoves or pumping by the child, each time the pendulum swings upward it reaches a point lower than the one from which it had previously swung downward. In the absence of external and internal force on the pendulum, friction and air resistance will prevent the cycle from continuing indefinitely. As shown by the damped oscillation at the bottom of the figure, the amplitude of each successive cycle diminishes until the swing stops completely.

The salesman's job is a similar succession of ups and downs, a series of experiences resulting in alternating feelings of exhilaration and depression. Although in his daily work he calls on receptive, pleasant, and courteous people, he also meets with considerable friction and sales resistance from people who are disinterested and frequently unpleasant. He must often accept many nos in exchange for one yes. His attempts to overcome the objections of prospects and compete against the proposals of rival salesmen are often frustrating. As indicated previously, he may perceive certain company actions as abuses. For example, the firm may withdraw territories as commissions build. It may fail to ship orders and provide quality products and customer services, resulting in continual returns and loss of commissions. The firm may not respond to salesmen's needs for literature, samples, and sales aids. It may fail to pay commissions or to pay them promptly, or it may recover commissions when customers are delinquent in payments.

Moreover, some salespeople must travel, work weekends and evenings, and otherwise spend considerable time away from their families. A salesman may have to work in the same territory or call on the same customers year after year. He may be called upon to perform menial tasks, such as counting inventory, rearranging displays,

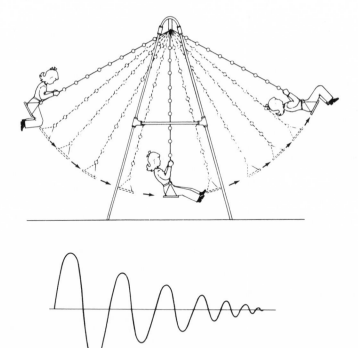

Figure 10.1 The selling pendulum

filling out call reports. His job may lose its challenge as the product line becomes static and his sales calls degenerate into a routine order taking.[1]

As in the case of the swing, the damping of energy can be averted by both internal forces (those of the salesman) and external forces (those of management).

UNDERSTANDING THE SALESPERSON'S NEEDS

Hierarchy of Needs

Although a salesperson's motivations come from within, management is in a position to offer inducements, challenges, incentives, and direction which are capable of guiding, impelling, and inciting the salesman to productive performance. The noted psychologist, A. H. Maslow, has offered a general model for understanding the behavior of salespeople. He suggests that man is a perpetually wanting unit. As certain needs are satisfied, the next most important needs in a prescribed sequence tend to dominate the individual's conscious life.[2]

As concerns salespeople, the hierarchy of needs would be as follows:

1. Physiological needs such as for food, clothing, shelter, and health, and the need for the financial resources to satisfy them.
2. Security needs, such as for job and income continuity and provisions for retirement and old age.
3. Belonging needs, such as for love, affection, and acceptance by family, friends, customers, management, and other associates.
4. Esteem needs, such as for status, prestige, self-respect, and recognition.
5. Self-actualization needs, such as the need to succeed, serve, acquire power, and lead.
6. The need to gain knowledge and understanding, such as to learn, to acquire skills and instinctiveness, to organize one's life, and to develop one's self.
7. Esthetic needs, such as the need for beauty and pleasure.

According to Maslow, when a higher-priority need is satisfied, the next most important need will prevail until it is fulfilled. Thus, a salesman who is not earning enough money to feed and clothe himself and his family (needs 1 and 2) is not likely to be concerned about his acceptance (need 3), his status (need 4), or serving his customers (need 5), and so on.

Management can position sales-force members along the need continuum and study each person's location in the hierarchy. Satisfaction can thus be customized to help each one to fulfill his unmet needs, and incentives can be personalized. This explicit positioning (preferably in writing) will tell management which people need guidance with personal problems, which would benefit from a pat on the back or a shoulder to lean on, which are in need of retraining, which can absorb more responsibilities, and which would improve their productivity under a modified compensation plan.

The Paradox of Needs

Financial and security needs are found among all types of employees. Most people are not totally satisfied with their earnings and many feel insecure and uncertain about the future. Other needs are tied more closely to certain types of people. Strangely, the described hierarchy of needs does not apply to all salespeople. For example, a salesman may be desperately in need of cash to pay hospital bills, buy furniture, and repair his car (need 1), but he may not necessarily exert himself to increase his productivity and earnings. Instead, he may spend his selling hours drinking beer, going to the movies, or chasing females or golf balls (need 3).

Many a salesman would gladly give up a comfortable commission of $50,000 a year to become a field sales manager at a salary of $30,000 a year. This is true despite the fact that the new manager may have to struggle to maintain his living standards because of the income reduction. In essence, he is willing to sacrifice income for security and prestige. However, the move into management is accompanied by a more prestigious title, more power, an office, and a secretary.

MOTIVATING SALES PERSONNEL

Urges to satisfy needs are called drives or motives. Since management is perpetually concerned with the actions that stem from a salesman's motives, sales managers are expected to help satisfy the salesman's range of needs. Salesmen can be divided into three groups: those who make things happen, those who watch things happen, and those who wonder what happened.[3] It follows that a salesman can falter or fail for only one of two reasons—either he doesn't work or he doesn't work right. The first has to do with will-do, the second with can-do.

Dynamic Inner Drive

Let's look at the salesman who won't work, who lacks will-do characteristics. Such a person is lacking in needs, impulses, emotions, inner drive, or motives that are necessary to incite him to action. He may have the ability to succeed but he cannot get started. He's like a beautiful car with a dead battery. When he's riding out on the highway, he performs quite well. But quite frequently, after he stops, his battery goes dead. The more often his battery goes dead, the longer it takes to charge it up. Eventually the battery will be beyond repair.

Dynamic inner drive refers to start-up power in addition to continuous energy, competitive spirit, anxiousness to excel, self-pressure, and goal-oriented behavior. It has been shown that those who drive too hard burn themselves out and are subject to ulcers, heart attacks, insomnia, and other unfavorable reactions.[4] The secret of the self-starter is that he has mastered the knack of getting started each day, and also of restarting after each unfavorable sales call. After he gets started, he seems to be propelled along by an inner "want to" rather than a coercive "ought to." [5]

Demotivating Forces

How does one start the car with a dead battery? There are several methods, but one is to give it a push and another is to connect the dead battery to a good one. These are precisely the methods used by management in handling the salesperson with low motivation.

A necessary prerequisite to the correct approach is management's understanding of demotivating forces as they apply to each sales-force member. Often the steady decrease in productivity of the once successful salesman is traceable to a mental attitude rather than to a diminution of his facilities and capacity for work.

The absence of the RMA (right mental attitude) is frequently related to nonbusiness factors which were not apparent during the selection process. These include domestic and romantic problems, money needs, and personal and family health problems. Some sales managers refuse to become involved in the salesman's personal problems. Others offer the troubled employee a shoulder to lean on and serve as marriage counselors, financial consultants, and medical advisors.

Many successful salesmen develop an occupational disease in which job tension is created by conflict between their role as delineated by organizational factors and their role as delineated by the selling job itself.[6]

There are a number of symptoms of occupational diseases. Experienced producers may begin to tire easily either from physical fatigue or emotional exhaustion. Senior salesmen may begin to lose interest in their work. Feelings of inadequacy, insecurity, and anxiety may appear. The effects are often self-perpetuating since tensions and loss of confidence reduce the ability to solve customers' problems, and the inability to solve problems increases tensions and insecurity. The salesman may begin to rationalize, to denigrate himself, or to withdraw psychologically or physically.[7]

> "It's not my fault. Economic conditions are bad."
> "The territory is poor."
> "The product is inferior to the competitor's."
> "I guess I'm not cut out to be a salesman."
> "It's too hot to work today."
> "I'd better stop and have a few drinks."
> "I'm going to look for a different job."

Management is often inadequate in terms of understanding salesmen's needs and personal goals and detecting dissatisfactions, their causes, and their levels of intensity. Even though they lack the self-discipline to help themselves, many sales-force members will not share their frustrations with management. They wait for their troubles to blow away in the wind. They wish and wait for the magical event to improve their lives. Meanwhile, time runs out and they are failures. In transactional analysis, this is called "waiting for Santa Claus." [8]

Role conflict and dissatisfaction may also result from management's failure to maintain an organizational climate that demands the salesman's best effort. As the unfavorable attitudes of individuals spread throughout the organization, the one-on-one motivational problems can be multiplied, resulting in a full-blown situation of low sales-force morale.

Improving the Selling Climate

Diagnosis is the fundamental step in assessing the motivational climate in which the sales force operates.[9] The search for causes of low motivation or poor morale can be preventive, if management continuously probes for cues, symptoms, or indications of problems that are barely beginning to emerge. Even though a favorable climate may exist, management should solicit the input of sales-force members with respect to plans for organizational changes. More often, diagnostic activities are actually remedial, in that a serious problem already exists and management is seeking to learn why it happened and how it can be corrected. The investigation can be on behalf of individual sales-force members or it can apply to the sales force as a whole.

Some demands on management are periodic and repetitive, such as getting the sales force back to work after the Christmas and New Year holiday season and firing up the staff to introduce a completely new product. Others are unique or one-time actions, such as dealing with a disenchanted top salesman who has been bypassed for promotion.

A healthy selling climate calls for a prevailing set of company conditions and managerial actions that stimulate achievement by sales-force members. Many have already been discussed in previous chapters, such as the compensation plan, the training program, quota setting, etc. The next chapter concentrates on field supervision and the control of sales-force members. The balance of this chapter deals with communications, sales meetings, contests, and other types of recognition that produce incentive and stimulation.

WRITTEN COMMUNICATION WITH THE SALES FORCE

When the sales organization is small and/or concentrated, the sales manager is in a position to meet with or speak to each sales-force member quite frequently, perhaps even daily. This type of salesman-management interaction allows the sales manager to observe a slowdown in the selling pendulum and a weakening of the salesman's battery. The necessary push or recharging can thus take place when it is most needed.

Although there is no acceptable substitute for two-way eyeball-to-eyeball or telephone contact, organizations employing wide spans of control must rely more heavily on such forms of written communication as regularly scheduled house organs, newsletters, or bulletins. The company house organ is motivational and morale building, informing employees about company policies and activities, maintaining group cohesiveness and generally fostering the competitive spirit and keeping salespeople excited. This is done by listing the leading offices and sales producers, circulating success stories, and describing how outstanding accomplishments came about. All employees, especially salespeople, enjoy seeing their pictures and names in print since this satisfies their need for recognition and praise.

The company house organ can also be a form of continuing education for sales-force members. Many firms publish a professionally done magazine or journal developed by a full editorial staff. For example, the Northwestern Mutual Life Insurance Company has published *Field Notes* every two months for the past seventy-five years. This is a seventy- to ninety-page magazine containing articles by managers, field sales-force members, and the editorial staff. They cover such topics as telephone techniques, dollar averaging, the value of the salesman's time, and doing business with self-employed people. The avowed objective of *Field Notes* is "to provide information, inspiration, and practical sales messages to members of the company's field force." [10]

The house organ need not be elaborate or professionally done, however. Some of the most well-received newsletters are mimeographed. Often a decentralized company will distribute a mimeographed weekly bulletin from the district or regional office and mail a professionally prepared monthly magazine from the home office.

SALES MEETINGS

Clinics, sales meetings, and conventions are important inspirational and motivational tools in all sales organizations. Although each type of meeting serves a specific purpose for each sales organization, the major broad purposes are to (1) exchange information with salespeople; (2) strengthen the employee's identity with the firm, its leaders, and fellow salespeople; (3) kindle the competitive spirit; (4) provide specialized training; (5) provide sales-force members with a change of pace.

General Purposes

Exchanging Information. There is something very impersonal about sending sales-force members a written notice about major policy changes, new product introductions, or changes in prices and compensation methods. Such information is more appropriately distributed at impromptu local clinics, regularly scheduled regional sales meetings, or annual national sales conventions. Moreover, when the sales force is large, a meeting offers the opportunity for detailed discussions, question-and-answer sessions, and clarification of issues that are confusing when handled by mail or on the telephone.

For example, at a sales meeting a product-line price rise may be packaged attractively and presented in such a way that salesmen are convinced that increased commissions and earnings will be forthcoming. Compare this procedure with a dismal notice in the company house organ about an across-the-board increase in prices.

Typically, salesmen are inspired by an audience and find much pleasure in sharing their selling techniques with their peers and their leaders. This is particularly true at the small local clinic where the salesperson of the week is called upon to tell everyone "how he did it." It is also comforting for salesmen to learn, firsthand, that other salesmen have been confronted with and overcome problems similar to their own.

Identity with Company, Leaders, and Peers. Generally, salespeople welcome the opportunity to have a rap session with the big boss and to "swap a few lies" with their counterparts from other areas. More than most other employees, salespeople form close friendships with other salespeople in the firm. The sales meeting is almost like the college reunion where friends talk about the good old days and exchange information about their present progress, their families, and so on.

Salesmen are frequently suspicious of such statements by sales managers as "Harry made 200 percent of his quota in Paducah," and they welcome the opportunity to see Harry and get it from the horse's mouth. Furthermore, bringing salespeople to a posh resort tells them (and their spouses, too, if they're invited) that the company is successful and holds them in high esteem.

Competitive Spirit. The sales meeting provides management with an excellent opportunity to recognize sales accomplishments, to announce the names of sales leaders and to award trophies, plaques, and other rewards to outstanding salesmen and sales managers.

One company holds a three-day annual sales convention for district and division sales managers and their spouses. On the final evening, a formal dinner is held where manager-of-the-year trophies are given out in an "Academy Award" style, including requests for "the envelope please." Throughout the year, the company house organ builds up to the momentous occasion when the envelope will be opened by the president's wife and the name of the manager of the year will be announced.

Another firm awards stock options to sales-force members and uses the weekly sales meeting to announce the paper dollar gains of salesmen who own a substantial number of company shares. Their sales meetings on Saturday morning start out with coffee and doughnuts and take on the atmosphere of a pregame pep rally. At one point in the meeting, all attendees stand on their chairs and the salesman of the week stands on a table to lead the following cheer which increases in intensity with each line:

> To be enthusiastic, you must act enthusiastic.
> To be enthusiastic, you must act enthusiastic.
> To be enthusiastic, you must act enthusiastic.
> OH, BOY! AM I ENTHUSIASTIC!

Specialized Training. Often the national or regional sales meeting will offer management an excellent opportunity to train all sales-force members simultaneously in how to handle a newly required sales technique or company function. For example, the company may seek to introduce an audiovisual sales presentation or to teach de-marketing skills, that is, how to handle orders that cannot be filled because of limited supplies or curtailed production.

One manufacturer of inexpensive costume jewelry held a training session at a national sales meeting to help company salesmen handle a delicate problem. As the firm's merchandise was being sold off its racks, retail clerks were filling in the racks with jewelry purchased from competitors. In turn, company salesmen were removing competitive products from its displays. Store buyers instructed the clerks to put the items back on the racks. Company salesmen argued that if competitors didn't furnish racks, they should be discontinued as suppliers. Discussions among all the salespeople at the sales meeting were fruitful in uncovering a company-wide method of handling this troublesome matter.

Some firms hold weekly clinics to analyze the activity or call reports of sales-force members. Copies of a salesman's call reports are distributed, discussed, and criticized under the watchful eye of the sales manager. The effect is helpful and stimulating since many sales-force members share common problems.

Companies will often bring in well-known speakers or specialized sales trainers to handle sessions of the sales meeting. If the meeting is held in the same city as the firm's factory, salesmen may enjoy the benefits of additional technical training.

Change of Pace. The regional or national sales meeting is often a vacation with a purpose. Getting away helps salespeople unwind. Many firms hold their sales meetings at resort sites, where salespeople (and their spouses) can enjoy golf, tennis, swimming, horseback riding, winter sports, and health-club facilities in between business meetings.

Burlington Industries reports that its salesmen are excited about the company's use of resorts for sales meetings.[11] The announcement of a resort site, accompanied by handsome brochures, will usually cause prospective attendees to look forward to the meeting. It also tells them there will be more to the meeting than business.

Planning the Sales Meeting

Obviously the subjects, themes, schedules, speakers, and programs of sales meetings must be planned to fit particular situations. All too often, the meeting plan is unidirectional and does not generate audience participation. As a result, attendance at frequently held local sales meetings is often poor and those who do attend are generally listless and passive rather than inspired, involved, and excited.

It behooves management to use creativity and originality in planning meetings that salesmen are anxious to attend and contribute to. One approach is to assign a role or duty to each sales force attendee. A few methods for doing this are:

1. Organize salesmen into teams who compete against each other in contributing solutions to difficult selling situations.
2. Organize discussions based on real or fictitious sales cases in which the leader elicits a solution from the experiences of the attendees.
3. Provide participants with a meeting outline with blanks for taking notes. Include a list of relevant and provocative questions to keep participants thinking during and after the meeting.
4. Elicit feedback from salespeople by using questionnaires. Discuss results openly and solicit recommendations that will lead to improved selling and working conditions.
5. Use props for driving home key points to be remembered.

The use of props can be very effective. One company developed a circular dart board with the caption "The Reason for Poor Selling Results." The wedge-shaped subdivisions included small spaces with answers such as Bad Territory, High Prices, Competition, Economic Conditions, and Poor Leads. A very large space in the center of the board read ME. After a few darts were thrown, a discussion was held on the subject of passing the buck for lost sales. Each salesperson was given his own dart board.

Costs of Sales Meetings

When planning a major sales meeting or convention, management must contend with two types of costs. First are the obvious out-of-pocket costs of transporting salespeople to the meeting, paying for their hotel bills and meals, and financing meeting activities. Second, it is not uncommon for the opportunity costs of lost sales (due to removal of salespeople from the field) to exceed the out-of-pocket costs. These opportunity costs are extended when sales-force members find it difficult to rebound from a few days of "living it up" during the festive social functions at meeting headquarters.

Another intangible cost of sales meetings demands the attention of sales managers. National or regional meetings offer the opportunity for informal conversations among salesmen and field sales managers of intrafirm districts and branches. Despite the advantages inherent in such fraternization, disenchanted sales-force members are not reluctant to compare notes, thus reassuring each other of faulty products, unpopular company practices, and disturbing market conditions. Moreover, the sales meeting is a breeding ground for proselytism in that good producers are frequently persuaded to request a transfer to a better sales territory within the company. These activities create clashes among the company's managers and

CONTESTS

A sales contest is a special selling event during which sales-force members (or managers) are offered incentives beyond that of normal compensation if they reach certain specified levels of productivity. The contest period is normally limited and the rewards may or may not be of a monetary nature.

Objectives

It was reported in 1969 that the most popular objectives of sales contests are finding new customers, promoting special items, increasing volume per sales call, overcoming seasonal sales slumps, and introducing new products.[12] Although these will always be worthy contest goals, the astute contest planner will coordinate contests with current market conditions or company needs of the moment. For example, during the tough economy of 1975, the consensus of sales executives was that "using sales incentives merely to increase sales volume is passé."[13] Instead, marketers used sales-contest incentives to zero in on specific sales targets, such as selling a more profitable product mix, cutting costs, adjusting quotas, reordering salesmen's priorities, and boosting morale.

Hallmark Cards continuously holds contests that encourage its own sales representatives to sell retailers a training program to develop better sales clerks. Loctite, an adhesives and specialty chemicals marketer, ran a contest aimed at shifting salesmen's efforts from developing long-term business to selling to the faster payout plant-maintenance-and-repair market. Dictaphone conducted an incentive program with the purpose of getting field sales managers to improve their cost-control measures.

Contests have been held for easing an overstocked-inventory condition, encouraging salesmen to recruit and train newcomers, developing new prospecting methods, writing neater orders, preparing call reports more carefully, and for numerous other purposes.

Value to Salesmen

Seemingly, the major purpose of contests is to stimulate sales-force members to put forth a special effort to help achieve the firm's short-run objectives. An attendant result is a marked improvement in the individual salesman's performance during the contest period. Yet, there is little research evidence that contests result in a sustained level of improvement in the average salesperson's productivity.

In fact, postcontest letdown by salesmen often results in an overall reduction in progress toward the firm's long-run goals. Yet, a properly organized contest can offer opportunities for salesmen to fulfill personal needs, such as the desire for recognition by management, peers, and family.[14] Contest winners and leaders are often glorified in house organs and at sales meetings. Many salesmen delight in showing off plaques, pins, and home furnishings won in company contests.

Contest Structure and Promotion

The success of a contest is closely tied to the level of precontest enthusiasm among sales-force members. In turn, enthusiasm is a function of the contest theme, the perceived desirability of the prizes, and the methods used by the company to introduce the contest. Throughout the contest, promotion must continue and interest must be intensified, and the names of leaders and prize winners must be publicized at sales meetings and in company house organs and special written releases.

The theme can be annual, such as a summer contest or a Christmas contest, both of which can be designed to persuade salesmen to put forth special efforts during vacation or holiday seasons. The rules may be as uncomplicated as awarding points to correspond with unit or dollar sales volume, which in turn are converted into prizes that are described in a merchandise catalog. Points or prizes can be tied to quotas or past accomplishments, and awards can be based on competition among sales-force members.

For any contest incentive to be effective, the reward must be something the contestant regards as valuable and within his capability to achieve. Otherwise, the salesperson is actually demotivated. He finds the task so hopeless that he loses what previous incentive he had. Each salesperson should feel that he has an excellent chance of winning worthwhile awards, and he must be convinced of the fairness of the rules.

Sometimes the design of the contest is to foster friendly competition between rival groups within the company, such that merchandise or cash awards are less than appropriate. For example, two nearby district offices might compete against each other in a contest based on dollar sales as a percentage of assigned quota. At the completion of the contest, a dinner could be held with the members of the winning team eating steak and the losers eating beans. There is much to be said on behalf of competition among groups rather than among individuals. Group rather than individual competition among salespeople offers the opportunity for mediocre sales producers to be part of a winning team and also develops team spirit, cohesiveness, and shared and contagious enthusiasm.

The design of a unique contest to accomplish a one-time company objective demands much creativity on the part of the contest administrator. Novelty themes can be related to the contest objective, to current events, to seasonal sports, or to other appealing common denominators. One firm held a very successful "strip the brass" contest which had the effect of fulfilling the recognition needs of salesmen. In this company, the president wore a very unusual digital watch, its marketing vice-president was recognized by his elegant leather attaché case with raised edges, and the sales vice-president had a wardrobe of designers' shirts. During a two-week contest, replicas or reproductions of these three items were awarded to winners by the three executives (in person) in accordance with a formula that related productivity to the value of the prizes.

Members of the $2 billion incentive industry practice what they preach in that sales-force members of companies such as Maritz, Sperry and Hutchinson, E. F. McDonald, Carlson, and Top Value Enterprises run contests for their account executives with both merchandise and travel awards.[15] Travel awards tend to be extremely glamorous and popular among salespeople and their spouses. However, they suffer from the same disadvantages as national sales meetings in that top salespeople are removed from the field and subjected to the threat of postcontest lethargy.

Limitations of Sales Contests

As in the case of sales meetings, the costs of contests are both measurable and intangible. The costs of cash, merchandise, and travel awards are obvious. However, for the most part, these are variable expenses in that the firm pays for these awards in proportion to the productive benefits received.

The indirect costs relate to unfavorable effects on motivation, on morale, on customers, and in achieving the desired company objectives. These major ill-effects can be summarized as follows:

1. Contests are habit forming in that they become expected forms of additional compensation. Once a periodic contest is established it is difficult to discontinue it.
2. Contests may encourage undesirable conduct by salesmen including high-pressure selling, overstocking customers, and

"sandbagging" orders which should have been processed prior to the contest.

3. Due to special selling efforts put forth during the contest period, postcontest letdowns and sales slumps often result.
4. Contests consume so much interest that various important non-selling activities, such as servicing customers, may be neglected during contest periods.
5. The design, rules, and administration of contests are always subject to criticism by some sales-force members, especially by those who perceive their rewards to be insufficient. Moreover, whenever there are losers or those who win less than others, the likelihood of morale problems increases.

Surely, a contest is not a substitute for good management and inspiring leadership by sales management. Moreover, the effectiveness of a contest is apparent only when management is in a position to compare contest-inspired results with those that would be forthcoming in the absence of such an event. Expert studies are very much needed in the area of contest evaluation.

RECOGNITION AND HONOR AWARDS

Contests and sales conventions are short-lived methods of stimulating salespeople, although each has certain positive carry-over effects. Recognition of selling accomplishments is often more permanent and less costly when methods such as the following are used: [16] titles, such as Salesman of the Month; trophies; congratulations from high-ranking officials; recognizing spouses of successful salespeople; memberships in honorary clubs or organizations; recognition in house publications; pins, rings, certificates, diplomas, etc.

The reader will recognize that a single award can include several of the foregoing forms of recognition. For example, the Salesman of the Year may be simultaneously congratulated by the firm's president, presented with a trophy or ring, and featured in the company house organ. Such awards are reasonably low in cost and enduring, in contrast to the cash, travel, and merchandise prizes acquired in a short-term contest. A trophy, a photograph with the president, or a copy of a printed testimonial is permanently stimulating as it rests on the salesman's desk or shelf or hangs on the wall of his den.

Often recognition in a given industry takes the form of membership in an exclusive society reserved for outstanding sales producers. As an illustration, in the life insurance industry, every sales-

SUMMARY AND CONCLUSIONS

Selling slumps or failures are related more to one's unwill-ingness to succeed than to one's inability to succeed. As salesmen meet with resistance in the general, operating, or internal environments of the firm, their drives toward achievement often attenuate and sometimes cease.

Some salespeople have the inner capacity to bounce back. Others will respond to the "carrot" of compensation. Still others require a push or continued reassurance and recognition by management. Diagnostic activities may be preventive or remedial, and the appropriate form of stimulation may be either a kick in the pants or a pat on the back.

A healthy selling climate demands incentives and communication that will motivate salespeople to move as quickly as possible in the direction of superior performance. These include written messages, sales meetings, contests, and other forms of recognition and reward.

NOTES

1. Several of the sales-force demotivators mentioned in this and the previous paragraphs were mentioned by Richard R. Still and Edward W. Cundiff, *Sales Management: Decisions, Policies, and Cases* (Englewood Cliffs, N.J.: Prentice-Hall, 1969), pp. 244–45.

2. A. H. Maslow, "A Theory of Human Motivation," *Psychological Review* 50 (1943):370–96.

3. Adapted from Peter F. Tague, III, and Kevin G. Barbera, "Marketing the Professional Service," *Marketing News* 9 (21 November 1975):4.

4. Viktor E. Frankl, *Man's Search for Meaning* (Boston: Beacon Press, 1963).

5. Robert A. Whitney, Thomas Hubin, and John D. Murphy, *The New Psychology of Persuasion and Motivation in Selling* (Englewood Cliffs, N.J.: Prentice-Hall, 1965), pp. 246–47.

6. Richard T. Hise, "Conflict in the Salesman's Role," *University of Washington Business Review* (Winter 1968):18–22.

7. Daniel D. Howard, "What to Do When Salesmen Run Out of Steam," *Management Review* 56 (September 1967):6–7.

8. Muriel James and Dorothy Jongeward, *Born to Win* (Reading, Mass.: Addison-Wesley, 1973), p. 134.

240

9. Robert M. Olsen, "The Liberating Motivational Climate—An Essential for Sales Effectiveness," in Thomas R. Wotruba and Robert M. Olsen, eds., *Readings in Sales Management: Concepts and Viewpoints* (New York: Holt, Rinehart, and Winston, 1971), p. 247.

10. See *Field Notes* (Milwaukee, Wis.: The Northwestern Mutual Life Insurance Company, November–December 1975), p. 2.

11. "The Fun Never Sets," *Sales Management* 115 (3 November 1975):65.

12. Albert Haring and Malcolm C. Morris, "Sales Contests as a Motivating Device," *The Southern Journal of Business* 4 (April 1969):178–83.

13. Sally Scanlon, "A New Role for Incentives," *Sales Management* 114 (7 April 1975):41–44.

14. Thomas R. Wotruba, *Sales Management: Planning, Accomplishment, and Evaluation* (New York: Holt, Rinehart, and Winston, 1971), p. 452.

15. Sally Scanlon, "Selling Smarter in Incentives," *Sales Management* 113 (23 September 1974):35–44.

16. Albert Haring and Malcolm L. Morris, *Contests: Prizes, Awards for Sales Motivation* (New York: Sales and Marketing Executives—International, 1968), p. 18.

QUESTIONS FOR DISCUSSION AND REVIEW

1. "The balkiness, the sulking, the rebelliousness we frequently encounter in our salesmen is closely akin to the same behavior we encounter in our children. Attention is being sought; the relationship with the boss is being tested; reassurance of his acceptance is unconsciously being striven for."

   Do you agree with the above statement? If so, should sales managers handle salespeople as parents handle children?

2. Does the field sales manager have the right or qualifications to intercede in highly personal matters that are interfering with a salesman's performance?

3. One of your salesmen, Henry Stone, who was a better-than-average producer last year, complains that his production has dropped off due to unstable economic conditions, an increase in competitive offerings, and a rise in procrastination on the part of prospective buyers. Your investigation uncovers the fact that Henry has been going to the movies two afternoons a week, thus explaining why he has delivered fewer sales presentations in recent months. As Henry's field sales manager, how would you approach this situation? What might have caused Henry to behave this way?

4. Should the company house organ publish absolute productivity figures in terms of unit and dollar sales of representatives and offices? Or, should only relative figures and rankings be communicated? These questions arise since some organizations are reluctant to disclose sales figures when

business is generally poor because of the fear of reducing sales-force
morale.

5. This chapter identified five major purposes of sales clinics, meetings, and conventions. For each of the following sales organizations, rank these objectives and describe the meeting mix which you feel would be most appropriate.
   a. An aggressive discount appliance retailer who employs one hundred commissioned floor salesmen in an eight-store local operation.
   b. A national pharmaceutical firm that employs eighty-five salespeople throughout the country.
   c. A manufacturer of men's pajamas whose sales force sells directly to department stores.
   d. A producer of computer equipment and software that sells to government and industry.
   e. A major life insurance company.
   f. An organization that sells vacuum cleaners directly to homes.

6. Comment on the following statement: When contests occur regularly, they become routine, expected events; they do little to elicit extra effort and increased productivity from the sales force. Thus they represent an added cost that has little incentive value.

7. Should contest scoring systems be tied to individual sales quotas?

8. If you were the marketing manager for a firm employing four thousand salespeople in fifty states, to whom would you delegate the responsibilities for the company house organ, company sales meetings, the planning, implementation, and control of contests?

Case 10.1 Monitoring Systems, Inc.

Controlling Proselytism at National Sales Meetings

Monitoring Systems, Inc. sells telephone-answering equipment to commercial accounts through thirty district offices throughout the country. All offices are company owned, and district managers are credited with 32 percent of sales out of which all promotional expenses including sales commissions are paid. Since each district manager employs only five or six salespeople, who are difficult to replace, the loss of a key salesman is a substantial blow to a district manager.

For the past ten years, the company has held a sales convention at national headquarters with all salesmen and managers invited at home-office expense. Postmeeting surveys have indicated that the meetings are very beneficial to sales-force members in terms of technical and sales training, providing employees with a sense of belonging, relaxing sales-force members, and allowing salesmen to benefit from informal rap sessions with their colleagues from other parts of the country.

However, following the 1975 and 1976 meetings, a serious problem evolved. The sales convention proved to be a formidable breeding ground for intracompany transfer requests. For example, following the 1975 meeting, Elaine Landover, a top producer in the Toledo district office, requested a transfer to the Los Angeles office. Mike Barber, the Toledo district manager, was furious since he felt Kevin Knapp, the Los Angeles district manager, had wined and dined Elaine at the sales convention and had persuaded her to transfer by offering her under-the-table compensation, an increased flow of sales leads, and an opportunity to move into management. Mike also gave home office officials evidence of romantic shenanigans between Knapp and Landover. Los Angeles was a larger territory, offered the advantages of better weather and preferred living conditions, and was quite appealing to 26-year-old Elaine Landover.

Knapp indicated that he made no overtures to Elaine and claimed that she had approached him indicating she was tired of Toledo winters and the constraints of a small territory. Elaine supported Knapp's statements. Barber claimed that he had hired Elaine three years ago when she was earning $125 a week as a department-store sales clerk and that he had worked very hard to develop her into a $22,000-a-year earner. While awaiting the home-office decision, Elaine was very lethargic and her production fell to one-third of its original level. She was quite disturbed that Mike was attempting to block her transfer. She indicated she would resign and move to a competitive organization if her transfer was denied.

Several weeks later, the vice-president of sales visited Toledo with the news that the transfer had been denied and that intrafirm transfers would require written permission from the releasing manager. True to her word, Elaine resigned in a rage, and both Knapp and Barber submitted official grievances to the home office.

Later it was discovered that Elaine was writing orders "under a flag" in Los Angeles, that is, orders were being processed under the name of a bogus salesperson named Shirley Brown. This was considered an unethical practice on the part of Kevin Knapp, and his and Elaine's employment was accordingly terminated.

When a similar transfer request was received following the 1976 national sales meeting, the company decided to discontinue the annual sales meetings. Sales-force members throughout the country were very much concerned.

QUESTIONS AND ASSIGNMENTS

1. Should the national sales meetings be discontinued?
2. What type of transfer policy should be implemented?
3. Criticize the actions of Knapp, Barber, and Landover.

11

Supervising
Sales Personnel

The previous chapter focused on the firm's methods of providing an environment that satisfies the needs of the sales force as a whole. The approach of this chapter is to emphasize the ongoing personal relationships between the sales manager and the individual sales-force members.

THE MEANING OF SUPERVISION

The overriding importance of supervision is accepted by most sales executives. Yet, there is limited agreement as to the precise meaning of supervision in a selling framework. Some view supervision as synonomous with management, that is, the act of getting things done through people. Such a viewpoint includes almost all the subject areas covered in previous chapters including planning, coordinating, directing, and inspecting activities.

In a somewhat narrower context, supervision has been looked upon as a process whereby sales managers influence salespeople in much the same way as salesmen influence prospective customers. In this sense, the purpose of the supervisory relationship is to guide the behavior of sales-force members in a direction that is compatible with the goals of the firm.[1] One weakness of this approach is that the employee is seen as a passive object being manipulated to carry out mandates of others rather than as an active seeker of goals.[2] This is analogous to a seller who fails to reconcile his own interests with those of the prospective customer.

Chapter 10 stressed the need for compatibility between the goals of the firm and those of sales-force members and described the typical macromechanisms, such as house organs, sales meetings, contests, and special awards, which assist in attaining this harmony. Such formulalike approaches have the same shortcomings as highly structured sales presentations have—they bring about a desirable response from one group of salespeople and an undesirable or less than optimal response from others.

A Personalized Technique

Therefore, this chapter treats supervision as a one-on-one technique to guide and motivate the individual salesman and to provide him or her with continued help in planning activities, utilizing time and efforts more effectively, and developing the instinctive skills to deal with unique situations. Effective supervision improves the salesman's can-do and will-do characteristics, with emphasis upon the latter.

Ideally, the salesman's initiative should come from within. Management's job is to help salespeople develop their self-motivation, realize their growth potential, increase their capacity for assuming responsibility, and achieve a readiness to direct behavior toward the goals of the organization.[3] Yet, it has been found that even in an ideal organizational climate, many salesmen when left to their own devices do only the minimum which they believe will be acceptable. Even money, the well-known silent supervisor, will not inspire all salespeople. It is the sales manager who determines what his salesmen will accomplish.

Supervision Purposes

Supervision takes place in the field and is oriented to the salesman's daily activities in front of prospects. Supervising sales-force members is aimed toward (1) improving the salesman's morale; (2) uncovering selling deficiencies; (3) providing additional training; (4) enforcing company needs; and (5) stimulating improved performance.

An examination of these aims reinforces the notion, first introduced in Chapter 9, that supervision involves directing and controlling the activities of the salesperson to be sure he does not wander too far from the plan of action that was prescribed in the training program. The larger portion of this chapter discusses the supervisory activities required to achieve these aims.

Neglect of the Supervision Program

There is little doubt that one-on-one supervision of sales personnel is a neglected function in many organizations. Five reasons are offered for this neglect: it's not needed, it's too costly, too time consuming, too difficult, and resented by salesmen.[4]

There is a tendency on the part of some sales managers to dichotomize sales-force members into two groups—those who have it and those who don't. The first group consists of the self-starters who require little supervision; the second group is made up of the helpless and hopeless weak sisters who could not make the grade even with supervision twenty-four hours a day. This sink-or-swim approach neglects the fact that the largest group of people on any sales force are neither topflight nor weak. Most salespeople are in the development phase of the salesman's career cycle (SCC) and may be required to make many sacrifices, work long and possibly odd working hours, and sustain numerous refusals and substantial chastisement.[5] They have the capacity to learn and the willingness to endure negative situations, but they have a periodic need for tender care by management.

One cannot dispute the fact that it is costly and time consuming to supervise the individual salesman. The reader is surely aware that the field sales manager wears many hats. He is frequently engaged in administrative functions and in recruiting, training, and acquiring personal sales. He often writes the house organ, conducts local sales meetings, and designs and administers contests. In terms of profitability, he often questions the wisdom of working in the field with a salesman or paying a field supervisor to perform this function.

Sales-force members are frequently so scattered geographically that it is difficult for the supervisor to spend much time with each subordinate. In addition, due to the unpredictability of human beings, every demand upon the supervisor is unique. The active field supervisor may spend time with a different salesman each day. Each salesperson may face a different problem and react in a different way. The supervisor is under pressure to uncover the deficiencies and recommend an instant solution. He has a new audience every day, somewhat like the baseball star who is expected by every new group of spectators to hit a home run.

Often, it is the salesmen who need help the most that are least receptive to supervision. They are convinced that the supervisor is there to appraise, evaluate, spy, and criticize rather than to assist. They became salesmen to enjoy freedom from close supervision and control. They may employ questionable selling techniques which they do not want management to discover. Finally, they may not be sold on the supervisor's ability to be helpful and may regard his visit as destructive and wasteful in terms of preventing the salesman from making his planned number of customer contacts.

THE SALESMAN'S MORALE

For every salesperson who is helpless and hopeless, there are many who can be developed into outstanding performers if their weaknesses are spotted and corrected in time. This is particularly true of inexperienced salesmen who have yet to accustom themselves to the rejections and disappointments that are a part of selling. In the absence of proper supervision, they may resort to flight tactics, fight tactics, or other "coping devices." [6]

Flight Tactics

Outward manifestations of emotional flight by the salesperson can be recognized in behavior such as the following:

1. He avoids prospecting for new customers.
2. He avoids contact with difficult customers.
3. He is willing to spend considerable time in waiting rooms or driving in his car in order to avoid customer contact.
4. Instead of asking for orders, he develops a sizeable group of people who want to think it over, thus creating a list of imaginary future buyers.
5. His apathy towards prospects turns to sympathy.

Under stress conditions, the salesman may become so nervous that he may remove himself from the field and resort to such coping devices as sleep, drugs, alcohol, sex, golf, movies, and so on.

Fight Tactics

In contrast to those who attempt to escape from the tensions of the sales job, there are those who display fight reactions. For example, a salesperson may behave as follows:

1. He finds fault with his company and with its products, promotional methods, prices, service, methods, etc.
2. He complains to and about sales supervisors, exaggerating and falsifying to strengthen his attack.
3. He may speak against the company when dealing with customers or prospects, criticizing products, services, prices, methods, management, and policies.

4. He may display hostility in dealing with customers or prospects.
5. He may not get along with people and this may result in disputes, violence, and dismissal.

Reasons for Low Morale

When the salesperson's work assignments provoke intolerable anxieties in him, it may be the result of the inherent disappointments of selling, described in the previous chapter by the selling pendulum. There are also more specific reasons. The salesperson may have been assigned to duties beneath his capabilities, with resultant routinization and boredom. On the other hand, he may have been placed in a job that is clearly over his head, in terms of his ability to function and to engage in the required personal relationships. For example, a salesman may be quite successful when he is supplied with qualified prospects by his employer, but he may find it difficult to create leads by his own efforts, that is, by telephone solicitation, cold canvassing, and other creative prospecting methods.

The company may fail to provide a strong, compatible supervisor. Instead, the latter may be weak, incompetent, vindictive, punitive, unreliable, and/or authoritarian. Management may fail to structure and define the salesman's duties, goals, responsibilities, and scope of authority, with the result that he is afloat in a sea of ambiguity. He does not know what his job is, how well he is doing, or where he is going.

The salesperson may be placed in a work environment where he is not accepted, either covertly or overtly, and where his past history or present inadequacies may be sources of rejection or conflict. Even when the salesperson is not subjected to open attack, he can be deprived by the in-group of support, membership, and acceptance and can become, in essence, an outcast.

In addition, salesmen fear slumps, layoffs, and discharges when the general outlook for the health of a company or an industry is not favorable.

Low morale is fostered by the absence of a shoulder to lean on, someone in the firm to answer the salesman's job-related questions and also help in solving his personal problems.

UNCOVERING AND CORRECTING
SELLING DEFICIENCIES

Although the previous section may suggest to some sales managers that many salespeople are neurotic lethargic moaners whose heads are not screwed on properly, it also indicates that emotional reactions by salesmen may often be justified.

Clearly, many grievances or concerns of the salesman are fancied, but even these call for coaching and counseling by sales managers.[7] Coaching is a teaching technique for imparting facts and methods, or ways to accomplish a task. The personality of the salesperson is not affected. Coaching involves instructional aid while the salesman is performing or immediately following performance of the task. Counseling is called for when a salesperson's personal feelings become involved and when his attitudes come into play. It is used when the salesman cannot view his own actions with the objectivity necessary for learning, when he views these actions through the lens of his own personal feelings, self-image, and prejudices.

Counseling

Consider the case of the salesman who complains of a sales slump that has persisted for two weeks. Such a salesman requires understanding and support by his sales manager. The manager should listen carefully to the salesman's account of his experiences and encourage the salesman to disclose why he feels the slump has occurred. The manager should not attempt to judge the salesman or to offer unsolicited advice. The aim of counseling is to render the salesperson independent so that he will be able to solve similar future problems by himself. Thus, the competent sales counselor will help the salesman to help himself.

Presume that in this case the sales supervisor uncovers no serious flaws in the salesman's work habits or sales techniques. He should seek to build confidence in his subordinate by showing him that the slump is the result of nothing more than the "law of averages" in action. The following is one way a supervisor could convey these thoughts:

> John, suppose I were to toss a coin in the air a thousand times and record the result of each toss on a sheet of paper. No doubt the final tally would work out to somewhere near five hundred heads and five hundred tails, right? However, if I examined the results very carefully, I would likely discover certain streaks of ten heads in a row

or eight tails in a row. These streaks are quite normal as is the streak of "no sales" that you are now encountering. In other words, there is absolutely no pattern to occurrences of heads and tails or sales and nonsales. All we know with certainty is that, in the long run, about half of the tosses will result in heads. Similarly, in your own case, about 25 percent of your sales presentations over the past three years have resulted in sales and, as you continue to improve your skills, your conversion rate will also improve over time.

The important thing to remember is that the "head" on the coin does not become upset when "tails" comes up ten times in a row. Similarly, you have little to worry about when you run into a negative streak. Think of yourself as a coin that accepts nos as well as yeses in a sequence that is impossible to predict.

Coaching

As shown in the above example, counseling may be the ideal solution for an imagined sales problem. Often, however, the concern is quite real and the salesman has truly developed certain bad habits or weaknesses that must be spotted and corrected. Chapter 9 has already discussed various methods of retraining experienced salesmen by use of refresher courses, role-playing sessions, field-observation sessions, and curbstone conferences.

Many sales managers are of the mistaken impression that coaching in the field means that the sales manager should pick up a sales kit and take the slumping salesman out on a few calls to show him how easy it is to make a sale. This may prove that the firm's product can be sold, but it will not prove that the salesman can sell it. Therefore, it must be repeated that it is insufficient to just tell or show the salesperson how to do it. He must be taught how, and this calls for the supervisor to alternate calls with the salesperson and observe him until he masters the techniques being taught. Only then will the supervision process bring about self-development.

Activity Reports

Despite the acknowledged importance and effectiveness of field supervision, it is quite costly in terms of demands upon the sales manager's time and energy. Moreover, selling deficiencies can often be uncovered in the office with equal effectiveness. In fact, there are certain continuous inside methods of supervision that may be more effective than field supervision, which is necessarily occasional.

One such technique is the proper use of activity reports, or call reports. Unfortunately, the literature has stressed the use of these reports for evaluation and for assisting management rather than as tools for uncovering the salesman's deficiencies and improving his performance.

This author prefers to call them activity reports rather than call reports since the report, properly designed, develops more data when it includes all the activities and not just the results of sales calls on prospects or customers. This need is properly emphasized when one remembers that selling is more than what happens in front of the prospect.

Consider the following sample report of the past week's activities prepared by a salesman who obtains all his prospects by use of the telephone:

Number of telephone calls	110
Number of telephone contacts with prospects	73
Number of appointments made by telephone	26
Number of sales presentations completed	4
Number of sales	1

The salesman earned only $90 in weekly commissions even though his sales conversion rate, one sale in four presentations, was approximately equivalent to the company average. The problem is that only four sales presentations were delivered despite twenty-six appointments.

There are two possible explanations for this performance: either the salesman did not bother to keep most of his appointments or the appointments were so poorly set up that the prospects were unwilling to keep them. A detailed review of each appointment would reveal which of the explanations is valid. If a poor work habit is uncovered, counseling may be called for. Otherwise, coaching in the technique of making solid appointments by telephone may be required. In either case, there is little need for the sales manager to accompany the salesman on field calls, at least until the results of the present counseling and coaching have been studied.

Providing Additional Training

The salesman's activity report and its subsequent analysis may pinpoint the need for improving the salesman's sales presentation or his closing techniques. He may require additional training in technical aspects of the product, in preparing proposals, or in analyzing customer requirements.

He may be referred to various books or technical manuals, asked to reread material published by the company, enrolled in company refresher programs, or otherwise retrained as described in Chapter 9. Some firms supply sales-force members with programmed learning materials to be studied or played at home. In all cases, a plan of action must be developed to offer direction to the salesman. An important part of this plan is the follow-up procedure, which makes sure that the additional training results in improved performance.

STRESSING COMPANY NEEDS

Supervision is much more than altruistically serving the needs of sales-force members. This and the previous chapter have focused on improving the company's selling effectiveness by developing a thorough knowledge of the salesman's needs and behavior. However, the achievement of company goals is the sought-after reward for the skillful development of happy salespeople.

In most cases, the company plan requires that the salesman be disciplined to do the company job the company way. The salesman's needs must necessarily be servile to those of the company. Accordingly, management is often willing to tolerate such negative situations as high turnover of salespeople, low sales-force morale, and numerous customer complaints if such conditions are required for the achievement of company objectives. Happy salesmen and a low turnover rate are of little comfort to a company in distress.

The pattern of supervision should be adjusted to the needs of the firm. Frequently, salesmen's priorities must be reordered to generate a prescribed product or customer mix. Management may compel salesmen to concentrate on slower-moving items in the product line or to focus on larger rather than smaller customers. Sometimes salesmen are required to submit detailed expense accounts or the company places a limit on travel and entertainment expenses.

The company might also impose certain credit restrictions or adjust its minimum down-payment requirements, advertising allowances, or billing terms. These techniques can be considered to be "automatic supervisors" in that they control the salesman's actions and exert constant pressure on him to conform to the overall sales plan set forth by management.[8]

It may also be in the company's best interest to control the content of the sales message to prevent inaccurate or unethical statements by sales-force members. As was indicated in Chapter 6, the memorized or otherwise structured sales presentation is a highly effective method of accomplishing this objective. This type of sales message also assists the sales supervisor in troubleshooting the poor producer. Many firms that depend on standardized or canned sales presentations argue that supervision boils down to seeing that the salesman does not deviate from "the standard pitch."

The demands of consumerism have persuaded many sales managers to step up the intensity of monitoring the sales calls of new or questionable salespeople. A number of firms, especially those who sell directly to consumers, have initiated a postsale system of verifying the sales transaction with the new customer (by telephone) for the purpose of uncovering misunderstandings, complaints, or buyer's remorse. The order is not processed until all customer grievances have been settled. One firm, which sought to control sales misrepresentations and irregularities, supplied salesmen under surveillance with the names of bogus prospects in whose premises tape recorders had been planted. The latter plan was costly in that those who assisted in the detective work were well compensated for their cooperation. It was, however, quite effective since several unethical salespeople were caught red-handed and either were reprimanded or terminated.

STIMULATING IMPROVED PERFORMANCE

Some readers may question the need for this section in the chapter on supervision. They may say, "If the salesman's morale is improved, if his selling deficiencies are uncovered, if the appropriate additional training has been provided, and if the company needs have been stressed, improved performance by the salesman will be an automatic result. They may further point to superb design and administration of the macromechanisms described in Chapter 10 as additional aids to assuring improved sales performance. Sadly, in many cases even the brilliant execution of all of these plans simultaneously may not result in the improved performance of a given salesperson.

Why Salesmen Fail

Perhaps the salesman shouldn't have been hired in the first place. Perhaps he was oversold in the job interview, accepted the job as a temporary stopgap, recognized early that the job did not suit him, and is floundering because he never did have his heart in it.

Perhaps the salesman was inadequately trained for his particular job assignment.

On the other hand, presume that the selection and training functions were performed properly. The salesperson may still flounder or fail for two major reasons: (1) incompatibility with management, and (2) a lack of positive and constructive leadership.[9] Personality conflicts are often difficult to resolve. Extreme sensitivity, as well as a strong sense of self-righteousness, often lead to incompatibility and friction. Early exposure and a frank discussion of differences are usually quite helpful. But what is meant by that intangible something called "leadership"? Of the thousands of definitions that have been advanced over time, the most meaningful one in a sales management context is "that ingredient of personality which causes people to follow."

Leadership

Burton Bigelow once described the sales manager's leadership as "a priceless ingredient that turns the effort of ordinary salespeople into extraordinary results." These ordinary people are characterized by similar attitudes and motives which the sales supervisor must understand and know how to deal with. According to Bigelow, mediocre people—

prefer to avoid making decisions;

are lukewarm and uncertain in their enthusiasm;

lack faith in themselves and have little native confidence in others;

are afraid of responsibility and inhospitable to any suggestion that they accept it;

are undecided as to where they are going—even as to where they want to go.

If one is mindful of the old Chinese proverb which says "knowledge, like water, takes the form of the vessel into which it's poured," one will no doubt argue that the sales leader who can transform mediocre people into productive producers is a rare genius. Alexander Hamilton rejected the notion that the expert leader is a genius when he observed:

Men give me credit for some genius. All the genius I have lies in this: When I have a subject in hand, I study it profoundly. Day and night it is before me. I explore it in all its bearings. My mind becomes pervaded with it. Then the effort which I have made is what people are pleased to call the fruit of genius. It is instead the fruit of labor and thought.

Sales leadership is the process of shaping a human being, molding him, as if he were clay, into what the leader wants him to be, until he is capable of performing as the leader wishes him to perform. Fortunately, what a sales leader *does* is considerably more tangible than what a leader *is*. Past experience and current practice indicate a number of guidelines, of varying degrees of importance, for the effective leadership of sales personnel: [10]

1. Keep salesmen excited.
2. Expect enough—not too little—not too much.
3. Establish clear-cut objectives.
4. Set up a step-by-step program to reach sales objectives.
5. Sell the program enthusiastically.
6. Plan ahead for yourself and your sales force.
7. Coach salespeople in the *how* as well as the *what*.
8. Continually inspect and promptly correct.
9. Sell the sales force on the importance of the job.
10. Challenge the fighters—bolster the timid.
11. Tell salespeople how they stand.
12. Use the power of incentives.
13. Bestow praise when earned.
14. Be the boss through thick and thin.
15. Set the pace.
16. Encourage and assist salespeople, one at a time.
17. Display wisdom, fairness, and human understanding.

The above list was succinctly summarized at Willy Loman's funeral in the play "Death of a Salesman":

> The job of the sales manager is to help the salesman to keep the smile and the shoe-shine, to avoid the earthquake, to keep the spots off his hat, to make the salesman dream the right dreams, and then help to make these dreams come true.

SUPERVISORY TECHNIQUES

"Many salesmen can outsell me but none can outtry me."

The above statement, made by a salesman of construction equipment, is a tribute both to the man who made it and to his supervisors who provided the spark that started the motivational process within him. Such an attitude is indicative of collaboration and interdependence between the salesperson and management through the development of mutual target setting. How does such mutuality come about?

Managing by Objectives

One way of promoting greater sales efficiency, raising sales-force morale, and blending the goals of the organization and the individual so that the achievement is mutual is management by objectives (MBO).[11] This process features management's use of input from the salesman in every phase of the selling job. The specific goals of the salesman and the firm are discussed openly so as to establish common targets and agree upon strategies for reaching these targets. This will be achieved only if the planning sessions are of the give-and-take variety. The salesman can benefit from management's broad experience in dealing with other salesmen. Conversely, management often has much to gain by granting the employee equal time to inject his intimate knowledge of the marketplace into the discussion.

In MBO, criteria are agreed upon for the appraisal of sales results. This opens the door for supervision because the sales manager can focus his supervisory efforts on areas where the salesman is failing to meet mutual objectives. In turn the sales-force member will expect and receive help in the form of advice, reprimands, retraining, etc., when needed. Deviations from the planned selling results provide automatic feedback which, in turn, serves as meaningful input for the planning of future goals, strategies, methods of appraisal, and rewards for both parties.

The give-and-take exchange between management and the sales-force member becomes more fruitful and acceptable to the salesman when at least a portion of the input from management is objective and based on hard data. For example, one author describes the computer-based system used by an industrial marketing firm to help the salesman use field time more effectively.[12] In this system, the salesman feeds the computer data on each of his accounts, such as number of calls made in the current three-month period, number of expected calls in the upcoming quarter, average time per call, expected annual sales, expected sales for each account, and the sales-adjustment factor based on the account's impact on profitability due to purchased products or commissions. With such data, the computer is then programmed to fit sales-response curves through expected sales volumes of different call frequencies. It then prints optimum call policies designed to maximize sales, profits, and commissions. This approach relieves the salesperson of arduous calculation chores while helping to coordinate cost control and time-management factors.

Sales-Force Segmentation

In essence, the MBO approach compels the sales manager to study each salesperson and customize the goal-setting and supervision package to satisfy each employee's unique set of needs and expectations. Instead, management may discover that the sales force can be subdivided into a few groups of employees who have common needs and goals. This alternative method of "sales-force segmentation" calls for applying different motivation, communication, administrative, goal-setting, and supervisory principles to each group in order to achieve maximum performance from each.[13]

Mossien and Fram suggest several bases for sales-force segmentation.[14] First, salesmen can be segmented *by job title* so that a person would be classified as a trainee, salesman, senior salesman, or master salesman, depending upon his level of productivity. In segmentation *by financial recognition,* some salespeople would be on salary plans, others on commission programs, and still others on mixed plans. Commission and bonus rates and salary levels would be geared to the needs and productivity of each group.

Other bases for segmentation are *by peripheral benefits* and *personal recognition.* For example, company cars would be available to certain groups and not to others and there would be separate sales contests, award incentives, national sales meetings, and retraining sessions. Segmentation *by communications differences* is based on the belief that it is inappropriate to address the top professional in the same manner as one addresses the neophyte. Accordingly, it is not far-fetched to consider the preparation of separate house organs, newsletters, and local sales clinics for each of the sales-force segments.

The underlying value of this motivating method is that it provides a system by which career salespeople can grow in status, financial remuneration, and level of communication with management. The differing needs and motivational requirements of various sales-force members are recognized without the need for the extensive customization that is demanded in the MBO process.

Sales Manager as Educator

One authority has stated that education may be one of the greatest forces for motivating sales-force members.[15] No salesman will ever live long enough to learn all he needs to know about selling through his personal experiences alone. That's why salesmen read books, watch other salesmen, and exchange ideas by participating in meetings and seminars. Knowledge drives out fear. The absence of fear creates confidence. Confidence is based on understanding, which must be assiduously cultivated if it is to bear good fruit.

Teaching salesmen is quite different from teaching students in the college classroom. The key to this difference is the subject's readiness to learn. Often the bright college student will not learn because the material is not meaningful to him and the instructor has done little to make it meaningful. Only a grade is at stake. The sales supervisor or trainer is more fortunate than the professor in that he is in the position of being able to make all of his material meaningful to his salesmen. Most salesmen are ready to learn. They are totally involved.[16]

The best way to motivate a customer to place reorders is to sell him a product that produces favorable results. Similarly, the best way to motivate a salesman to learn is to offer him instruction and guidance that is convertible into productive sales results.

Prescription for the Ailing Salesman

Every salesman must be handled differently. The "can't" salesman needs a boot. The "won't" salesman needs a needle. The wounded salesman needs a band-aid. Finally, the producing salesman needs a blue ribbon which may prevent him from becoming ill at a later date.

The diagnosis or troubleshooting process can take place in the office, in the car, on the curbstone, on the golf course, in the lunchroom, or any place that the salesman and his supervisor can meet on a one-on-one basis. A useful troubleshooting tool is the checklist or a "why I didn't get the order" form. The checklist should consist of a lengthy list of items covering every facet of the selling program, from prospecting to closing. The checklist is a sequential inventory of techniques or characteristics which are necessarily possessed by the "ideal" salesman. By periodically discussing and observing the items on the list, the supervisor is in a position to note a salesman's points of strength and weakness relative to a given selling situation or over a period of time. The salesperson may also use the checklist as a self-improvement tool by evaluating his own strong and weak points.

Too often selling errors are not permanently corrected by the sales supervisor. One sales researcher suggests the use of "dialogue analysis" as a method of reorienting experienced salesmen.[17] In this approach, transcriptions of conversations between salesmen and prospects are analyzed. The dialogues recreate real situations involving communications between people. These conversations are analyzed for proper use or misuse of techniques, ideas, concepts, and strategies in selling. Although the best method of collecting dialogues is by use of concealed tape recorders, some managers, salesmen, and prospects may find this method objectionable and even unethical. An imperfect but useful alternative is dialogue material contributed by salesmen or sales managers as a result of their recall of selling experiences. Dialogues illustrating specific points are easily remembered by salesmen and are, therefore, more beneficial than most methods in developing an understanding of the important principles of good selling.

SUMMARY AND CONCLUSIONS

Supervision involves the creation of an atmosphere of mutuality between the sales-force member and management by improving the salesman's morale, uncovering selling deficiencies, providing additional training, stressing company needs, and stimulating improvement in performance. Although an effective program of supervision will surely improve the salesman's skills and knowledge, a frequently sought result is an improvement of his mental attitude.

The sales supervisor is often expected to be a messiah who can administer instant cures to ailing salespeople. Although this is seldom possible, this chapter has suggested a number of approaches for improving sales-force productivity. The MBO process features the joint establishment of goals, strategies, and appraisal methods by employees and management. The sales force can also be subdivided into subsets or groups, which are, in turn, subjected to differing motivational modes.

Checklists are useful tools for supervisors who seek to keep a perpetual inventory of skills of each sales-force member. Finally, dialogue training is recommended as a method of permanently correcting field errors or weaknesses of salesmen. This method develops instinctiveness by allowing salesmen to analyze and criticize previously recorded conversations between salesmen and prospects.

NOTES

1. Kenneth R. Davis and Frederick E. Webster, Jr., *Sales Force Management* (New York: Ronald Press, 1968), p. 70.

2. Charles S. Goodman, *Management of the Personal Selling Function* (New York: Holt, Rinehart, and Winston, 1971), p. 363.

3. W. Cameron Caswell, "Marketing Effectiveness and Sales Supervision," *California Management* Review 7 (Fall 1964): 43.

4. William J. Stanton and Richard H. Buskirk, *Management of the Sales Force* (Homewood, Ill.: R. D. Irwin, 1974), pp. 442–43. These authors discussed several of these reasons for neglect of supervision.

5. For a description of the phases of the SCC, see Marvin A. Jolson, "The Salesman's Career Cycle," *Journal of Marketing* 38 (July 1974): 39–46.

6. Several examples of flight and fight behavior are taken from *Supervising Salesmen in a Competitive Market* (Chicago: Dartnell Corporation, 1968), pp. 69–70.

7. Ibid. The work has an excellent discussion of coaching and counseling from which this chapter draws heavily.

8. Stanton and Buskirk, *Management,* pp. 452–53.

9. Wilbert J. Miller, "Why Salesmen Change Jobs," *Sales and Marketing in Australia* (February 1974): 2–3.

10. Burton Bigelow, "Tested Ways to Improve Manpower Leadership," in *Solving Manpower Sales Problems* (New York: Sales Management, Inc., 1959), pp. 7–21.

11. Donald W. Jackson, Jr. and Ramon J. Aldag, "Managing the Sales Force by Objectives," *MSU Business Topics* (Spring 1974), pp. 53–59.

12. Robert Haas, *Industrial Marketing Management* (New York: Petrocelli/Charter, 1976), p. 190.

13. Herbert Mossien and Eugene H. Fram, "Segmentation for Sales Force Motivation," *Akron Business and Economic Review* (Winter 1973): 5–12.

14. Ibid. Much of this section is based on material provided by these authors.

15. Joseph W. Thompson, *Selling: A Behavioral Science Approach* (New York: McGraw-Hill, 1966), p. 323.

16. Ibid.

17. Thompson, *Selling,* pp. 321–38.

QUESTIONS FOR DISCUSSION AND REVIEW

1. Do you agree with the author's statement that in many instances selling deficiencies can be uncovered in the office without the need for the sales supervisor to accompany the salesman on a field selling trip?

2. Suppose it was discovered that a highly productive salesman was employing honorable but nonstandard methods of selling to achieve his results. What steps would you take before granting his wish to be promoted to a supervisory position?

3. Dialogue analysis is often compared to the case method. In what ways are they similar and dissimilar? Would the case method be effective in improving a salesman's performance?

4. A floundering salesman is asked to deliver his sales presentation in the

office in front of his sales supervisors. He complains that he cannot get in 261
the mood to perform unless he is in front of a live prospect. Defend or
support the salesman's reasoning.

5. Form two debating teams to argue in behalf of and in opposition to MBO
   and sales-force segmentation as motivation techniques.

6. Can a salesperson be successful by merely going out in pursuit of sales
   without giving much thought to the objectives of the firm?

7. How should the sales manager train the supervisors under him to develop
   leadership qualities?

8. What is the right way to reprimand a nonproductive salesperson?

Case 11.1 The Salvation of Philip Bates

Dealing with Salesmen's Personality Problems

Phil Bates was fifty-six years old and had spent sixteen years with his
firm, a Boston-based producer of a line of industrial building materials. For years he had been productive working independently as a
representative in an isolated territory where his contact with management was limited to an occasional phone call and a letter or two a
month relating to a specific order. Phil was an excellent man in his
industry. He was experienced, totally familiar with his product and
with its benefits to customers, and a devoted, hard worker.

When Phil's wife passed away, he requested and was granted a
transfer to Boston where he continued as a salesman and also began
to supervise a few junior salespeople. It was at this point that his difficulties became apparent. Phil was anxious, impatient, overcritical
in his dealings with his men, his customers, and management. He
fussed over trivialities, worried far too much, shifted the blame
when things went wrong, and claimed all the credit when things
turned out right. He was overdependent on his superiors and
needed too much praise. He irritated everyone and generated a negative atmosphere.

He was found to be markedly undertolerant, overtempered, un-
derhumble, very impulsive, overly pessimistic, greatly lacking in a
sense of humor, overanalytical, very irritable, and basically unsure.
His difficulty was all in the realm of human relations. In every other
way he had all that was needed to do his work and advance in it.

The following alternative methods of dealing with Philip Bates
were proposed by various company executives:

Proposal 1

Executive vice-president Lawrence Wiley was furious about the disturbing and dampening effect that Bates had on the entire sales force. One promising young salesman had quit because Bates "had driven him bananas." Several others had remarked that "business must be awful bad if management was willing to put up with anyone as morose and antagonistic as Phil Bates." Wiley remarked that "when Bates arrived in Boston, it was as if the company had been struck with a dreaded, incurable disease." He recommended that "the only way to cut out the cancer was to give Bates ninety days' severance pay and dismiss him."

Proposal 2

National sales manager Oliver Munro indicated that the only mistake that the company had made was to move Bates into Boston. He indicated that because of Bates's potential value based on his experience, intelligence, good qualities, and long service with the company, termination would be too drastic a course of action. He also reasoned that because of Bates's temperament, he would be incapable of making a comeback following dismissal.

His suggestion was to return Bates to his original remote territory where he could serve the company as he did before. Munro recognized that Bates would feel he was demoted, would not want to return to the scene of his past personal sorrow, and would object violently to such a decision. He proposed to handle the matter delicately and with every consideration for Bates's feelings. However, if the ensuing discussion became too heated, he was prepared to tell Bates to "take it or leave it."

Proposal 3

President Ray Moore was prepared to sit down with Phil and diplomatically convey to him a detailed documentation of the catastrophic sequence of events that had taken place since he arrived in Boston and took on supervisory duties. It was apparent to him that Bates had displayed fight tactics and had generally impeded the company in its efforts to implement and maintain a favorable climate for supervisory sales-force members. He was destroying sales-force morale, diverting company attempts to uncover selling deficiencies, setting up roadblocks to enforcing company needs, and stimulating widespread deficiencies in sales performance in Boston.

In essence, he felt that Bates should be informed of his faults and given a reasonable opportunity to correct them. He wanted to show Phil a new world, a new self, a new practical philosophy, and lead him out of the darkness. He argued that "any bully can fire a man or put him down, but it takes a real man to turn tension, anxiety, and negation into an atmosphere of warmth, creativity, and harmony."

Proposal 4

Senior vice president of marketing Melvin O'Mara, was of the opinion that "reminding a man of his faults intensifies them." He felt that Bates was worth saving and the company had an obligation to try. It was apparent to him that Phil would resist any company move to "lay it on the line."

Accordingly, he devised a unique strategy to point out Bates's faults in an indirect way. He decided to write a Harvard-type case which told the story of a hypothetical salesman whose behavior paralleled that of Bates. In disguised form, the case would demonstrate the impact of the salesman's conduct on his associates and on the interests of the firm.

O'Mara was confident that he could write the case in a clever enough way so that Bates would never suspect he was the intended target of the exercise. O'Mara proposed that this case, along with two other unrelated cases should be the subjects of a series of managers' sales meetings in which attending managers, including Bates, would discuss the facts of the cases and the alternative solutions. O'Mara was confident that the recommendations of Wiley, Munroe, and Moore would be included in the discussion. In other words, O'Mara's course of action was to devise a unique scheme that would allow Bates to look at himself through a window and see himself as others see him. The plan was designed to deliver the message to Bates while allowing him to save face.

QUESTIONS AND ASSIGNMENTS

1. Offer an explanation for Bates's behavior.
2. Rank the four proposals in order of perceived effectiveness.
3. Can you offer an alternative proposal?

12

Evaluating Selling Performance

In a general sense, the evaluation process consists of comparing actual performance with planned performance. These comparisons take place on both macro and micro levels in that management has the dual task of appraising the performance of each individual sales-force member and the sales force as a whole.

Evaluation implies a process of systematically uncovering deviations between goals and accomplishments. When weaknesses are identified, the firm will devise and implement corrective methods through supervision and other control devices. When strengths are indicated, by the discovery of deviations in a favorable direction, management will use this information as a valuable aid in anticipating and dealing with problems in future periods. This may take the form of revising performance standards and generally reappraising present policies, procedures, marketing communication methods, and potential opportunities for the firm. Thus, the evaluation process aims at "both prognosis and diagnosis and is considered to be a preventive and curative marketing device." [1]

In summarizing the sales-management process, significant steps can be identified: (1) establishing standards of performance; (2) assembling and preparing resources for performance; (3) directing sales performance; (4) measuring actual performance results; (5) comparing these results with established standards; and (6) taking appropriate action in response to measured deviations. The reader will observe that step 5 is, in essence, the evaluation step and step 6 is management's attempt to react to the observed gap between expectations and actual results.

It will also be noted that previously discussed processes of stimulating and supervising the sales force are important parts of step 6 in that they are designed to maintain and improve sales-force performance. This chapter will fill in the missing links in steps 5 and 6 and will concentrate on the methods for measuring sales-force performance and minimizing dysfunctional activities.

APPRAISING OVERALL PERFORMANCE

The company audit is the summation of the audits of each of the firm's functional areas, that is, marketing, engineering, manufacturing, etc. Similarly, the marketing audit is an after-the-fact analysis of each element in the marketing mix, that is, selling, advertising, pricing, distribution, product policy, packaging, etc., and also of the linkages among these elements. Obviously, conducting company or marketing audits is such a sizeable task that few firms schedule them regularly.

The sales audit is a bit more manageable and considerably more popular. Basically, it consists of analysis of sales volume and costs expended to achieve that volume. If advertising, product planning, and other audits in the marketing area are conducted simultaneously, the resultant coordination of findings is often quite useful in pinpointing conflicting goals and strategies and costs that should be corrected.

Sales Analysis

Since sales analysis is the process of comparing actual sales with some established sales standard, it would seem that the analyst should do nothing more than see whether the company has met its forecast. In many firms, this is exactly what happens. If the analysis takes place at an interim period in the fiscal year, deviations between forecast and actual sales will dictate either a revision of the forecast or a revision of sales policies, strategies, or tactics.

Ordinarily the analysis will be considerably more complex. For example, actual sales volume may be compared simultaneously to forecasted sales, sales potential, last year's sales at the same date, average sales or some other criterion. Sales may be defined in terms of orders received, cash receipts, or shipments. As shown in Figure 12.1, sales may be measured in dollars, units, as a percentage of the year's sales, or in relative terms. Sales volume may be broken down by product categories, customer types, territories, salesmen, order sizes, etc.

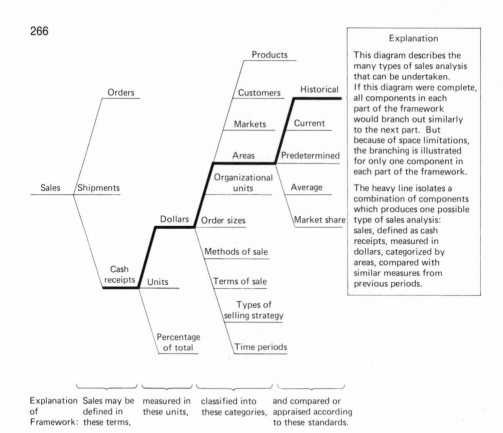

Explanation of Framework:

Explanation of Framework: Sales may be defined in these terms, measured in these units, classified into these categories, and compared or appraised according to these standards.

Figure 12.1 Framework for identifying and combining components of sales-analysis information

SOURCE: Thomas R. Wotruba, *Sales Management: Planning, Accomplishment, and Evaluation* (New York: Holt, Rinehart & Winston, 1971), p. 472. Reprinted with permission.

Obviously, the most readily available company sales figure is the combined sales of all products in all territories to all customers. However, this figure may be of limited value in that it does not disclose relevant weaknesses among products, territories, sales-force members, or customer types.

For example, let us say a hypothetical firm, the World-Wide Record Club, based in Geneva, reports actual annual sales in United States currency of $1,203,700 which is 13.3 percent beneath forecast sales volume. This information might stimulate company comparisons against sales of previous years or those of competitors. Assuming industry-wide trends are favorable, the firm's need is to pinpoint the specific sources of weakness within the company. Such inadequacies may be traced to certain products, specific territories, or other entities of the firm.

An analysis of sales by product and territory is found in Table 12.1. The United States territory is found to be right on forecast with negative deviations appearing in the reference books and children's books divisions. The Orient territory is the weakest in the firm except for outstanding performance in the reference books division. Management must ascertain whether the deficiencies in the Orient territory stem from exclusive concentration on reference books and musical records or whether consumers in the territory are not receptive to the other products. Also, since the United States operation is the only division that performs well in marketing children's records, it may be that the product design is not appealing to European and Oriental consumers.

Conceivably, there is a need to transfer some of the selling methods of the United States to other territories. Despite the detailed information conveyed by the data of Table 12.1, the reason for the relative performances will not be readily apparent without further in-depth investigations of local operations. However, the described data provide a fruitful base for more penetrating investigations by company personnel during visits to the territories.

Cost Analysis

It was indicated in Chapter 4 that sales production and cost-control mechanisms operate in unison to achieve the firm's hierarchy of selling goals. There is little purpose in achieving sales goals in the absence of profitability. Therefore, a meaningful sales audit may have the ultimate purpose of detecting deviations between forecast and actual profit figures within the same segments studied by the sales analyst. For example, Table 12.1 could be reproduced using profit dollars rather than sales dollars.

Historically, sales managers are not cost oriented. This is not to say that they do not recognize the need for profitable sales volume. However, they often make the mistake of treating volume development and cost control as two totally disassociated, separate entities. Some sales leaders are so motivated to generate sales that they give little thought to the costs of obtaining those sales. Others are myopic with regard to cost/volume relationships.

For example, consider the sales manager who regards the straight-commission plan as least costly to the firm, since the firm incurs no compensation costs unless sales are produced. This viewpoint disregards the direct costs of excessive recruiting, hiring, training, and the intangible costs of lost sales. Sales managers, in pursuit

Table 12.1 Analysis of territorial sales volume by product World-wide Record Club

	Area											
	Europe			Orient			United States			Total		
Product	F	A	D %	F	A	D %	F	A	D %	F	A	D %
Musical records and tapes	261.2	194.8	25.4	79.3	71.8	9.5	183.8	194.1	+ 5.6	524.3	460.7	12.1
Children's records and tapes	112.4	90.0	19.9	60.0	12.7	78.9	112.1	110.6	1.3	284.5	213.3	25.0
Educational records and tapes	61.2	60.0	2.0	16.3	8.4	48.5	66.3	80.1	+20.8	143.8	148.5	+ 3.3
Reference books	56.8	50.4	11.3	12.9	22.3	+72.9	80.0	70.0	12.5	149.7	142.7	4.7
Children's books	112.9	100.8	9.4	62.4	41.3	33.9	110.1	96.4	12.4	285.4	238.5	16.4
All products	604.5	496.0	17.9	230.9	156.5	32.2	552.3	551.2	0.0	1387.7	1203.7	13.3

NOTE: F designates forecasted annual sales volume in thousands of United States dollars.
A designates actual annual sales volume in thousands of United States dollars.
D designates deviations from forecast; all deviations are negative unless otherwise indicated.

of sales, are often reluctant to delete unprofitable products, drop unprofitable customers, or eliminate unprofitable territories.

Whereas sales managers may be receptive to reports or computer printouts from the financial department that deal with cost elements of the sales audit, cost analysis is rarely initiated by sales management.[2] They presume, often correctly, that the preparation of cost and profit analyses is a broader marketing function and, in fact, an area of concern to all functional areas of the firm. As such, the sales manager is willing to delegate the duty to financial and accounting people. The sales manager is typically concerned solely with costs over which he has control such as recruiting, selection, training, supervision, and compensation expenses.

Product sales managers in multiproduct companies are sensitive to company methods of allocating various distribution costs to specific product areas. Many of these costs are common rather than separable as in the case of rents, office equipment, advertising, computer services, administrative salaries, and physical distribution resources. Moreover, within the sales department, the sales manager finds it difficult to divide common fixed costs among products, territories, customer types, and sales-force members. Thus, in contrast to sales analysis, cost analysis is complex, time consuming, and often disturbing.

Speed of the Sales Audit

The value of the sales audit lies in the immediate availability of data to those who are in a position to respond to discovered weaknesses. In this age of the high-speed computer, many firms are in the position of being able to distribute instantaneous cost and sales information to decentralized decision makers.

In the retailing area, computerized cash-register systems are capable of feeding information on sales, costs, inventory control, stockturn, and margins directly to department managers on a daily basis. Yet, the majority of America's department stores restrict their analyses to broad merchandise lines and depend on vendors to supply sales, cost, and inventory information about individual products.

APPRAISING INDIVIDUAL PERFORMANCE

Management gathers information on the individual salesperson's performance for three major reasons—to reward him, to punish him, or to improve him.

Obviously the good performer should be properly recognized in the form of increased compensation, promotion, or awards. Similarly, the poor producer should be denied these forms of recognition and, when necessary, he should be dismissed. However, the ideal purpose of the performance evaluation is to uncover the areas where corrective measures will serve to improve the sales-force member's future results.

Evaluation Bases

The frustration of attempting to evaluate a group of sales-force members on the basis of field results was demonstrated in an article by Richard I. Levin.[3] Five hypothetical company salesmen were ranked by using, alternatively, gross sales, margin dollars, margin percent, controllable profits, net profits, new accounts, and percentage of sales protential. Each salesman was rated first and last at least once, indicating that a salesperson can look good or bad depending on the base used by management to evaluate him.

Quantitative evaluation standards can be based on the salesman's results or his efforts. Several result-oriented factors were given in the previous paragraph. There are others, including sales volume as a percentage of quota; conversion rate (orders/sales presentations); and number of orders cancelled, returns, misrepresentations, or claimed irregularities. Evaluation based on effort (input) rather than results (output) is justified on the grounds that favorable output is a function of favorable input. Among the input factors used in appraising sales personnel are number of sales contacts, number of sales presentations, amounts of time spent with existing customers, and contributions at sales meetings and clinics.

A salesman may be appraised qualitatively in terms of his attitudes toward and concern for company relations, such as:

1. Awareness of job requirements.
2. Attitudes toward the learning process.
3. Perceptions of customer-company-salesman relationships.
4. Understanding of personal relationships.
5. Coordination with other functional areas.
6. Activities as pacesetter, coach, field trainer.
7. Willingness and ability to acquire new capacities.
8. Willingness and ability to recognize problems and provide needed feedback such as information on competitive activities.[4]
9. Product-line concentration.

A salesman's relations with customers may also be judged on the basis of such skills as problem solving, general availability, and proficiency in providing service and assistance. An all-encompassing evaluation criterion is the representative's knowledge about his job as it relates to results. This includes such areas as his understanding of product features and applications, markets, customers, and competitive strategies; his prospecting talents; his ability to overcome objections; and his skills in delivering the sales presentation.

Numerous sale supervisors use a list of difficult-to-measure personal characteristics to intuitively discriminate successful from unsuccessful salespeople:

appearance	patience	empathy
verbal ability	dependability	ego drive
initiative	stability	enthusiasm
imagination	aggressiveness	willingness to listen
ambition	flexibility	judgment

The reader should be cautioned against thinking that all successful salespeople possess all or most of the above qualities. In many selling situations, several of these characteristics are unnecessary and even detrimental.[5]

The appropriate combination of appraisal criteria depends on the specific selling framework and on the broad corporate, marketing, and selling objectives. In establishing goals for individual salesmen, management must take care to avoid the condition of suboptimization referred to in Chapter 1. For example, it is not uncommon for the result-oriented high producer to be indifferent to company and customer needs, including ethical considerations and posttransactional requirements of regular customers.

Information Sources

Supervision and evaluation are interdependent and continuous processes. The field sales manager cannot work closely with a subordinate without being aware of his strengths and weaknesses. Salesmen discuss each other with members of management. Customers and prospective customers praise and complain about sales personnel. A certain amount of informal, subjective appraisal of selling activity is both inevitable and desirable. However, a major step toward the improvement of the evaluation method occurs when judging becomes systematic. A systemic procedure is one in which a framework is supplied to ensure that the evaluation is complete, free of personal bias, consistent over time, and comparable in scope for all those being assessed.[6]

The final rating of a salesman's performance should be a composite of information received from many sources, with each source appropriately weighted. The obvious source of quantitative information is the record kept by the firm, that is, the "bottom line." How did salesman Kelly do in terms of number of orders, sales volume, gross margin, and selling costs? Such information about "how much" is supplemented by information about "why" provided by other sources. The field sales manager is in a position to discuss the quality of Kelly's sales presentation, his work habits, his rapport with prospects, his devotion to his work, his mental attitude, etc.

Activity reports turned in by the salesman provide valuable information about effort such as prospecting methods, number and frequency of calls, number of presentations, time spent in entertaining clients, etc. These reports are especially useful when combined with informal comments and solicited remarks from prospects or customers. In this age of consumerism, input from buyers is easily obtained during order-verification phone calls or through frequently used mail questionnaires which seek information for improving the offerings and services of sellers.

The Salesman's Career Cycle [7]

It has recently been suggested that evaluation standards and supervisory measures should be related to the position of the salesforce member in his career cycle. Analogous to the product life cycle, the career cycle has been suggested as a continuum that ranges from the recruitment of a new salesman to his termination. Unlike with a product, however, a salesman's termination can be voluntary as well as being an action of management; a salesman can become tired, bored, disgruntled, disabled, or deceased at the peak of his productivity.

The salesman's career cycle (SCC) moves through the stages of preparation, development, maturity, and decline (Figure 12.2), and he can repeat any stage or the entire cycle any number of times. The time interval of each phase is determined by a complex interaction of variables based on personal, management, buyer, and environmental factors.

Training is the essential ingredient in the preparation phase. The experienced salesman who has just shifted to a new product or a new company will, in most cases, require less preparation in terms of indoctrination and initial training than the novice who is in his first selling job. If the trainee is new to the company, it is management's

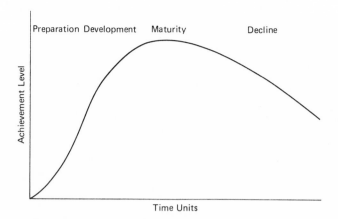

Figure 12.2 The salesman's career cycle

SOURCE: Marvin A. Jolson, "The Salesman's Career Cycle," *Journal of Marketing* 38 (July 1974), p. 39. Reprinted with permission.

responsibility at this early stage to integrate the company's requirements with the salesman's own needs and abilities as an autonomous agent.

The salesman who has survived the preparation phase must now convert his training into productive results. The salesman's productivity rises slowly in the development phase. Predominant management responsibilities consist of identifying and correcting evolving field problems and undesirable behavior patterns. Depending upon the size and dispersion of the sales force and the sales manager's span of control, sales-performance data will be obtained by written, telephone, or face-to-face communication with the salesman, or discussions with prospects and customers. When sales problems cannot be identified and corrected in the office, the sales manager must accompany the salesman in actual field selling situations, where on-the-spot coaching and curbstone conferences may take place. Supervision, field control, and retraining of the salesman must be carefully planned, staffed, activated, and controlled in order to close gaps between desired results and present performance.

The first sign that a salesman has reached the maturity stage is a leveling off of his productivity. Some salespeople seem to reach a "rated capacity" beyond which they are unable or unwilling to go. These salesmen may be content with their present sales volume and income, such that unusual efforts and sacrifices may not be perceived as worthwhile.

The dynamics of society call for a new level of management of established sales-force members. Retraining should be aimed at widening the perspectives of proven producers. Less paperwork may be required, and these salesmen may be given greater freedom in allocating their time and negotiating prices and other relationships with customers. In addition to the normal financial rewards and trophies, recognition, praise, and intense management involvement should be used to stimulate effort and productivity.

Mature salesmen can be used as pacesetters, teachers, and field trainers. Even the most successful sales representative has a tendency not to want to be a salesman all his life. Thus, top producers are logical targets for proselytism by rival firms who offer new challenges, more security, and prestige in the form of new and more exciting product and market opportunities, more or different compensation, and offers to enter management.

As salesmen enter the decline stage, management may take frenzied steps to inject belated doses of retraining and motivation. Yet there are few instances where management is able to help a rapidly declining salesman overcome the negative attitudes that limit his effectiveness. Resistance by prospects, low occupational status, inadequate intrafirm communication, neglected training, and poor earnings are difficult to reverse and usually result in a severely demotivated employee and, in some cases, impairment of health, alcoholism, and eventual termination. Recruitment of an energetic replacement retriggers the cycle.

Once a systematic evaluation scheme has been devised, each sales-force member may be placed in his appropriate SCC compartment. A salesman may be evaluated and assigned to phases in three ways: in comparison with established standards, in comparison with his own prior performance, and in comparison with other salesmen.

The Evaluation Sequence

The discussion that follows outlines the steps for implementing the SCC model while summarizing one suggested series of evaluation steps. Of significant importance is the method of combining the information from various evaluation sources.

The first step is to itemize and carefully define the criteria to be used in evaluating sales-force members. A given company may use all or some of these items or may substitute those which fit unique company objectives.

As shown in Figure 12.3, appropriate evaluation instruments are sent to selected raters after they have become thoroughly familiar with the relevant criteria and their intended use. If customers are used as a source of appraisal information, the questionnaire or rating form must be designed with unusual care in order to elicit the de-

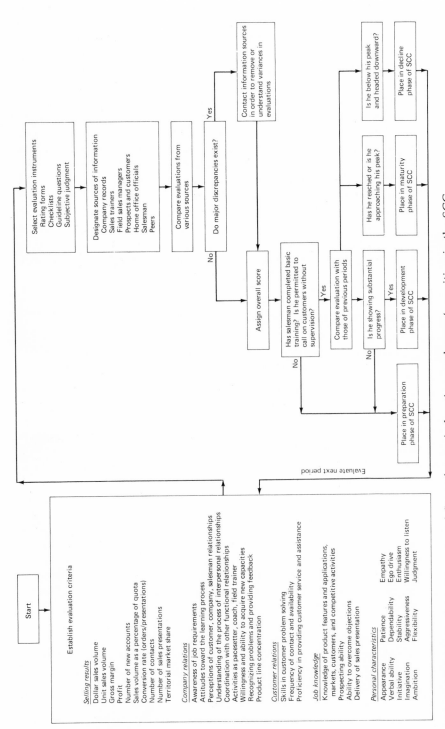

Figure 12.3 Evaluation sequence and flow of steps in locating a salesman's position in the SCC

SOURCE: Marvin A. Jolson, "The Salesman's Career Cycle," *Journal of Marketing* 38 (July 1974), p. 43. Reprinted with permission.

sired qualitative (how well) data in a constructive way. Company records supply quantitative (how much) information, while supervisory personnel, peers, and the salesman himself can provide both quantitative and qualitative data.

Once the evaluation data have been returned to the controlling office, information derived from the various sources should be compared to uncover rating biases and inconsistencies in the salesperson's behavior, skill, and production pattern. The controlling office will then convert the stream of appraisal information into a composite or overall score that reflects the weighting of the subjective and objective criteria employed. There are many methods for converting a number of selected performance measures into an overall rating or index. One is to compare the measure on every evaluation item for each salesperson with an "ideal" measure for that item, so that an "index of deviation from perfection" may be computed.[8]

The final step is to compare the current evaluation with those of previous periods. The direction and intensity of a given salesman's rating will govern his proper placement in the SCC.

USING EVALUATIVE INFORMATION

Developmental Rates

It was indicated earlier in this chapter that a salesman may be evaluated in comparison with established standards, in comparison with his own prior performance, and in comparison with other salesmen. In each case, the sales supervisor should recognize individual differences among sales-force members. Some of the best salesmen are slow learners. The fastest learners sometimes lack the instinctiveness to react to unique selling situations. If the evaluation process is to serve as a means for motivation and direction of selling efforts, the supervisor will be required to compare his findings over time and to use these findings constructively and in keeping with the selling goals of the firm and the potential of each individual sales-force member. The astute sales manager will use each salesperson's skills where they will both do the most good and prevent individual weaknesses from causing destructive effects. Where possible, this will call for the matching of products, territories, and customer types with salespeople who are capable of handling the respective assignments.

Transmitting Evaluation Information

There is nothing more motivational to a successful salesperson than earned praise from his boss. Recognition sets into motion new urges and often new and better accomplishments.

Conversely, even the poor or marginal salesperson should be promptly informed of his progress, standing, and need for improvement. Sales managers are often hesitant to dismiss an ineffective producer. A cautious approach while gathering information is commendable, but once it is determined that a salesman is unlikely to improve, termination should be prompt and efforts should be redirected to a more likely candidate. There are numerous examples of sales managers who are reluctant to fire a man because he was a highly touted recruit or because the firm has already invested a sizeable sum of money in training and compensating him. The necessity for eliminating salespeople with little chance of success was emphasized by the sales manager who, when congratulated upon his excellent sales staff, replied: "I had to hire and fire thirty-seven people over the past three years in order to build my present team of twelve fine salespeople."

It was indicated in Chapter 2 that a salesman's weakness in performing a single basic sales task can overwhelm his strengths in performing all other selling tasks. Thus, the salesman's value to the firm is signified by the totality of his effectiveness in performing his entire job rather than by a weighting or mathematical averaging of the various individual tasks. Accordingly, the skillful evaluator is not unlike the researcher who, in keeping with selling objectives, objectively analyzes and synthesizes each unit of information from each data source.

A Plan for Improvement

The intended purpose of appraising overall and individual sales performances is to provide management with valid guidelines for responding to observed deviations from established standards. Variations may be attributed to individual weaknesses of salespeople or to major weaknesses in the company selling plan.

It is sometimes quite difficult for management to admit that the company, rather than the sales-force member, is at fault. Numerous examples have been cited where selling goals were arbitrarily set at the outset of a new sales venture, and when these goals were not achieved, management failed to recognize the source of the weakness.

For example, Case 7.2 describes a firm that markets current

movies to apartment dwellers. This firm had operated successfully in the real estate industry in a major eastern city and had many contacts with apartment-building owners. The firm had no difficulty in securing the permission of building owners to install their equipment and consequently invested substantial sums of money in the new enterprise. A sales manager was hired and told that the selling goal was to enroll 30 percent of the tenants in each building. When the sales force fell substantially short of the estimated target, a marketing consultant was hired. When the consultant questioned the procedure for establishing the 30 percent figure, management indicated that they thought such a goal was obtainable in the paid-TV industry.

Another case of misdirected company standards has to do with a European mail-order house that decided to sell a thirteen-volume library of books on medical advice directly to consumers on a door-to-door basis, for over $500 a set. The firm hired an experienced encyclopedia sales executive who, in turn, recruited a number of former encyclopedia salesmen as the nucleus for the sales organization. Established overall standards and individual quotas were compatible with those that existed in the encyclopedia industry.

After three years of financial losses and substantial sales-force turnover, the firm became aware of the fact that mass selling of books on medical advice was significantly different from marketing encyclopedias. When widespread changes were made in the prospecting system, the sales-compensation methods, the recruiting procedure, and the sales presentation itself, the sales and profit trends were reversed.

When individual salesmen are being evaluated, the first step is to meet with the salesperson to discuss management's appraisal. Before the meeting, the sales manager should study each of the ratings and discuss them with the salesperson's immediate supervisor so as to build a listing of specific incidents that support the ratings.

The salesman must be willing to correct his weaknesses. He will do this only if he accepts the appraisal as being fair and constructive and intended for his development. The appraisal interview should be an informal, two-way exchange which focuses on the causes rather than the results of performance.

The salesman should be permitted to react to each segment of the appraisal, to suggest modifications of ratings, to explain any unique circumstances, and to recommend methods whereby he and management together can strive to improve his performance. In many ways, the appraisal interview is the beginning of an MBO plan in that the employee and management work together in developing a set of goals, including standards of performance for the next selling period. A final step is to establish the means for reaching these goals through self-development activities, formal retraining, or field-related supervisory actions by the salesman's immediate supervisor.

SUMMARY AND CONCLUSIONS

Evaluation, supervision, and stimulation are closely related functions of sales management. Evaluation is the process of systematically uncovering deviations between goals and accomplishments. Supervision serves a dual role in that it prevents and uncovers sales-force weaknesses and also helps stimulate improved performance after problem sources have been determined. Finally, stimulation consists of using incentives and interpersonal communications to motivate sales personnel to move as quickly as possible in the direction of superior performance.

In monitoring and appraising the overall performance of the sales force, sales and cost analyses are conducted to compare actual results with the firm's sales forecast and budget. If the analysis of results is to provide management with meaningful information for corrective action, the final data must be divided into categories for analysis such as by product, territory, sales manager, customer type, etc.

In appraising individual sales-force members, evaluation standards may be both quantitative and qualitative and also may be related to the salesman's results, efforts, personal characteristics, or attitudes. Evaluative information is available from company records, field sales managers, prospects and customers, the salesman, and his peers. Although informal appraisal information is acceptable and valuable, optimal judgments are dependent on systematic procedures that are free of bias, consistent over time, and comparable in scope for all salespeople being appraised.

Salesmen may be evaluated in comparison with established standards, in comparison with prior performance, and in comparison with peers. Although the evaluation process assists management in both granting and denying rewards, its most beneficial purpose is to uncover weaknesses and areas where corrective actions will result in improved performance.

NOTES

1. Abraham Schuchman, "The Marketing Audit: Its Nature, Purposes, and Problems," in *Analyzing and Improving Marketing Performance: Marketing Audits in Theory and Practice,* Management Report, no. 32 (New York: American Management Association, 1959), p. 14.

2. William P. Hall, "Improving Sales Force Productivity," *Business Horizons* 18 (August 1975):41–42.

3. Richard I. Levin, "Who's On First," *Sales Management* 93 (17 July 1964):53–56.

4. For example, see Dan H. Robertson, "Sales Force Feedback on Competitive Activities," *Journal of Marketing* 38 (April 1974):69–72.

5. Patrick J. Robinson and Bent Stidsen, *Personal Selling in a Modern Perspective* (Boston: Allyn and Bacon, 1967), p. 250.

6. Thomas R. Wotruba, *Sales Management: Planning Accomplishment and Evaluation* (New York: Holt, Rinehart, and Winston, 1971), p. 525.

7. This and the following section draw heavily from Marvin A. Jolson, "The Salesman's Career Cycle," *Journal of Marketing* 38 (July 1974):39–46.

8. Allan Easton, "A Forward Step in Performance Evaluation," *Journal of Marketing* 30 (July 1966):26–32.

QUESTIONS FOR DISCUSSION AND REVIEW

1. How can the SCC model be used to analyze and evaluate the sales force as a whole?

2. The World-Wide Record Club (see data in Table 12.1) is about to commence operations in Canada. The vice-president of international sales is uncertain as to which products should be made available in the new operation. How would the information in Table 12.1 facilitate his decision?

3. Following a sales/cost analysis by customer types, the management of the Dumbarton Corporation decides to eliminate all customers whose annual purchases are less than $5,000. All sales-force members are notified accordingly. One of the better salesmen, Tim Browning, develops a $6,000 overdraft in his drawing account within four months following the policy change. He complains he has been the lone profit generator with small accounts, and he is unable and unwilling to tolerate the red tape necessary in dealing with larger customers. How should management handle this dilemma?

4. H. P. Fruman is one of the Acme Company's best producers and highest earners. He is well respected by his peers and supervisors. However, when appraisal input is solicited from customers, the following summary statement is received:

> His attitude is wrong. He's cocky and smart, too patronizing, lazy, and takes customers for granted. He argues all the time, is a flatterer, a show-off, and persistent to the point of bad taste.

When confronted with this finding, Fruman is amazed. He claims that no one is more devoted to customers than he is and indicates that his unique style is what makes him successful. What further steps should management take?

5. Brown delivers an average of sixty sales presentations per month and averages twelve sales. Black averages nine sales per month and delivers twenty sales presentations. Which salesman is more valuable to the company? Would your response depend on the nature of the product, customer type, and selling environment?

6. The flow chart of Figure 12.3 suggests that following the establishment of various evaluation criteria and the receipt of information from several sources, an overall score should be assigned to the salesperson being evaluated. How does one calculate an overall score? In particular, how does one quantify qualitative items such as company relations, customer relations, job knowledge, and personal characteristics?

7. Discuss the relative advantages of evaluating a salesman
   a. in comparison with established standards,
   b. in comparison with prior performance,
   c. in comparison with the performance of peers.

8. Design a plan for the evaluation of field sales managers.

Case 12.1 Commonwealth Northern Life Insurance Company

Using A Salesman's Evaluation Matrix

The sales manager of a life-insurance company's branch office wishes to appraise the performance of each member of his fifteen-person sales force. The following salesman's evaluation matrix is filled out by field supervisors for each salesperson with the various sales tasks to be performed (see Chapter 1), weighted in accordance with the perceived division of the selling process in the insurance industry.

The major jobs of the life-insurance salesman are to locate new prospects and to hold on to them after the initial sale. The potential insurance purchaser seldom seeks out the seller. The insurance salesman is always seeking prospects. He is constantly calling on prospects. He must gain acceptance, win the confidence of the prospect, and convert the average prospect's latent desire for insurance into a "now need." Since there are few differences among life-insurance policies, the prime selling objective is to develop a company preference which, in essence, is a preference for a particular salesman and the services he can provide.

Once an insurance salesman establishes himself with a client, a steady schedule of seller-buyer contacts is required to assure that the client will not succumb to a competitive presentation. The market for life insurance is unsatiated such that substantial increases in sales volume are always possible. As more prospects are contacted and more sales presentations are delivered, sales volume rises.

In the following table, the salesman's proficiency in the performance of each sales task is rated by his supervisor who places an X in the appropriate column. Note that Kramer receives high ratings for the prospecting, contacting, and retaining functions and mediocre ratings for the stimulating and closing functions. The performance-rating value in each row is multiplied by each task weight and the products are listed in the last column. The final index of proficiency of .734 for Kramer is obtained by adding the values in the last column.

Before receiving the foregoing formal ratings of Kramer and Lawrence, the sales manager had written the following informal statements describing the two men:

> Kramer is a bear for work, always seeking new prospects, and constantly in touch with his clients. He is new

Salesman's evaluation matrix

Sales task	Relative weight	Performance-rating values (PRV)											Index (weight × PRV)
		1.0	.9	.8	.7	.6	.5	.4	.3	.2	.1	0	
Kramer													
Prospecting	.31			· X									.248
Contacting	.20		X										.180
Stimulating	.06							X					.024
Closing	.12							X					.048
Retaining	.24			X									.192
Other	.07					X							.042
												Total	.734
Lawrence													
Prospecting	.31					X							.155
Contacting	.20							X					.080
Stimulating	.06	X											.060
Closing	.12	X											.120
Retaining	.24						X						.120
Other	.07							X					.028
												Total	.563

in the industry, has limited product knowledge, has many flaws in his sales presentation, and is not a convincing closer.

Lawrence is totally familiar with all facets of insurance, is extremely articulate and most persuasive and convincing. He converts a high percentage of his presentations into sales. However, he delivers relatively few presentations because he is lazy, has too many outside interests, makes few appointments with new prospects, and often breaks those appointments that he makes. Furthermore, he does not keep in steady contact with people to whom he has sold. Therefore, a number of his policyholders have purchased new policies from competitive companies.

QUESTIONS AND ASSIGNMENTS

1. Did the evaluation matrix add to the information the sales manager already had?
2. Choose two associates or classmates to play the roles of Kramer and Lawrence and conduct an appraisal interview with each.
3. How should the proficiency-index numbers be interpreted?
4. What are the strengths and limitations of the salesman's evaluation matrix as a universal tool for appraising all types of salesmen?
5. Place Kramer and Lawrence on the SCC continuum.

13

Overview of Sales Management: Today and Tomorrow

The author has taken the time to reread the preface to make sure that the intended objectives of this text have been attained. Obviously, such a judgment must come from the reader rather than from the author. However, one of the author's primary express hopes was that the content of this book would stick to the reader's ribs and that the book would serve as a ready reference long after the reader had advanced beyond his present role in life. An underlying assumption was that the reader's thorough understanding of the conceptual framework for selling activities, for current problem areas in sales management, and for today's alternative approaches to these problems would help him comprehend and deal logically with the emerging needs of sales management in an unpredictable tomorrow.

This final chapter integrates the previously discussed elements of the selling framework, broadens the base for recognizing the differentiating features of sales management as compared to other forms of management, and offers some insights about probable future sales management activities, problems, and their solutions.

SUMMARY OF SALES-ADMINISTRATION FUNCTIONS

Although the first line of the income statement reads "sales," personal selling (as discussed in Chapter 1) is one of the last steps in the lengthy sequence of business activities designed to earn profits by providing goods and services to satisfy the unfilled wants of the marketplace. This sequence is summarized by the configuration of delicately balanced geometric figures shown in Figure 13.1.

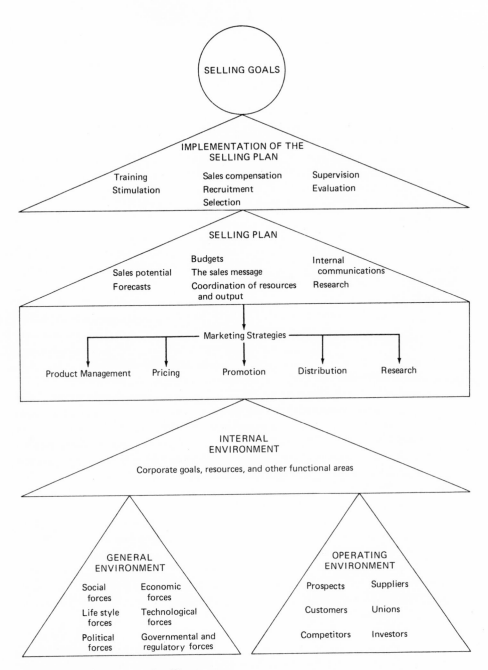

Figure 13.1 The personal selling system

286   The foundation of the structure is made up of the general and operating environments which provide cues that inform the firm about the available market opportunities and the external constraints to their realization. Clearly, a change in the composition of the bottom triangles (public policies, consumer attitudes, availability of supplies, competitive actions, etc.) will call for a rebalancing of the internal environment, for example, for a rethinking of corporate goals and/or a reshaping of company resources.

Once the three environmental layers are in balance, specific marketing goals can be established, and a strategic marketing plan can be designed to achieve these goals. Part of the marketing package is the promotional plan, of which personal selling is a formidable part.

Chapters 4, 5, and 6 describe the major component parts of the selling plan. The sales forecast is the planning document that predicts the firm's sales level for a future period, while the budget is the forecast of expenditures that will be required to buy the projected revenues.

The firm's total market is divided into groupings or territories, each of which consists of potential or actual customers who share certain characteristics which are relevant to buying behavior. Territorial and sales-force-size decisions are largely based on company efforts to simultaneously satisfy customers' service needs, sales-force income demands, and company profit requirements. However, in numerous firms, particularly under unsatiated market conditions, sales volume is predominant, rather than profits, in dictating sales-force size. In these situations, the objective is to develop as large a sales force as possible with no upper limit. Following the determination of territorial sales potential and the formulation of forecasts, budgets, territorial boundaries, and optimal sales-force size, quotas (motivational targets) are assigned to field units to assist management in creating incentives, controlling selling efforts, and evaluating the performance of salesmen and their field sales managers.

Although the design of the sales presentation (discussed in Chapter 6) may be viewed as part of the planning process, successful management of field sales-force members may depend on how well the sales message answers the sometimes diverse needs of prospects, sales-force members, and the firm. There is considerable disagreement among sales managers as to whether the company should make a major contribution to decisions about the content and/or mode of the selling message or whether the decisions should be made by the salesperson based on his intuition and perception of the best approach in a specific selling situation.

Even though current practices do not favor high levels of company input, there is substantial evidence that memorized talks, flip charts, visual aids, and audiovisuals are effective in preventing omissions, misstatements, and unethical selling methods and also facilitating the training and supervision of sales-force members. Yet, if one considers the sales call to be a problem-solving process, the customer-specific or relatively unstructured message offers the salesperson the flexibility to adjust his message to the mood, thinking, questioning, and specific needs of each prospective buyer.

SUMMARY OF FIELD SALES MANAGEMENT FUNCTIONS

Although Figure 13.1 is geometrically questionable, it does illustrate the interrelationships of the selling plan, as developed by sales administration, the implementation of that plan as carried out by sales-force management, and the ultimate achievement of the firm's selling goals. A toppling (due to poor conception) of the sales plan will obviously nullify impact of sales force management efforts in reaching selling goals. A solid plan improperly implemented will yield similar results.

Sales-force management or the implementation of the selling plan is the responsibility of field sales management. Field sales managers are those line officials who operate between the sales force and the home office. They are concerned with inducing qualified personnel to apply for employment and with selecting applicants who have the highest perceived probability of job success. Once hired, the sales recruits must be trained, and a productive selling team must be developed. This requires use of stimulation, supervision, and evaluation, all closely related.

The difficulty of the recruiting task is related to the perceived attractiveness of the job features by the prospective applicant. Because of both real and imagined undesirable job elements, many messages describing job offers will omit the mention of stigma-producing stimuli such as straight-commission compensation plans, excessive travel, and products that may be difficult to sell. In such cases, the person conducting the job interview is required to compose a persuasive presentation, disclosing the job requirements in a logical and psychological sequence that will trigger an application for the job opening.

When a sales manager selects an applicant from a group of recruits, he is forecasting that the chosen individual is able and willing to do what is necessary to be a successful salesman with the hiring firm. Will-do characteristics are considerably more difficult to predict than can-do qualities. The former include such intangible factors as character traits, habits, job motivations not already satisfied off the job, basic energy levels, and degrees of emotional maturity.

It was indicated in Chapter 7 that unless a prospective sales recruit is satisfied with the firm's level and method of compensation, he may reject a given job opportunity. Similarly, since monies paid to salespeople represent costs to the firm, training, supervision, and evaluation programs often affect the dual goal of generating productive selling results while controlling company sales costs. The fixed and variable components of sales-compensation packages have attractive and unattractive elements for both the employee and the firm.

Initial sales training has three major purposes:(1) imparting knowledge, (2) developing skills, and (3) shaping attitudes and work habits for the purpose of maximizing selling effectiveness. Training consists of telling, showing, and teaching the trainee, monitoring his results, and making constructive corrections. This is partially accomplished through classroom techniques; however, the key to creating and maintaining a climate for growth lies in field training, which demonstrates the true realism of contact with live prospects.

Effective sales-compensation plans and communication with the sales force (through written messages, sales meetings, contests, and recognition) are designed to stimulate and motivate sales personnel to move as quickly as possible in the direction of superior performance. Supervision serves a dual role in that it prevents and uncovers sales-force weaknesses and also helps stimulate improved performance after problem sources have been determined. Evaluation is the process of systematically uncovering deviations from goals in the accomplishments of individual sales-force members and the sales force as a whole.

WHY IS SALES MANAGEMENT DIFFERENT?

In one sense, management is management, whether it is of sales personnel, production people, administrators, baseball players, chorus girls, or any other group of employees. The previous chapters have utilized the traditional functions of all managers—planning, organizing, staffing, directing, and controlling—to build a logical framework which portrays the job of sales management as sales managers themselves perceive it.

On the other hand, the development of the sales manager has been along a different path from that of other corporate managers because of : (1) the people he manages, (2) the training he receives, (3) the visibility of his actions.

The People He Manages

More than most employees on the same company level, the salesman has been depicted as a "man in the middle." Incompatible demands as to how he should perform his job are being made by the sales manager and the customer, by the sales manager and family members, by the sales manager and members of other departments in the firm, and by other pairs of individuals and groups with opposing needs.[1] Chapter 10 introduced the notion of the selling pendulum and depicted the salesman's job as a succession of ups and downs and a series of field experiences resulting in alternating feelings of exhilaration and depression. In addition, the salesman must cope with the activities of competitive salesmen. He must often endure company failures to provide quality products, meet competitive prices, and ship orders on time. Management may decide to withdraw territories or alter compensation plans and quotas, and this may upset his equilibrium. He may have to sacrifice earnings when sales are poor, travel, work odd hours, and otherwise spend considerable time away from his family.

Some salesmen lack the needs, impulses, emotions, inner drives, and motives that are necessary to incite them to action. Since the salesperson's performance is necessarily more flexible and less observable by management than that of his counterparts in other functional areas, he is more difficult to manage.

Chapter 3 introduced a number of unfavorable comments about the occupational prestige of personal selling and presented several forceful criticisms by both outsiders and proponents of personal selling. It is within this environment of anxiety and unrest that the sales manager must assemble, train, supervise, and stimulate a group of stress-ridden human beings, molding them into an exciting, purposeful, cohesive, productive, selling unit.

The Training He Receives

Historically, top management's concept of the sales manager's role has been governed by their conception of the salesman's role.[2] Accordingly, in choosing someone to lead salesmen, management frequently selects a top salesman who has little or no training as a manager.

In examining the development of managers in other functional

13. Overview of Sales Management: Today and Tomorrow

areas, one management consultant concludes that companies try to instill the management point of view in their executives by (1) hiring graduates from the leading business schools, (2) putting managers through their own management-development program, (3) sending their managers to management courses and seminars, and (4) encouraging their managers to read and study modern methods of managing.[3] The same authority correctly reasons that relatively few sales managers have the capacity, the time, or the inclination to attend courses, read, or otherwise engage in intellectual self-development exercises. Thus, they engage in nonmanaging or "doing" activities rather than management activities. Companies train nonselling managers, and companies train salesmen; but sales managers are expected to learn their jobs by osmosis.

Sales managers are seemingly content with this unstructured learning process and top management is doing little to encourage these employees to think otherwise. This situation exists because of certain related attitudes about sales managers: (1) They are too busy stimulating, supervising, and evaluating salesmen to take time out to participate in a management development program. (2) Removal of sales managers from the field will have undesirable effects on sales productivity and profitability. (3) Emphasis of the sales manager's role as a manager will give a sales manager grandiose ideas of his job and insulate him from happenings in the field. (4) The sales manager does not need formal management training since the leadership skills he requires are developed out on the firing line rather than in the classroom. The validity of such reasoning is questionable.

In contrast to other managers, the sales manager is encouraged by his superiors to think in terms of direct, immediate action and attendant results. He is encouraged to be self-sufficient, flexible, instinctive, and autonomous. With this in mind, he often views company policy as a general guide, not an operational dictum.[4]

In the context of the several schools of management advanced by management theorists, sales management may be described by the empirical school which analyzes management by a study of experiences, including successes and mistakes, with intent to draw generalizations. The study of sales management also draws from the human behavior school which depends on the relevant social sciences to study the personality dynamics of individuals as the core of management.[5]

The Visibility of His Actions

More than most managers, the sales manager operates in a glass cage in that his actions and the results of his actions are subject to continuous scrutiny. Personal selling is one of the primary interfaces of business with society. Since the sales manager is responsible for the actions of his subordinates, he has certain social and ethical responsibilities.

The management of personal selling as a public communication medium calls for two socially oriented precautions by the sales manager. First, messages authorized by the company must be devoid of false, misleading, or exaggerated statements. Second, those who deliver the statements must be trained, supervised, and policed in such a way that the intent of the sales message and the delivery of the sales message are congruent.

Discrepancies between top management's expectations and the sales manager's performance are tangible, readily measurable, and rapidly available. The sales manager therefore works under conditions of continuous evaluation and pressure. Salespeople are not reluctant to complain to top management about perceived mistreatment by the sales manager. Credit managers, collection managers, financial managers, and production managers frequently object to the sales manager's judgment in selecting customers, disbursing funds, or making delivery commitments.

Since the work schedule of the sales manager is often irregular, and since his leisure hours are frequently subject to interruption by conditions perceived as urgent, his home and social life may be somewhat unlike that of his peers in other functional areas. The nonroutine demands of the sales manager also make him particularly susceptible to feelings of role ambiguity as brought about by conflicting questions by his wife:

"How come you won't be home for dinner again tonight?"

versus

"Our expenses are soaring. Why don't you spend more time with your salesmen so that sales will improve?"

THE FUTURE DIRECTION OF SALES MANAGEMENT ACTIVITIES

The dismal forecasting failures of the economists of the mid-seventies are ample evidence that speculations about the future direction of sales management are fraught with uncertainty. Yet, four virtually certain environmental factors have encouraged the author to include such speculation in the last part of this text: (1) greater variety of consumer choice, (2) improved data processing and communications technology, (3) the predominance of the large organization, (4) the continuing impact of consumerism.[6] The balance of this chapter will discuss the implications of these conditions for sales management.

Greater Variety of Consumer Choices

Despite certain scarcities in recent years, improved technology and world-wide growth of markets suggest that the number of available products and services will continue to grow. As choices become greater in number, consumers and organizational buyers will become less tolerant of supplier imperfections and less hesitant than before in making changes in their product selections, outlets, vendors, and other sources.

Buyers' choices will become more difficult because differences among competitive versions of products will be difficult to discern. Thus, selling resources will be solicited by resellers on the basis of their posttransactional proficiency rather than because of their product lines or sales talks. A salesman will be trained to "live with" a customer after the sale is made, for example, to help him move merchandise, to travel with the customer's salespeople, to educate the customer in merchandising techniques and profit-measuring methods. The industrial salesman will become an account executive who remains with his customers during and after the installation and/or delivery of equipment and materials to supply first-hand, full-time advice and consultation until the customer feels comfortable on his own.

Clearly, sales training will place less emphasis on product knowledge and selling skills. Instead, trainees will focus on customer needs, and the training site may well shift to the retail store or the customer's plant. Since more time will be spent with each customer, a salesman will be expected to give more tender care to fewer customers. Thus, territory size will be reduced and customers will be assigned to salesmen on the basis of the salesman's expertise in satisfying a specific set of customer-service needs.

Quotas, compensation, and evaluation will be tied more to the salesperson's efforts and overall customer satisfaction than to quantifiable measures of sales volume, orders, and profitability. The recruit's persuasive selling ability will be less important as a selection criterion. Instead, the applicant will be judged in terms of his capacity to "wear well" as a quasi-consultant to customers.

Improved Data Processing and Communications Technology

The increasing use of computer services will undoubtedly facilitate the sales-planning process, especially in the area of sales forecasting. One study reported that more than 60 percent of the respondent firms use computers for forecasting, and fewer forecasting errors were reported by those firms.[7] There is little doubt that the sales manager of the future will depend heavily on the computer as an aid in studying, manipulating, and synthesizing both historical and internally generated forecasting information.

EDP retrieval systems are already available to accumulate scattered employment information about sales applicants and gather data about the responses of prospects to selling efforts. Whole new fields of critical importance for evaluating the entire force have emerged, ranging from integrated data processing to systems engineering.

As has been previously indicated, many of today's sales managers do not have the time, skills, or temperament to use newer communications technology. Therefore, as companies upgrade their sales-management information systems, more sophisticated management must be made available to operate the systems. Otherwise, the quality of sales-management decisions may become poorer than ever as a result of the confusion and resentment created by management's inability to cope with the more intricate methods.

Predominance of the Large Organization

As the percentage of independent business operations continues to decrease, committee buying groups will replace many of the individual buyers and purchasing agents. A new breed of salespeople will be recruited to deliver group sales presentations and to become members of selling teams. The selling functions described at the outset of this text will be divided among selling specialists, for example, prospectors, demonstrators, closers, and customer-service experts. The resulting new bases for sales-force segmentation will call for a multiplicity of training and retraining systems, compensation plans, sales meetings, contests, and so forth. Supervision of these specialized functions will require more specially trained managers, with a narrower span of control for each manager.

Company bigness will be accompanied by more leverage by

buyers. This tendency will be directly correlated with the demands of buyers for services and consultations.

Even as retail chains expand, spatial considerations will limit the level of in-store selling. Pressures for sales output per square foot will compel department stores to diversify their selling methods. Mail order, telephone, and cable TV selling systems will grow in scope. Retail stores will develop specialized direct-to-home sales organizations to market such products as insurance, encyclopedias, home appliances, and other items requiring interactive communication processes between buyer and seller.

Continuing Impact of Consumerism

There is substantial evidence that government intervention in and regulation of selling activities will continue even though the effectiveness of many antiselling laws is in doubt. The predicted impact of the combination of public policy actions and the increased demands of more powerful buyers is a substantial loss of the seller's sovereignty.

Management's role in structuring sales presentations will increase, and the use of automated audiovisuals will rise. However, because of the customer's need for the seller's assistance in solving problems, salesmen will be granted considerable discretion in responding to consumers' needs for information. This approach will enhance the sales manager's ability to control the content of the sales message while simultaneously permitting the needed two-way communication between buyer and seller.

The future will undoubtedly see a gradual reduction of misleading and unethical statements by salesmen. Closer supervision by management will help reinforce the salesman's identification with his company, his clients, and society. As relationships become more permanent, salesmen will develop more enduring attitudes and will be less tempted to rock the boat with questionable behavior.

SUMMARY AND CONCLUSIONS

This chapter reemphasized the interdependence of personal selling and other entities in the business environment. From the viewpoint of classical managerial functions, sales managers and other company managers have much in common. There are, however, some noteworthy differences.

Because many salespeople are subject to more stigmas, stress, and anxiety than other employees, the sales manager must regard obstacles, complaints, and other interpersonal complications as challenges rather than problems. In terms of training and preparation for his role, the typical sales manager may be considered an "organizational orphan." The performance of the sales manager is observable by potential customers and other members of society and immediately measurable by his superiors. Also, his schedule is often objectionable to his wife and other family members.

The predicted future of sales management activities may be encouraging to some observers and highly disturbing to others. Seemingly, the emphasis of the personal selling functions is shifting from finding prospects and closing orders to providing professional service and counsel to established customers. This new consultative approach to selling will compel the sales manager to recruit and develop personnel who are more sophisticated, better educated, more devoted and patient, and broader in scope than salesmen of the past and present.

Improved communications technology will aid the sales manager in his planning, sales-force supervision, and evaluation duties. But, a new breed of sales managers will be needed to interpret the more elaborate flow of intelligence.

Sales management will respond affirmatively to the continuing wave of consumerism and new demands of society. The status of salespeople and their managers will be higher as members of the selling organization become less dissimilar from other company personnel on the same level.

Even though the sales manager will be managing more account executives and fewer creative order chasers than before, sales calls, presentations, and closers will still be required in all industries, particularly when the customer is the household consumer. However, more than ever, promises and commitments to the prospective customer will require sustained reinforcement by sales personnel if the customer is to be retained.

Despite the forthcoming challenges of environmental change and emerging marketplace needs, the sales manager and his team will respond instinctively to their new roles. Although their activities will change over time, their contribution to marketing in society will remain vital to the continued progress of the world economy.

NOTES

1. Neil M. Ford, Orville C. Walker, Jr., and Gilbert A. Churchill, Jr., "Expectation-Specific Measures of the Intersender Conflict and Role Ambiguity

Experienced by Industrial Salesmen," *Journal of Business Research* 3 (April 1975):95–111.

2. Leslie M. Dawson, "Toward a New Concept of Sales Management," *Journal of Marketing* 34 (April 1970):33–34.

3. Raymond O. Loen, "Sales Managers Must Manage," *Harvard Business Review* 42 (May–June 1964):108. Much of the material in this section is based on this.

4. Robert T. Davis, "A Sales Manager in Action," in Harper W. Boyd and Robert T. Davis, eds., *Readings in Sales Management* (Homewood, Ill.: D. Irwin, 1970), p. 265.

5. Harold Koontz and Cyril O'Donnell, *Principles of Management* (New York: McGraw-Hill, 1964), pp. 26–33.

6. These factors were either discussed in detail or mentioned in Charles S. Goodman, *Management of the Personal Selling Function* (New York: Holt, Rinehart, and Winston, 1971), pp. 449–66. Parts of this section were inspired by Professor Goodman's treatment.

7. Douglas J. Dalrymple, "Sales Forecasting Methods and Accuracy," *Business Horizons* 18 (December 1975):71–72.

Name Index

Subject Index